Walter Richards

Her Majesty's Army

A descriptive account of the various regiments now comprising the Queen's forces,

from their first establishment to the present time. Vol. 2

Walter Richards

Her Majesty's Army
A descriptive account of the various regiments now comprising the Queen's forces, from their first establishment to the present time. Vol. 2

ISBN/EAN: 9783337324995

Printed in Europe, USA, Canada, Australia, Japan

Cover: Foto ©ninafisch / pixelio.de

More available books at **www.hansebooks.com**

HER MAJESTY'S ARMY

A DESCRIPTIVE ACCOUNT

OF THE

VARIOUS REGIMENTS NOW COMPRISING THE QUEEN'S FORCES, FROM
THEIR FIRST ESTABLISHMENT TO THE PRESENT TIME

BY

WALTER RICHARDS

With Coloured Illustrations

VOL. II.

For the next four or five years they were constantly engaged in the fierce though desultory fighting which our position in India then entailed upon us, and in 1805 sustained heavy loss and gained fresh honours at Bhurtpore. So severely had the twenty years in India dealt with the regiment, that a month after their return home in 1807 "only forty-four men remained." The following year they discarded the Highland uniform, which was not resumed till 1882. They were not again engaged in any campaign of note till 1835, when in the small war at the Cape they earned "South Africa" as a distinction. Then again came a period of comparative quiet, to be terribly broken by the fateful mutiny in India. Early in that terrible time they were at Umballa, when the 5th Bengal Infantry mutinied; in June of the same year, nine companies were with the force under Barnard before Delhi. Early in the morning of the 8th of that month, the army having started at one o'clock in the morning, came upon a strong body of mutineers, with twelve pieces of artillery. The order was given, "Charge and carry those guns!" With a loud and hearty cheer—almost a hoarse roar of joy that they were about to grapple with the destroyers of so many innocent people —Her Majesty's 75th, or Stirlingshire Regiment, swept in line to the front under a storm of musketry, and carried the guns by the bayonet, driving back the Sepoys.

The 75th joined Sir Colin Campbell's force for the relief of Lucknow, and were placed in charge of the Alumbagh, where they repulsed an attempt made to take it by the enemy. Amongst the awards of the Victoria Cross was one to Ensign R. Wadeson,[*] of the regiment, for the gallant manner in which, at imminent risk to himself, he saved the lives of two men. Two other crosses were gained by men of the 75th at Budlee-ke-Serai. Private Corbett lay wounded and surrounded by the enemy. Sergeant Coghlan of the 75th did not "like" this arrangement, and forthwith, with three of his comrades to help him, entered the Serai where Corbett lay and brought him back to the British lines. Later on he displayed conspicuous coolness and courage, and attained the coveted honour of a V.C. The third cross fell to Private Green who, seeing a wounded comrade in imminent risk of being butchered, "went out into the open and under a heavy fire carried him back." Before the mutiny was finally quelled, the 75th did good service in Oude under Captain Brookes. With the exception of some desultory skirmishing with the Kaffir tribes in 1872—74, no further active service of note fell to the share of the 75th till the recent Egyptian campaign. Here they were in the Third Brigade under

---

[*] He was then ignorant of his promotion from the rank of sergeant. He subsequently became Lieutenant-Colonel of the regiment.

Sir Archibald Alison, and found plenty of opportunities for the display of their valour. After a period spent in more or less unimportant skirmishing, the Highland Brigade at the end of August were ordered to Ismailia, arriving there early in September, and in the march to Kasassin, which immediately followed, the columns were led by the Gordon Highlanders. At Tel-el-Kebir they, with the Cameron Highlanders, were for a time, as has been before observed, in the position of the "apex of a wedge" thrust into the heart of the Egyptian army, and being opposed by the 1st Guards of Arabi's force, experienced some severe fighting. Their loss was one officer * and five non-coms. and men killed, one officer and twenty-nine non-coms. and men wounded.† This phase of the war was now practically over, as predicted by Sir Garnet Wolseley, and the Gordon Highlanders had won "Egypt" and "Tel-el-Kebir" to the list of their honours. At the grand review, which was held in Cairo, it is related by a Scotch writer that the regiment was preceded by the "dog of the regiment, Juno," who went with it into Tel-el-Kebir, and was decorated with a handsome silver collar." ‡

The 75th remained in the army of occupation, and were accordingly ready when the need arose for renewed operations in 1884, and were selected to form part of the expeditionary force for the relief of Tokar, Colonel F. Daniell being in command of the regiment. On the occasion of the battle of El Teb they were in the First Brigade, and particularly distinguished themselves by their steadiness of movement, and by the brilliant manner in which they carried an important position held stubbornly by the enemy. They took part in the battles of Tamai and Tamanieh, and gained the latest addition to their many distinctions by the sterling service they rendered in the Nile campaign.

The Second Battalion of the Gordon Highlanders consists of the old 92nd, a regiment whose career has been as adventurous as its origin was romantic. The regiment was raised in 1794 by the Marquis of Huntly, afterwards the last Duke of Gordon, and the story is familiar to every one how the beautiful duchess, his mother, assisted to recruit her son's regiment, placing—when all other arguments failed—the given bounty between her peerless lips. To quote a somewhat hackneyed modern song, many were the stalwart Highlanders who gladly allowed themselves to be thus "bought and sold for a kiss."

* Lieutenant H. G. Brookes.
† It is recorded that, in the following October, a detachment of the Gordon Highlanders had to be sent to re-inter the dead at Tel-el-Kebir, whose bodies had been exhumed and stripped by the Bedouins.
‡ On the collar was the inscription, " Presented to 'Juno' (First Battalion Gordon Highlanders), the heroine of Tel-el-Kebir, by English and Irish admirers."

Concerning the uniform at this time, we read that the officers wore scarlet jackets, yellow facings, silver lace, with a blue silk worm in the centre, flat plated buttons, silver epaulettes, scarlet waistcoats, belted plaid of green tartan, the sword being the Highland claymore. The privates carried muskets; queues were worn by officers and men.

Shortly after its establishment the regiment sailed for Gibraltar, and for the next four years or so was engaged there and in Corsica, returning to England in 1798. Up to this date its regimental number was 100, but at the end of this year, 1798, it received the numerical distinction it at present bears.

The Gordon Highlanders joined the Russo-British expedition against the French in Holland, 1799; and at Oude-Sluys, at Alkmaar, and notably at Egmont-op-Zee, they displayed signal courage. After some unimportant services against the French in Minorca, Quiberon Bay, and Belle Isle, they joined the forces under Sir Ralph Abercromby in Egypt. With the rest of the troops they landed at Aboukir Bay on March 8, 1801, and made good their position under a heavy fire. At Mandora, five days later, the Gordon Highlanders led the left column, and during the course of the engagement made a brilliant charge, and subsequently captured a battery. They remained in Egypt till the termination of the campaign, when they returned to England; the next foreign service in which they were engaged being the expedition against Denmark in 1807,* and the year following found them amongst the forces with Moore at Corunna, at which famous action they served with distinction.

In the following year, 1810, commenced for the Gordon Highlanders a period as stirring as it was fruitful of honour, for then it was that they joined the army of Wellington. Under Cameron of Fassiefern the light company of the regiment was particularly distinguished, despite the untoward circumstances in which they were placed at Fuentes d'Onor.†

At Arroyo dos Molinos they were in the left column under Colonel Stewart, and commenced the attack upon the village. Attacking it in the early morning they spread terror amongst the defenders, their pipers, according to Lord de Ros's account, striking up "with some spirit of waggery the old Highland tune, 'Hey, Johnny Cope, are ye waken yet?'" At Almaraz they were in General Howard's brigade, and were led by Sir Rowland Hill in person to carry the town at the point of the bayonet. Noticeable here amongst much that was noticeable was the individual merit and gallantry of

---

* About this time a second battalion was formed.
† See *supra*, p. 159, note.

Privates Gall and Somerville, of the grenadier company, who, eager to capture Ragusa, "tossed aside their bonnets and muskets, flung themselves into the river, and daringly swam across," to fetch back the pontoon bridge which had become loosened. This exploit undoubtedly forwarded in a considerable degree the attainment of Lord Hill's object, and the gallant Highlanders were rewarded by the general for their service. Particularly did the 92nd distinguish themselves, too, at Salamanca, pushing steadily on through the "cloud of smoke and dust that rolled along, within which was the battle with all its sights and sounds of terror." They bear Vittoria on their colours; at Maya, under Major John Mitchell, they lost two-thirds of their number, so many being slain that "the enemy was actually stopped by the heaped mass of dead and dying; and then the left wing of that noble regiment coming down from the higher ground was forced to smite wounded friends and exulting foes alike, as, mixed together, they stood or crawled before its fire. The stern valour of the 92nd Highlanders would have graced Thermopylæ" (Napier). At the passage of the Nivelle the 92nd, at whose head rode Colonel Cameron, led the way. At St. Pierre "so furious was their attack that they routed the whole of the French skirmishers." But soon a storm of artillery was ploughing through their ranks. Colonel Cameron was nearly killed,* and the regiment had to fall back. Other troops now came up, giving the Gordon Highlanders time to reform; "and its gallant colonel, Cameron, once more led it down to the road with colours flying and music playing, resolved to give the shock to whatever stood in the way." The brilliant chronicler of the war thus comments on the incident—"How gloriously did that regiment come forth again to the charge, with the colours flying and its national music playing as if going to a review! This was to understand war. The man who in that moment, and immediately after a repulse, thought of such military pomp was by nature a soldier. The 92nd was but a small clump compared with the heavy mass in its front, and the French soldiers seemed willing enough to close with the bayonet, until an officer riding at their head suddenly turned his horse, waved his sword, and appeared to order a retreat. Then they faced about, and retired across the valley to their original position; in good order, however, and scarcely pursued by the allies, so exhausted were the

* The occurrence is thus described by a writer : "Cameron's horse, being wounded, fell, and nearly crushed him. A Frenchman rushed forward to bayonet him while thus disabled ; but before the blow had reached, Ewen (Macmillan, the colonel's foster-brother) came up and pierced him to the heart. He raised his master from his dangerous position, and conducted him to a place of safety, after which he returned and carried off the saddle on which Cameron had sat. All this was done with the greatest coolness, though the battle was at its height, and the bullets of the enemy were flying on every side. When Ewen rejoined his company, he displayed his trophy to his comrades, and exultingly exclaimed, " We must leave them the carcass, but they sha'n't get the saddle where Fassiefern sat."

victors. This retrograde movement was produced partly by the gallant advance of the 92nd."

On that day of fighting at St. Pierre it is officially recorded that the 92nd "made four distinct charges with the bayonet, and lost thirteen officers and a hundred and seventy-one rank and file." At Orthes they and the 50th Regiment routed the French under General Harispe, and took the town of Aire;* and when Napoleon's abdication gave the signal for peace, few regiments had earned a better right than the 92nd to the rest and honours that followed the temporary cessation of the war. At Quatre Bras, where they were in Pack's brigade, they came in for the thick of the fighting. At one time in the day matters looked serious for the British. The French Cuirassiers were working terrible havoc, and in their headlong career came "down the Charleroi road to Quatre Bras towards the ditch where the 92nd (the Gordon Highlanders) were lying. Wellington himself, who was trying to rally the Brunswick Hussars, only escaped from them by calling to the 92nd to lie down, and forcing his horse to jump the ditch. The instant he had cleared it the Highlanders sprang up, and discharged a volley which emptied the foremost saddles and stopped the onward career of the squadrons." Later on, the French infantry, supported by cavalry, advanced "in good order, drove back the disordered masses of the Brunswickers and Hanoverians, and moved towards the ditch where the 92nd Highlanders were still lying. The adjutant-general, Sir E. Barnes, rode up to the Highlanders, and waving his hat called, 'Now, 92nd, follow me!' The pipers struck up the 'Camerons' Gathering,' the Highlanders sprang from the ditch, leapt upon the French column, and flung it back with their bayonets. Under the shelter of a hedgerow the French again formed and fired on the 92nd. Their colonel, John Cameron of Fassiefern, fell mortally wounded; and with increased fury the Highlanders, regardless of the musketry, rushed forward and drove the enemy into the wood."

"Concerning this gallant soldier it has been well said that Cameron, of the 92nd, who fought and fell at Quatre Bras, was less the colonel than the chief of that gallant regiment, which was raised partly in Lochabar, his native district. He knew every

---

* For his prowess on this occasion Colonel Cameron received the unusual and marked honour of an heraldic grant, which was "above the cognisance of Lochiel, a representation of the town of Aire, in allusion to his glorious services on the 2nd of March, when, after an arduous and sanguinary conflict, he succeeded in forcing a superior body of the enemy to abandon the said town." He also received from the king "a crest of augmentation, viz., on a wreath a demi-Highlander of the 92nd regiment, up to the middle in water, grasping a broadsword and banner inscribed '92nd,' and in an escrol above, *Arrivette*, in allusion to the bravery he displayed at the passage of the river."

man in his regiment, and watched over their interests as if they had been his brothers or his sons. An angry look or a stern word from him was dreaded more than the lash. He was their father, and when he fell there rose from his mountain children that wild wail of sorrow which once heard can never be forgotten."

At Waterloo the work was even sterner, and the 92nd, thinned as they were by the fighting at Quatre Bras, were soon "reduced to less than three hundred men. A column of three thousand French was formed in front of the regiment. This was the state of affairs when Sir Denis Pack galloped up and called out, '92nd, you must charge, for all the troops on your right and left have given way.' Three cheers from the regiment expressed the devoted readiness of every individual in its ranks. The French column did not show a large front. The regiment formed four deep, and in that compact order advanced until within twenty paces, when it fired a volley, and instantly darted into the heart of the French column, in which it became almost invisible in the midst of the mass opposed to it."

"While the regiment was in the act of charging the Scots Greys came trotting up in rear of its ranks, when both corps shouted, 'Scotland for ever!' The column was instantly broken, and in its flight the cavalry rode over it. The result of this dash, which occupied only a few minutes, was a loss to the enemy of two eagles and two thousand prisoners, those that escaped, doing so without arms or knapsacks. After this brilliant affair, Sir Denis Pack rode up to the regiment and said, 'You have saved the day, Highlanders, but you must return to your position. There is more work to be done!'"

After Waterloo they remained for some time with the army of occupation, returning to England in 1816. For a long time now the Gordon Highlanders enjoyed a respite from "the stern joy that warriors feel," though for many years they were stationed in far-away, often unhealthy, quarters, and suffered frequently as much from fever as from the fiercest engagement. Jamaica, Gibraltar, Malta, Barbadoes, Corfu—such were some of the places where they served between the close of the Peninsular War and the Crimea. They joined the forces before Sevastopol in September, 1855, after the more memorable battles had been fought, and early in 1858 went to India, where, under Sir Hugh Rose, they did good service in the Central Provinces, and notably at Surat and Pojein. They remained in India till 1863, returning there again in 1868, after a sojourn at home. In 1879 two companies formed part of the escort which accompanied the fated Cavagnari to the Shutargardan Pass, where he was met by the Ameer's troops, "who received him with every honour." In September of the same year the Gordon Highlanders were attached to Roberts's column in its march to avenge our envoy's treacherous murder. They were actively engaged at Charasiah, under Major White. "The advance of the 92nd," writes Major Mitford, in his account of the campaign, "was a splendid sight. The dark-green kilts went up the steep rocky hillside at a fine rate, though one would occasionally drop and roll several feet down the slope, showing that the rattling fire kept up by the enemy was not all show. . . . Still the gallant kilts pressed on and on, and it was altogether as pretty a piece of light infantry drill as could be seen." At Takt-i-Shah Lieutenant Dick Cunyngham gained the Victoria Cross for saving, at great personal risk, the day, which was beginning to look threateningly for the British. "A short but desperate struggle ensued. . . . The mass of Afghans in front, with flashing eyes and fierce aspect, waved their swords and threatened a terrible charge. Their bullets searched the ground around the Highlanders. These wavered slightly, but in a moment Lieutenant Dick Cunyngham rushed forward full in the fire of the enemy, shouting to his men to follow. The Afghans' shots whistled past him in hundreds, but, as if he bore a charmed life, he went forward unhurt. Then with a cry of revenge, the Highlanders, with bayonets at the charge, hurled themselves upon their foes, carried them back in the rush, and won the first position."* Major White, again, won another Victoria Cross for a signal act of readiness and courage. "With two companies of his regiment he came upon a body of the enemy strongly posted, and outnumbering his force by *eighteen to one*. His men being much exhausted, and immediate action necessary, Major White took a rifle, and, going on by himself, shot dead the leader of the enemy." Throughout the campaign the 92nd well sustained their high reputation. At its close it fell to Captain M'Callum and two hundred of the regiment to secure booty valued at about £90,000. Acting "on information received," they "surrounded a building said to contain a vast amount of treasure. A search was made, and soon a couple of rooms were found piled up with boxes; these, on being opened, were found to contain all sorts of miscellaneous articles, from soap to brilliants and gold, besides beautiful china, silks, satins, and costly furs, handsome guns, swords and pistols . . . . over nine lacs' worth of treasure, most of it in the gold coin of the country."

The last war service in which the 92nd have been engaged was the deplorable campaign in South Africa in 1881. They were attached to Sir Evelyn Wood's column, about a hundred and fifty being present on the fatal occasion of Majuba Hill. Here

* Elliott, "The Victoria Cross in Afghanistan."

Majors Hay and Singleton, and Lieutenants Hector Macdonald, Ian Hamilton, and Ian Macdonald behaved with signal courage and devotion to duty in the whirlwind of destruction that enveloped the devoted band of seven hundred. Hamilton, with the thirty men under him, held his position longer than appeared possible against the hail of bullets that fell amongst them; Ian Macdonald tried in vain, revolver in hand, to check the rout that seemed imminent; above the gunshots and hoarse cries of pain and shouts of triumph, Major Hay's voice was heard, calmly and cheerily as ever, "Men of the 92nd, don't forget your bayonets!" The exhortation was well heeded. Again and again "the Boers, with fierce and exultant shouts, swarmed up the side of the hill and made furious attempts to carry it at a rush, but each time were driven back by the bayonets, many of which were dyed with blood." Then came the end. The *Times'* report stated that "the handful of Highlanders were the last to leave the hill, and remained there throwing down stones on the Boers and receiving them at the point of the bayonet." * Since South Africa, the 92nd have not been engaged in any hostilities.

THE HAMPSHIRE REGIMENT † (Regimental District No. 37) consists of the 37th and 67th Regiments. The former were raised in 1702, in Ireland, and forthwith departed to "seek the bubble reputation" in the wars under Marlborough. They fought at Schellenberg and famous Blenheim, at Neer Hespen and Ramillies, at Oudenarde and Malplaquet. As "Ponsonby's Regiment" they fought at Dettingen, soon after returning to Scotland on the occasion of the rebellion, during which they fought at Culloden, where they were hotly engaged. On the suppression of the rebellion the regiment returned to Flanders, and served throughout the whole of the subsequent campaign, notably at the battle of Val, where they sustained serious losses.

The next name on their colours—Minden—recalls the share they had in the important campaign in Germany. At Minden the 37th (with the 12th and the 23rd) were the first to advance, which they did with great boldness and rapidity. Their attack was directed against the French left, where were posted the flower of the enemy's

* After the battle it was found that of the officers of the 92nd, Majors Hay and Singleton, and Lieutenant Hamilton were wounded; Captain Macgregor and Lieutenants Wright, Hector Macdonald, and Staunton, prisoners. Major Singleton, who had been in the regiment for twenty years, subsequently died of his wounds.

† The Hampshire Regiment bear as badges the Hampshire Rose in the Garter, surmounted by the Imperial Crown on the cap, and the Rose on the collar. On helmet plate, waist plate, and buttons is the Royal Tiger. The motto is that of the Garter. On the colours are: "Blenheim," "Ramillies," "Oudenarde," "Malplaquet," "Dettingen," "Minden," "Tournay," "Barossa," "Peninsula," "Taku Forts," "Pekin," "Charasiah," "Cabul, 1879," "Afghanistan, 1878-80." The uniform is scarlet, with facings of white.

cavalry. Undoubtedly the regiment was one of those on which the heaviest of the fighting fell, and which may be said to have won the victory, a victory so decisive that, "after five hours' incessant firing, the whole French army literally fled in the greatest disorder, with the loss of forty-three pieces of cannon, ten stand of colours, and seven standards."

Under the Hon. J. Stuart they took part in the expedition, commanded by General Studholm Hodgson, against Belle Isle, in which they evinced great courage and sustained considerable loss. They then served in America, fighting at Brooklyn and in other early affairs, during the latter part of the war being stationed at New York. After a short sojourn at home, the 37th went to Flanders at the commencement of the war with France, speedily distinguishing themselves at Dunkirk, and particularly in the disastrous conflicts near Tournay on May 18th and 22nd, 1794, and in the capture of the village of Pontichon. Later in the same year the 37th again won deserved credit at Druiten, on the Maes, a credit nobly sustained throughout that terrible winter, with its engagements at Nimeguen and Guildermalsen, and especially in the fearful retreat to Bremen, where "the high keen wind carried the drifted snow and sand with such violence that the human frame could scarcely resist its power; where the cold was intense; the water which collected in the hollow eyes of the men congealed as it fell, and hung in icicles from their eyelashes; the breath froze, and hung in icy incrustations about their haggard faces, and on the blankets and coats which they wrapped about them." From that time for many years the service that fell to the lot of the 37th was more solidly useful than exciting. They assisted in various ways the cause of their country in the war then raging, but did not till early in 1814 join Lord Wellington's army; earning, however, the distinction of "Peninsula" on their colours.

After the peace of 1814 they went to Canada, and remained there until 1826, a second battalion—which had been raised in 1811, and was disbanded four years later—being stationed in Holland, and forming part of the garrison of Antwerp during the battle of Waterloo. They served in Malta, the Ionian Islands, Jamaica, and North America. After a short stay at home they went, in 1846, to Ceylon, remaining there ten years. In 1857 the regiment served in India, and undoubtedly contributed not a little to the safety of Calcutta, surrounding the palace of the ex-King of Oude, whom rumour—subsequently confirmed—asserted to be in league with the mutineers. They were present at the first relief of Azemghur and in the night attack on Arrah, subsequently earning considerable praise for the effective and arduous service of clearing the Jugdespore jungles. No further important services of a warlike nature have been required of the gallant 37th, who, with short intervals at home, have been chiefly stationed for the last thirty years in India.

The second battalion of the Hampshire Regiment is the 67th, which was originally constituted in 1756 as the second battalion of the 20th Foot, acquiring its present numerical position in 1758, and having James Wolfe, of Quebec fame, for its first colonel. The first service of the regiment was at Belle Isle in 1761, and subsequently in the short campaign of 1762 against the Spaniards. Service in the West Indies decimated their ranks by the deadly climate as fatally as a series of the fiercest engagements, and a considerable period was necessary for recruiting both the corporate and individual strength of the regiment. In 1805, however, when they were ordered to India, they had their full complement of 1,200, exclusive of officers. In India the regiment remained for more than twenty years, during which it had its full share of arduous and valuable, if not widely known, services. Dinapore, Benares, Ghazeepore, Cawnpore, Meerut—such were some of the places whither they were despatched, and where often enough sharp fighting awaited them. They formed part of the Army of Reserve under Major-General Sir David Ochterlony. Subsequently they were engaged in the siege and capture of Ryghur, and at Surat, Nunderbar, Cokermundaye, Tonloda, and Kopriel. In March, 1819, the flank companies of the regiment joined the force detailed for the attack on Azeer, and particularly distinguished themselves for their hardihood in the face of tremendous odds; proceeding, in February, 1819, to Asseeghur to join the force under General Doveton. Throughout the latter part of the campaign under General Doveton they were actively engaged, and remained in Bombay until 1826, returning to England later in the same year, having earned by their long and loyal service in the Peninsula the distinction of the "Royal Tiger" and "India."

Meanwhile a second battalion, which had been raised in 1803, had been participating in the warfare that raged almost incessantly on the Continent of Europe. Under Sir Thomas Graham they were present at the defence of Cadiz, where, though our forces were not strong enough to raise the siege, yet the loss and annoyance they inflicted on the enemy was so great as occasionally to suggest to the latter that "they were besieged, rather than besieging Cadiz." The name "Barossa" on the colours of the regiment testifies to their participation in one of the most brilliant victories of the war. Subsequently they were engaged in the operations against Tarragona and Barcelona, and were thus prevented from sharing in the later battles of the war, though their distinguished service was recognised by the granting of "Peninsula" as a distinction. The second battalion was disbanded in 1817, and the first battalion remained in England until 1833, subsequently being stationed at Gibraltar, in the West Indies, and Canada. During the Russian War the regiment was stationed in Jamaica, afterwards coming in for the latter part of the Indian Mutiny. The North China campaign of 1860 brought them once more within the welcome sphere of active service. Here they were in the fourth brigade of the second division, which was the first to land at the Taku Forts, and worked splendidly in the hard work of road-making which preceded the assault. On the occasion of the assault itself, the 67th, under Colonel Knox, particularly distinguished themselves, forcing their way through the narrow breach and planting the colours of the regiment on the cavalier. The credit of this piece of *esprit de corps* must be given to Lieutenant Burslem, Ensign Chapman, and Private Lane. On the occasion of the capture of Pekin a wing of the 67th was told off to storm the breach when made, a necessity which the timely yielding of the Chinese obviated. They were the first British troops to enter, and on the termination of the war were left for a time to garrison the Taku Forts. Two years later we find them again in China, on the occasion of the Taeping rebellion, and a few years afterwards doing duty at the Cape and Natal. After a short sojourn in England, the 67th went to Burmah in 1872, and six years later took part in the Afghan campaigns of 1878-80.

On the occasion of the third Afghan campaign of 1879 the 67th formed part of the column under General Roberts. At Charasiah the main body of the regiment was not present, though they shortly after joined the troops under General Baker. At Cabul they narrowly escaped severe loss from the explosion at Bala Hissar,* their quarters being in an adjacent garden. In the November following, a company of the regiment, under Captain Poole and Lieutenant Carnegie, had a sharp affair with a large body of Afghans. The force of the Hampshire consisted only of twenty-eight men, and "overwhelmed by numbers, the slender company had to retreat, leaving three of their force behind. One who was wounded in the hip had to be abandoned, and was dreadfully mutilated before death. His companion seeing this, flung himself into the Cabul river to avoid a similar fate, and perished miserably, despite the efforts of Captain Poole and others to save him." In this skirmish Captain Poole was himself wounded, as well as five privates. Throughout the campaign till, on the 12th of August, 1880, they found

* In the magazine were stored 820,000 shot and shell, and 250,000 lbs. of powder. A private of the Hampshire was killed.

themselves in the third brigade (Brigadier Daunt) of General Stewart's division, preparing to retire from Kabul, the 67th availed themselves of all the opportunities that offered—and these were not few—to add still more to the high reputation they already possessed. Since then, if we except the expedition into Burmah in 1885, and those now pending, in which they have done splendid work, no active service of importance has fallen to the lot of the Hampshire Regiment.

The HIGHLAND LIGHT INFANTRY * (Regimental District No. 71), the next regiment in the alphabetical order of territorial nomenclature, consists of the 71st and 74th Regiments. The present first battalion is the third regiment that has borne the number 71, and was raised in 1777, and known as Macleod's Highlanders. It was originally numbered the 73rd, under which designation it acquired its early fame in the Indian wars, nine years after its incorporation receiving the present number. In 1779 the 71st embarked, under Colonel Macleod, for India, and were soon actively engaged in the campaigns against Hyder Ali and Tippoo Sahib.† At Conjeveram the flank companies of the regiment, under Captains Lindsay and Baird, were sent to the assistance of Colonel Baillie, who found himself "surrounded by the whole of Hyder Ali's army, and a fire opened upon him from sixty pieces of cannon." Despite the terrible odds, it seemed at one time as though the heroic courage of the little band of British was to achieve a victory. Hyder's cavalry were already in retreat, when an accidental explosion in the British lines threw them into confusion, and the overwhelming mass of the enemy closed in. They were reduced to about four hundred men, who defended themselves to the last on a little eminence, even the wounded making shift to turn their bayonets against the wave of fierce horsemen. In the hope of avoiding further sacrifice of life, the British at last surrendered, only to learn that in many cases the most painful death in battle would have been, by comparison, easy and pleasant. The tortures inflicted anticipated the horrors of a later day in India. "No sooner had the troops laid down their arms than they, the sick, and the wounded were all attacked with remorseless fury, and the most dreadful

* The Highland Light Infantry bear as badges the letters H. L. I. surrounded by a horn, on a star of the Order of the Thistle. Above the horn is an Imperial Crown, and below an Elephant, with "Assaye" on cap and collar. The motto is that of the Order of the Thistle. On the colours are the names "Hindoostan," "Assaye," "Seringapatam," "Cape of Good Hope, 1806," "Roleia," "Vimiera," "Corunna," "Busaco," "Fuentes d'Onor," "Ciudad Rodrigo," "Badajoz," "Almaraz," "Salamanca," "Vittoria," "Pyrenees," "Nivelle," "Nive," "Orthes," "Toulouse," "Peninsula," "Waterloo," "South Africa, 1851—2—3," "Sevastopol," "Central India," "Egypt, 1882," "Tel-el-Kebir." The uniform is scarlet, with facings of yellow.

† A second battalion, which was raised in 1778, served at Gibraltar and was present at the famous battle off Cape St. Vincent. It was disbanded in 1783.

butchery ensued. .... The young soldiers of Hyder Ali amused themselves by fleshing their swords and exhibiting their skill on men already helpless and dying, on the sick and wounded, and even on women and children." There were eighty-six officers of Baillie's little force; of these thirty-seven perished and thirty-four were dreadfully mangled. Of Macleod's Highlanders eighty-eight were killed and a hundred and fifteen, of whom only twenty-three were unwounded, taken prisoners. Amongst them—as has been before mentioned[*]—was Captain Baird, who was selected for an especial exhibition of the tyrant's cruelty, as "much of the slaughter in Hyder's force was attributed to his company of grenadiers." It is impossible fully to realise the tortures to which the unfortunate captives were subjected, tortures rendered the more diabolical, as in their stead were proffered wealth and pleasure if only they would "curse Christ and embrace Islam." Many of these Highlanders were at the very dawn of manhood, when life even for itself is lovely, and the passions and powers of enjoyment strongest. They were chained each to the other in filthy dungeons, rendered more awful still by the presence of the dead and dying, and by the foul atmosphere, reeking in the sweltering heat of a tropical clime. Without were riches and pleasures and beauty—sweet cool streams, soft luxurious couches for their wounded limbs, delicious foods, and dainty drinks. To the credit of the brave regiment, let it be recorded and held in lasting memory, that "not one could be prevailed upon to purchase life on these terms."

At the siege of Cuddalore the 71st—Macleod's Highlanders—were again the only European regiment of Eyre Coote's little army of 7,000 men which was to confront the force under Hyder, consisting of "twenty-five battalions of infantry, four hundred Europeans, nearly fifty thousand horse, more than a hundred thousand matchlock-men, peons, and polygars in chain armour, with helmets and round shields, spears and sabres; and he had forty-seven pieces of cannon." The 71st were under the command of Colonel Crawford, their late colonel, Lord Macleod, having returned to Britain in consequence either of some disagreement with the Commander-in-Chief, or of his considering the rank of colonel not a sufficiently exalted one to be borne longer by one who had been Lieutenant-General in the Swedish army. At Cuddalore, Perambucan, Sholinghur, and Vellore the 71st did right valiantly, at the first-named place undoubtedly giving a decisively favourable turn to the then doubtful day by the adroitness with which they occupied some redoubts evacuated by the enemy in a premature pursuit.

Later on we find them engaged in the yet more serious hostilities which included

[*] Page 190.

the engagements at Palghautcherria, Nundydroog, Savendroog, Outredroog, Ram Gurry, and Sheria Gurry, and the crowning exploits of Seringapatam and Bangalore. At Bangalore the 71st found themselves fighting with their present "linked battalion," the 74th, and together the regiments experienced severe work. In the storming of one of the redoubts Captain Sibbald was shot; the assaults made by Tippoo's followers waxed fiercer as their master's cause grew more desperate; at last the stately palace and gardens of delight were in the hands of the warriors of a mightier monarch, and the lord of the countless armies of the East had to yield to the handful of which the 71st was part. Pondicherry and Ceylon experienced their prowess; then after a short respite came the expedition under Sir David Baird to the Cape, when the 71st were brigaded under General Ferguson, and joined in the charge, which "was irresistible." Under Sir Home Popham they were the only complete British regiment which commenced the reduction of Buenos Ayres in 1806, sharing the fate of being made for a short time prisoners, owing to the force not being adequately supported. In 1808, shortly after having received the title of "The Glasgow Regiment," the 71st proceeded to the Peninsula and shared in the conflict at Rolica. At Vimiera they took part in the magnificent bayonet charge which shattered the flower of the French army. A contemporary account has given a graphic description of the charge. The French "came up to the charge like men accustomed to victory, but no troops, however brave, however accustomed to victory, have ever withstood the charge of the British bayonet. In a moment their foremost rank fell, like a line of grass beneath the scythes of the mowers."* Even after the decisive charge had been given the 71st were called upon to resist a determined attempt on the part of the enemy to "turn the doubtful day again;" with terrific fury the French, under the gallant Kellerman, swept on to the valley where, panting from their past exertions, the 71st and 82nd were resting. The British fell back a little, but their object in doing so was soon evident. Arrived at a rising ground they poured a withering volley into the ranks of the enemy, and once again did the bayonet, like the Roman broadsword of old, "cleave deep its gory way." As they advanced to the charge their piper was shot through the thigh. He refused to leave the field, and, sitting down, continued to play, with the cheery asseveration, "Deil hae me, lads, if ye shall want music." In the struggle, the French General, Bernier, was taken and would have been killed had not Corporal Mackay of the 71st intervened. To the General's intense astonishment, Mackay refused the proffered purse; the explanation given by Colonel Pack

* *Edinburgh Register*, 1808.

to the bewildered inquiry, "What manner of man is this who saves my life and refuses my money?" was typical of the spirit of British warfare, "Sir, we are British soldiers, not plunderers."* The corporal, one is glad to record, was, at Lord Wellington's special direction, immediately promoted to the rank of sergeant. After Vimiera came Corunna, at which they were engaged, and after that, at a short interval, the expedition to Flushing. The year 1810 saw them in Portugal, commencing an era of surpassing fame. At Fuentes d'Onor they fought stubbornly and long with the columns of Massena; at Arroyo dos Molinos the charge made by them and the 92nd lives in the brilliant pages of Napier; they shared in the Homeric struggle at Ciudad Rodrigo; in the blood-coloured canvas on which the siege of Badajoz is portrayed some of the combatants are seen to be men of the 71st. At Almaraz they took a standard from the enemy; at Salamanca they fought and conquered; at Vittoria, where their leader, General Cadogan, fell, they avenged right grimly his death, "three hundred remaining fit for duty out of a thousand who drew rations that morning." We can mention but the principal of the many engagements in which the 71st were engaged. They shared with their countrymen of the 92nd the glory of the combat at Aratesque; they number Nivelle and Nive amongst their exploits; at St. Pierre they well atoned for the inexplicable error which, in the early part of the fray, had withdrawn them from action; at Orthes and Toulouse they bore themselves right valiantly; they bear—and the name tells of their historic gallantry on the day—the crowning honour of "Waterloo." After Waterloo the 71st served with the army of occupation, and from that time till the Crimea they were quartered at home, in Canada, and the Bermudas. On their colours are "Sevastopol" and "Central India," the tale of which has been often told before. Their subsequent services have been confined to home and garrison duty, though during the Umbeyla campaign of 1863, a body of sharpshooters, formed by Lieutenant Fosberry from the ranks of the 71st and 101st regiments, performed most valuable service.

The Second Battalion of the Highland Light Infantry is the 74th Highland Regiment, which was raised in 1787 with a view to service in India. Their record runs on much the same lines as does that of the First Battalion: we find the same accounts of stubborn daring in India, crowned by conspicuous valour throughout the Peninsular War.

* A similar reply was given a century and a half later, when the French, at the sack of Pekin, wondered why the British Commander-in-Chief took nothing. "I should like a great many things which the Palace contains," said the Earl of Elgin, "but—I am not a thief."

The regiment arrived at Madras in 1789, and forthwith engaged in field service against Tippoo Sahib in the Mysore Territory. They took part in the attack on Seringapatam, in May, 1791, and, on that project being for the time abandoned, found full outlet for their energies in the capture of various hill forts. At Seringapatam, in 1792, the 74th particularly distinguished themselves. In the defence of the Sultan's Redoubt, a detachment of the regiment, with about fifty Sepoys—in all about a hundred and fifty men—held out all day, resisting the attacks "of thousands upon thousands, repelling not less than five assaults, each undertaken by a body of fresh troops."[*] They shared in the attack against Pondicherry in 1793, and in the expedition against Manilla of 1797. At the Battle of Mallavelly, in 1799, we again read of the 74th as having "greatly distinguished themselves." When at last Tippoo's hour had come, and through the dark night pressed on the avenging British, it is recorded that the 74th were the first regiment to enter the tyrant's palace, and that the general orders issued to the troops spoke of the "unparalleled valour" of that regiment. At Ahmednuggur, in 1803, we read that their conduct was the "admiration of Major-General Wellesley." At the Battle of Assaye, the following September, so fiercely were the 74th engaged that at its close *every officer was either killed or wounded.* None amongst the regiments who bear it have better earned the badge of "The Elephant," and for long afterwards it enjoyed the proud sobriquet of "The Assaye Regiment." Argaum, Bareuda,[†] Chandore, and Gaulnah were to be included in the triumphs which they bore with them to Europe on their return in 1805. After five years' rest, the 74th were ordered to the Peninsula, and (Busaco offering the first opportunity) gave evidence that the fame of India was to gain additional lustre in Spain. They "acquired fresh laurels at Fuentes d'Onor," joined in the second and third attacks on Badajoz; gained particular praise by their conduct at the storming of Ciudad Rodrigo. On the occasion of the third siege of Badajoz, amongst other incidents affecting the regiment, it is recorded that the piper, McLachlan, was foremost in the escalade, playing "The Campbells are Coming," and encouraging his comrades by mien and gesture, when he was shot dead through the bag of his pipes, and martial music and gallant heart-beats ceased together. At Salamanca they fought most gallantly, were present at the siege of Burgos, at the battle of Vittoria in 1813, and at the subsequent actions in the Pyrenees. Nivelle, Orthes, and

---

[*] Gleig. It is recorded that Captain Campbell of the 74th was instrumental in saving the Commander-in-Chief from capture.

[†] Amongst their feats they marched on one occasion sixty miles in twenty hours.

Toulouse closed for them the experience of the Peninsular War, as during Waterloo they were in Ireland. From that time till 1851, though they have been quartered in numerous places, including Canada, the Bermudas, and West Indies, they have not been actively engaged. In the latter year, however, they proceeded to South Africa to take part in the Kaffir War. In the march against Sandilli the 74th were the first to move, and "the pipes struck up 'Over the Border' and played us across the frontier into Kaffirland." * No troops could have fought better than did the 74th in the wild country of the Kaffirs—wading through rushing streams, scrambling up stony precipices, plunging into the thick gloom of tangled forests, wherein from unthought-of corners the fire of the enemy would be poured destructively on their line. At the attack on the Waterkloof a rumour arose that the 12th Regiment was cut off, and the 74th rushed back and rescued their comrades. It was no child's play, that savage warfare. Capture meant mutilation of the most awful kind,† the nature both of country and climate was against us, death lurked behind every bush, and from every boulder might come the fatal assegai. On one occasion the rearguard of the regiment was attacked and one man killed. Captain Gordon sprang to the aid of another who was wounded, and the foe were driven off, but "not before the wretched man had been severely mutilated." Later on Colonel Fordyce was shot, dying with the words "Take care of my Highlanders" on his lips. His successor, Colonel Seton, with sixty-six men, went down in the *Birkenhead* transport. After the Kaffir War the 74th went to Madras, where they remained till 1864, returning then to England. Their next actual service was in Egypt, where in 1882 they won the latest of their distinctions. Here they were in the Third Brigade under Sir Archibald Alison. During the action at Kasassin they were at Ismailia, soon, however, arriving at the point of concentration. At Tel-el-Kebir they came in for probably the fiercest fighting of the battle. The redoubt which faced them baffled all efforts at a front attack, and they had to try to force a way in at the sides. Time will not permit us to more than mention that, as might be expected, they suffered more severely than any other regiment, having three officers ‡ and fourteen non-commissioned officers and men killed, fifty-two non-commissioned officers and men wounded, eleven missing. A correspondent of one of the papers reported that in front of one of the bastions he saw

* Account of the expedition, by Captain King.
† Captain King describes the fate of a bandmaster of the 74th, who had been taken prisoner. "He had been brutally tortured for three days, cut with assegais, crucified, and daily deprived of a joint from each finger and toe till he expired; prior to which some of his own flesh was cut from him and thrust into his mouth, Kaffir women dancing round him the while."
‡ These were Major Thomas Colville and Lieutenants Hays and Somerville.

six men of the 74th all lying in a row, heads and bayonets pointed forward, while immediately in front of these was the body of young Lieutenant Somerville, who had been leading, claymore in hand, when a volley laid them all low."

THE ROYAL INNISKILLING FUSILIERS* (Regimental District No. 27) consist of the 27th and 108th Regiments. The former date from 1689, when they were formed by William III. out of the forces which had so distinguished themselves in the war then being waged in Ireland. The first "badge," that of the Castle, commemorates the gallant defence of Inniskilling in 1691 by Colonel Z. Tiffen's regiment, as the 27th were then named. Throughout the Irish wars which followed the accession to the throne of William III., from the passage of the Boyne to the fall of Limerick, the 27th fought gallantly for the new order of things. Their next important employment was in the sister kingdom of Scotland, where the adherents of the Stuart cause again endeavoured to restore the throne to the hereditary owners, and it was not until 1739 that the Inniskillings had the opportunity of experiencing foreign service. In this year they embarked for the West Indies, and were engaged in the melancholy fiasco of Carthagena in 1741. Though there was little enough of actual fighting, such was the fatal effect of the climate on our troops that the 27th alone lost 591 officers and men out of 600! Not long after their return to England and the completion of the necessary recruiting, they fought at Culloden, ten years or so later exchanging the uncongenial service of bearing arms against their fellow-countrymen for the more natural occupation of fighting the French in America and Canada. They fought at Ticonderoga and Crown Point, and in the subsequent engagements which completed the pacification of Canada under British government. They were at the capture of Martinique and Grenada in 1762, and at the siege and capture of Havanna. The War of Independence in America provided the same sort of unsatisfactory warfare for the Inniskillings as that wherewith they commenced their regimental career, but though "someone had blundered"—at the cost of a colony, with the Inniskillings, as with the other troops engaged, it was plainly "theirs not to reason why;" so at Brooklyn, White Plains, and Germantown they did their duty like

---

* The Royal Inniskilling Fusiliers bear as a badge the Castle of Inniskilling on a grenade on cap and collar, on the waist belt the White Horse of Hanover and the Sphinx with "Egypt." The motto is the one common to all regiments bearing the "White Horse" (given for services in Scotland, 1715)—"*Nec aspera terrent.*" On the colours are "St. Lucia," "Maida," "Badajoz," "Salamanca," "Vittoria," "Pyrenees," "Nivelle," "Orthes," "Toulouse," "Peninsula," "Waterloo," "South Africa, 1835," "South Africa, 1846–7," "Central India." The uniform is scarlet, with facings of blue and "racoon skin" caps.

brave men, and left the responsibility for other shoulders to bear. They served at St. Lucia in 1778, at the relief of Grenada in 1779, and with the Duke of York in Holland in 1793 and 1794, where they experienced the full horrors of war at Nimeguen and Guildermalsen. In the West Indies, in 1796, the 27th were with the force under Sir Ralph Abercromby, and gained the first distinction on their colours. The honour paid to the regiment at the time—an honour as effective as it was rare—adds an additional brilliancy to the emblazonment of 'St. Lucia.' So splendidly did they acquit themselves that, when the citadel surrendered, Sir Ralph Abercromby, " in recognition of the steady and intrepid bearing of officers and men, ordered that the French garrison—2,000 strong—should lay down their arms to the 27th, and that the 'King's' colour of the regiment should be displayed for the space of one hour previous to the hoisting of the Union Jack." Their next engagements were in 1799, when they fought at Bergen, Egmont-op-Zee, and Alkmaer. A second battalion, which was formed in 1800, went to Egypt with Sir Ralph Abercromby, and shared in the actions fought at the landing in Aboukir Bay, before Alexandria, the first battalion joining in time to take part in the siege of Alexandria. The first battalion subsequently served in the expedition to Naples, and afterwards in Sicily, taking part later on in the descent on Calabria. At the battle of Maida the 27th were on the left of our line, and greatly distinguished themselves, being afterwards represented by a detachment under Captain Jordan in the romantic defence of Scylla.

After serving for some time in Sicily the 27th joined Wellington's army near Badajoz in October, 1809, and soon had an opportunity of gaining fresh honours at Albuera, at Badajoz, and at the battles of Salamanca and Vittoria. They fought at Sebastian, at the passage of the Bidassoa, in the various actions in the Pyrenees, and on the Nivelle; Orthes and Toulouse complete the category of their deeds of prowess in the Peninsular War. After various services—always well performed, and which space alone prevents us from enumerating—they proceeded to Belgium, and joined Wellington's army on June 16th, marching through Brussels without halting, and arriving on the field of Waterloo on the 18th. It was well for the gallant Inniskillings that they made that forced march, for no regiment gained greater honour in that tremendous conflict. They were in Lambert's Brigade, the Sixth, and at one time, we are told, " So heavy was the fire on the 27th regiment that in a few minutes it was reduced to a mere cluster, surrounded by a bank of the slain." After Waterloo they remained in the army of occupation, returning to England in 1817.* The Kaffir War of 1835 was the next important service in which they were engaged, and in 1841 a detachment was sent overland from Graham's Town to assist in the difficulties at Port Natal, a service which entailed on the regiment heavy loss and privation. They subsequently served in the Kaffir War of 1846—47, returning the year after to England, and embarked for India in June, 1854. During the Mutiny they were in India, and were actively engaged on the north-west frontier. After some years' interval they were employed at the Straits Settlement in 1876, where, and in China and South Africa, their subsequent service has been passed.

The Second Battalion of the Royal Inniskilling Fusiliers is the 108th Foot, that regiment having been the third which has borne that number. The 108th of which we are now speaking was originally the "East India Company's 3rd Madras European Regiment," and as such did splendid service in Central India during the Mutiny; indeed, from 1854 to 1858. The opportunity has not yet occurred for the 108th—the Second Battalion of the Inniskillings—to take part in any important warfare. If continuity and tradition is to be trusted, should such occasion arise the Second Battalion may be relied on to warrant the epithet being applied to the regiment—"Par nobile fratrum."

The Princess Victoria's (Royal Irish) Fusiliers † (Regimental District No. 87) consist of the 87th and 89th regiments. The former dates from 1793, when they were raised by Colonel Doyle, numbering an effective strength of six hundred rank and file. Shortly after their incorporation they embarked for service in Flanders, and distinguished themselves in repulsing a vigorous attack upon Alost. At Bergen-op-Zoom a considerable number were taken prisoners by the French; later on they took part in the abortive attempt on Porto Rico in 1797. In 1804 they returned to England, and it gives a graphic picture of one phase of the hardships of a soldier's life, when we find it recorded that during the eight years they served in the West Indies they lost "by the diseases

---

* The regiment has been treated as a whole, reference to the creation, services, and disbandment of additional battalions being omitted.

† The Princess Victoria's (Royal Irish) Fusiliers, bear as badges "The Prince of Wales' Plume over the Irish Harp on a grenade; above the grenade the Coronet of the Princess Victoria on cap; and an eagle with 'S' below it in a laurel wreath on a grenade, the monogram and Coronet of the Princess Victoria, and above them the Sphinx over the word 'Egypt,' on the collar." The mottoes are "Ich Dien" and "Honi soit qui mal y pense." On their colours are the names of the following battles:—"Monte Video," "Talavera," "Barossa," "Tarifa," "Java," "Vittoria," "Nivelle," "Orthes," "Toulouse," "Peninsula," "Niagara," "Ava," "Sevastopol," "Egypt, 1882-1884," "Tel-el-Kebir." The uniform is scarlet with facings of blue and Fusilier's cap.

incident to the climate many officers and between seven and eight hundred men." At Monte Video, in 1807 the 87th gained great praise. They were posted near the north gate, which they were directed to enter when the storming party had forced them open, "but their ardour," so runs the General Order, "would not allow them to wait; they scaled the walls and opened themselves a passage." Again, at the regrettable conflict at Buenos Ayres in 1807 did they show the stuff they were made of. Lieutenant Hutchinson captured a couple of guns, and turned them on the enemy with most effective results; Sergeant Byrne distinguished himself by his bravery; Sergeant Grady performed a feat which, under another commander, would have been productive of distinct advantage both to him and to the army. Left with a score of invalids to guard the baggage, Grady repulsed an attack, and took prisoners a couple of officers and seventy men. These he sent to the Commander-in-Chief. A couple of hours later they returned triumphant, bearing an order from General Whitelocke that their arms were to be returned and themselves set at liberty, with an injunction to Grady that he was not to hinder or fire upon any one wishing to enter or leave the town, whether they were armed or not! As a result of this extraordinary direction, Grady and his helpless band were shortly surrounded by some five hundred of the enemy, taken prisoners, and subjected to every conceivable hardship and insult. It is mentioned in the official records that—a somewhat alarming incident—many of the enemy were dressed in the uniform of the 87th, a fact which must have considerably exasperated the gallant "County Downs." The explanation of this was that a store-ship, in which were supplies of uniforms for the regiment, had been captured by a privateer, and the contents sold in Monte Video. In 1815 they were in India, serving under General Ochterlony in Nepaul. The 87th were in the Third Brigade under Colonel Miller, and at Mukwanpoor materially assisted in gaining a brilliant victory, chiefly by a bayonet charge, before which the brave Ghoorkas—now amongst the most valuable soldiers of Her Majesty—fled "with howls of rage and dismay." In 1826 they fought at Burmah, gaining the distinction of "Ava" by their gallant conduct at Prome, Melloone, and Moulmein. On their return to England, after an absence of thirty-three years, the 87th received particular compliments from the King, receiving the title of "Royal" in "consequence of the extraordinary distinction that has marked the career of the corps on all occasions." This distinction, it may here be noted, was extensively shared in by the Second Battalion, now disbanded, whose honours the First Battalion inherited. Pursuing the career of the First Battalion, we find them again in India in 1849, and doing good service at the time of the Mutiny in Peshawur, aiding in the timely suppression of the mutinous 55th regiment, the execution of whose ringleaders was sternly superintended by the 87th. After a prolonged stay in India and China they returned to England in 1876, where they remained till the Egyptian War of 1882, when they were in the Second Brigade—General Graham's—of the First Division. They fought at Tel-el-Kebir with conspicuous courage, joining in the "Irish charge" which, carrying the inner line of redoubts, practically decided the victory. The loss of the regiment on this occasion was two killed, and thirty-seven wounded and missing. Shortly after they repaired once more to India, where, at the time of writing, they still are.

The Second Battalion of the 87th, to which is due the Peninsular honours borne by the regiment, was raised in 1804, and commenced a career of unsurpassed glory at Talavera. Here they were in Mackenzie's division, and an idea may be formed of the important part they played when it is mentioned that their loss in killed and wounded was fourteen officers and three hundred and forty men. At Barossa, "by a firm, rapid, and resolute charge, the 87th overthrew the first line of the French . . . on and yet on went the brave Irish with their bayonets," until first and second lines alike were swept away together and fled. The first Eagle captured in the Peninsular War fell to Sergeant Patrick Masterson, of the 87th, who was rewarded by a commission. It is in commemoration of that achievement that they bear the Eagle, with the number '8' of the French regiment they despoiled. We can well realise that it was with genuine enthusiasm General Graham wrote home to General Doyle, the Colonel of the Irish Fusiliers: "Your regiment has covered itself with glory." As illustrative of the utter contempt for danger which animated our troops in the Peninsula may be mentioned the following incident. During a short halt on one occasion a shell from a howitzer fell among the men of the 87th, who were sitting down, resting. James Geraghty, a private, jumped up, and, observing that he "would show them how they played football at Limerick," kicked the live shell with its burning fuse over the edge of the hill. At Tarifa, the 87th, under Colonel Gough—afterwards Field-Marshal Lord Gough, of Indian fame—defended the breach, and from their fire the French fell back, literally shattered, "the killed and shrieking wounded filling all the slimy hollow below." The officer who led the storming party fell, pierced with wounds and dying, against the portcullis, through which he handed his sword to Colonel Gough, the while that the drums and fifes of the 87th played familiar Irish airs. The report made of their conduct on this occasion equals the eulogy paid them by General Graham: "The conduct of

Lieutenant-Colonel Gough and the 87th Regiment surpasses praise." At Vittoria the baton of Marshal Jourdain was taken by the 87th, who lost in the memorable victory —chiefly in the desperate charge by which they carried the village of Hermandad— two hundred and fifty-four killed and wounded. At Nivelle they went into action numbering three hundred and eighty-six. At the close of the action only a hundred and seventy remained alive and unwounded, and from the commanding officers came the "animated praises"—"Gallant 87th!" "Noble 87th!" At Orthes they lost two hundred and sixty-four; at Toulouse a hundred. So ended the Peninsular campaign, after which the second battalion was disbanded, leaving to its natural heritors a record second to none for glory and dauntless courage.

The Second Battalion of the Royal Irish Fusiliers—the 89th—was raised in 1793, and was, according to a recent sketch of its career,* the third regiment so numbered. In 1794 the 89th served in Holland under Lord Moira, and four years later fought against the Irish rebels at Vinegar Hill. The following year a nobler strife awaited them in the operations in Egypt, where they gained the cognisance of the Sphinx borne by the regiment. They were in the brigade under General Doyle, and at the battle of Alexandria were in the second line. In 1810 they were engaged in the capture of the Isles of France and Bourbon, three years later being ordered to America, where they experienced some sharp service. In the Mahratta War of 1818—19 the 89th served with great distinction, and the Burmese campaign of 1824 added yet more to their Eastern laurels. Under Colonel Godwin they fought in the attack at Prome, in which the mystic Burmese Amazons found that their charms—magical—were no proof against the bullets of the British soldier, though their charms feminine secured tender, gentle treatment for the poor girl who fell into our hands, wounded to death. After the Burmese War the 89th were employed in various uneventful duties till the Crimea, when they joined the Third Division, and served with the heroism common to all our soldiers in the painful and dangerous duty in the trenches. Then came the time of the Indian Mutiny, during which, though not actually engaged in the more stirring scenes, their presence in the great Peninsula tended greatly to strengthen the position of the British authority. After another interval of comparatively uninteresting quiet, we find the 89th well to the fore in the Egyptian campaign of 1884, when they were represented in the force under Sir Gerald Graham. At El-Teb they were on the right of the square; at Tamai they were in the First Brigade under Buller, which, while the Second—which

* Colonel Laurent Archer. The official records of the regiment were lost.

had been leading—was thrown into temporary confusion, came on " in perfect order, and with the steadiness of troops on parade." The incidents of the recent Egyptian campaign are too recent to need any detailed reference here: it only remains to be said that the 89th ably performed their share of this, the latest warfare in which they have been called upon to take part.

THE ROYAL IRISH REGIMENT,* consisting of the old 18th Foot, was raised in 1684 from various companies of pikemen and musketeers which had previously to that date been on the Irish establishment. After King James's abdication, the regiment underwent a complete change in its *personnel*, twice as many officers and men leaving as remained.

The 18th fought throughout the Irish campaign; then, in 1602, took part in the expedition to Ostend, and the following year joined the Allied Armies in Flanders. At the siege of Namur they particularly distinguished themselves, planting their colours on the breach. For their " conspicuous valour " on this occasion they received the title of " The Royal Regiment of Foot of Ireland," and the King also conferred on the regiment the privilege of bearing his own arms, " The Lion of Nassau," on its colours (on which the Cross of St. Patrick had previously been displayed), also the " Harp in a blue field and a Crown over it," and the motto, " Virtutis Namurcensis Præmium." They fought at Venloo, Ruremonde, and Liege. At Schellenberg they had fifty-one of all ranks killed and wounded; they shared in the operations which led to the fall of Huy and Limburg, of Rayn and Ingoldstadt. At Blenheim they fought with marked determination and valour, leaving on the memorable field sixty-one killed, and numbering in their ranks a hundred and four wounded, as witnesses to the stubborn nature of the fray. At Ramillies they were " for some time spectators of the fight, but at a critical moment they were brought forward," and joined in the mighty effort which overthrew " the forces of France, Spain, and Bavaria." Many are the fierce skirmishes and sieges in which the gallant 18th participated, of which the names and objects alike are now forgotten, but in dealing with a regiment possessing such a record, we can but refer to the more memorable engagements in which they took part. At Oudenarde they were under the

* The Royal Irish Regiment bear as badges the Irish Harp and Crown on cap, and the Arms of Nassau on the collar. The motto is " Virtutis Namurcensis Præmium " (the reward for valour shown at Namur). On the colours are inscribed "Egypt" with the Sphinx, the Dragon, superscribed "China," and the Harp and Crown, with the names of the following battles : " Blenheim," " Ramillies," " Oudenarde," " Malplaquet," " Pegu," " Sevastopol," " New Zealand," " Afghanistan, 1879—80," " Egypt, 1882," " Tel-el-Kebir," " Nile, 1884—85." The uniform is scarlet with facings of blue.

brave Cadogan in the leading brigade. Their first achievement during the day was, with three other regiments, to attack seven Swiss battalions. Three of these were made prisoners *en bloc;* "the remainder," says the official record, "were either killed or intercepted in their attempt to escape and made prisoners." The fact recorded by Colonel Stearne, who commanded the regiment at Ramillies, is somewhat remarkable: "Our regiment, though the first that engaged, had only one lieutenant and eight men killed, and twelve men wounded."

At Malplaquet, by a curious coincidence, they found themselves engaged in a sort of duel with the other "Royal Irish Regiment" which had adhered to the service of James II. The chroniclers of Her Majesty's Royal Irish Regiment describe the affair, as might be expected, as a case of "Eclipse first and the rest nowhere." Colonel Stearne, who has been before quoted, says, "We marched into the wood after them, and when we had got through we found . . . . our brother 'harpers' scouring off as fast as their heels could carry them." The 18th served with distinct renown during the remainder of the campaign, returning to England in 1715. From that date till 1775 they were not engaged in any particularly important operations—a detachment, however, took part in the defence of Gibraltar in 1727—but in the outbreak of the rebellion in America they were amongst the regiments ordered to join the royal forces under General Gage, and fought at Lexington and Bunker's Hill. Returning to England in 1776 they were employed at home, and at Jersey and Gibraltar, till the outbreak of the war with France, when they were ordered to garrison Toulon, in which service they suffered some considerable loss. They achieved great success in Corsica and Italy, and in 1800 joined Abercromby's army in Egypt, where they were brigaded under General Cradock. Under Colonel Montresor they distinguished themselves at the landing, and subsequently at Mandora, the brigade in which they were eliciting from Sir Ralph Abercromby an expression of his most perfect satisfaction with their steady and gallant conduct. These qualities they displayed in a marked manner at the final battle before Alexandria and throughout the rest of the campaign.

After the final overthrow of the French power in Egypt, the 18th were engaged for well-nigh forty years in garrison and similar duties wherever British interests required the presence of an armed force. Malta, Ireland, Jamaica, Curaçoa, St. Domingo, St. Elmo, the Ionian Islands, Corfu, Ceylon, were amongst the places where they served. With the year 1840 came the war with China, in which they gained deserved distinction. Under Sir Hugh Gough, the 18th, in August of that year, landed on the island of Amoy. Two companies of the Royal Irish, under Major Tomlinson, had been sent to make a lodgment under cover, and, before many minutes had elapsed, marched through the gate which had been opened by the storming party. At Chusan the wing of the regiment that was engaged was under the command of Major Adams, and experienced some severe fighting. "The fire of the Celestials was very heavy, and many small parties were so resolute that after the masses had fled, they stood till every man of them was shot down or bayoneted. Though their loss was great, ours was small." Shortly afterwards Colonel Mountain, with a detachment of the 18th, attacked Chapoo, an important town about eighty miles from Chusan. It did not take long to capture the place, but unfortunately some loss chequered the success. Amongst others who fell was Captain Tomlinson before mentioned, an officer of the Royal Irish, who is described by a narrator of the events as "a plain, straightforward, English soldier, an honest, gallant fellow, and much beloved in his regiment." Again at Chiang-Kiang did the British forces encounter a more stubborn resistance than is often credited to the soldiers of China, and though the fierce Tartar garrison was ultimately driven out, the 18th lost another officer, Lieutenant Collinson. In referring to the services of the Royal Irish the names of Captain John Grattan and Lieutenant Armstrong, who were reported as having distinguished themselves by their singular courage, must not be omitted.

The 18th arrived in the Crimea shortly after Inkerman, and served from that time till the close of the war. On the occasion of the attack on the Redan, in June, 1855, Captain Thomas Esmonde gained the Victoria Cross. He "repeatedly went outside the trenches and brought in wounded men from exposed positions, under a perfect storm of shot and shell. Two days later, while in command of a covering party, he perceived that a fireball had alighted close by. In another moment the position of the working party would have been discovered, but in an instant Esmonde had reached the spot and extinguished the fireball. Scarcely had he done so when a murderous fire of grape and shell tore up the ground where it had fallen."*

In 1858 a Second Battalion was formed which added yet another " distinction "—that of " New Zealand "—to the colours of the Royal Irish. Whatever may be the opinions respecting the military operations against the Maories—and they have been expressed with a candour which 'Bret Harte' would describe as " frequent and painful and free " —there can be no question as to the gallantry displayed on all occasions by the 18th. On one occasion Captain Ring, with about fifty men, was attacked by a body of the

* " The Victoria Cross in the Crimea." Major Knollys : Dean and Son, Fleet Street.

enemy three times his strength; he charged and effected his retreat to a neighbouring house which he occupied till rescued, losing four men killed and ten officers and men wounded.* A few days after, the same officer and Lieutenant Wrey, and Ensigns Jackson and Butts, distinguished themselves by rescuing a party of settlers who were surrounded by a very large force of the enemy. Within a very short period the regiment were constantly engaged, and it is difficult to select representative incidents from a history which is one continuous record of gallantry. On one occasion Ensign Dawson was left in charge of a detachment consisting of two sergeants and sixty rank and file. Before long they were attacked in the rear, and, after dispersing and pursuing their assailants returned to find their onward path occupied by the enemy. " The men were perfectly steady before an enemy which appeared in great force, remaining in skirmishing order and keeping up a steady fire." They were rescued before long, and Ensign Dawson, Captain Noblett, and Lieutenant Croft—the two latter of whom were in the relieving party—were favourably reported for their " zealous services." The " Thames " Expedition was under the command of Colonel Carey of the 18th, who had recently arrived with reinforcements, and amongst those who distinguished themselves in the engagements that followed were Lieutenant-Colonel Sir H. Havelock and Captain Baker of the Royal Irish. At Orakan, where a hundred and twenty of the regiment were engaged, Captain Ring fell mortally wounded,† and Captain Baker again showed great gallantry, while Captain Inman was recommended for favourable notice. At Nukumaru the regiment were again engaged. The chronicler before referred to says of this engagement: " Nothing like this fight had ever before occurred in New Zealand," the Maories fought with great courage and skill and evoked the admiration of our troops. Of the 18th Major Rocke, and Captains Shaw and Dawson were especially mentioned, and throughout the remainder of the campaign officers and men of the Royal Irish elicited unqualified praise for the manner in which they carried out their multifarious and dangerous duties.

The next important service in which the Royal Irish—this time represented by the First Battalion—took part was the war in Afghanistan in 1879—80, where they shared in the operations of the Khyber line, and though not participating in any of the more

* " The conduct of Ensign Bricknell and that of the men was admirable under most trying circumstances." - Sir J. E. Alexander.

† Sir J. Alexander says, " Captain Ring had mentioned previously that he had a presentiment he was to fall at this place."

stirring engagements of the campaign, well merited the addition of its memorial to their colours.

The concluding distinctions are those gained in the recent Egyptian War. Here the Royal Irish (Second Battalion) were in the Second Brigade of the First Division under General Graham. At Tel-el-Kebir they were on the extreme right of the infantry, and in the " grand advance " which the brigade made lost an officer and two men killed, two officers and seventeen men wounded. Their subsequent achievements are commemorated by the addition " Nile, 1884—85," to the distinctions they had already won.

THE ROYAL IRISH RIFLES* consist of the 83rd and 86th Foot. The former were raised in Ireland in 1793, and the following year were ordered to the West Indies, where they served, taking part in the Maroon war, till 1806. " During its short service in the West Indies the corps lost by death twenty-six officers and eight hundred and seventy men." In this latter year, according to Colonel Archer, whose *résumé*, in the absence of a published record, we have followed, the 83rd went to the Cape of Good Hope, where they took part in the operations of the force commanded by General Baird. The numerical strength of the Dutch troops was about equal to ours; they had, however, the advantage over us in artillery, having twenty-seven pieces against our eight. Their position, moreover, was strategically a strong one. The 83rd were not engaged in the actual fighting that first ensued, and further hostile action was rendered unnecessary by the surrender of the colony to the British Crown.

A short time previously to this a Second Battalion had been formed, and it was by this part of the regiment that the Peninsular renown was gained. In Portugal, where they were ordered in 1809, the 83rd were placed in Cameron's Brigade, and at Talavera gave indubitable evidence of their sterling merit. The action was a fierce one, and in it the 83rd had three hundred and sixty-six, including eighteen officers, killed and wounded; at Busaco they were under Picton, and again shared to the full in the losses and triumphs of the day; at Sabugal they joined in the splendid charge which decided the eventful struggle. They fought at Fuentes d'Onor, and remained with the other troops—'victors of a well-fought day'—when " evening closed in and Massena withdrew his broken

---

* The Royal Irish Rifles have as a badge the Irish Harp surmounted by a Crown, on glengarry. On the helmet-plate the Sphinx with " Egypt," and a bugle with a scroll, having the motto "Quis separabit," and the record of the battles, which are " India," " Egypt," " Cape of Good Hope, 1806," "Bourbon," " Talavera," " Busaco," " Fuentes d'Onor," " Ciudad Rodrigo," " Badajoz," " Salamanca," " Vittoria," " Nivelle," " Orthes," " Toulonse," " Peninsula," " Central India." Being a Rifle regiment, the Royal Irish Rifles carry no colours. The uniform is green with facings of dark green.

columns." They took part in the desperate onslaught on Ciudad Rodrigo, where the previous preparations gave to the sanguinary conflict a solemnity intensely dramatic. Within two hundred yards of the fortress had our trenches been pushed, in the pits along the glacis were the riflemen placed, while over their heads poured a continuous hail of deadly missiles on the breaches through which the attack would soon be made. An effort was made by Lord Wellington to avoid the slaughter that must ensue; he sent to the garrison a summons to surrender, receiving a reply which increased the estimation in which our foes were held by all chivalrous British soldiers. "Sa Majesté l'Empereur m'a confié le commandement de Ciudad Rodrigo," wrote General Barnier, "je ne puis pas le rendre. Au contraire, moi et le brave garrison que je commande nous nous ensevelirons dans ses ruines." Then came the Spartan direction, "Ciudad Rodrigo must be stormed to-night!" "Darkness came on, and with it came the order to 'Stand to your arms!' With calm determination the soldiers heard their commanding officer announce the main breach as the object of attack, and every man prepared himself promptly for the coming struggle, each one after his individual fancy fitting himself for action."—(*Maxwell.*) At length, by dint of terrible, magnificent fighting, the citadel was taken. At Badajoz, where the carnage was such that when it was told to Wellington, "the pride of conquest sank into a passionate burst of grief for the loss of his gallant soldiers," the 83rd were the first to rush to the assault, their bugler, though grievously wounded, sounding the "advance" as he lay helpless beside the headlong rush of furious men. The regiment lost at Badajoz forty of all ranks killed and seventy-six wounded. They fought at Salamanca; at Vittoria they lost twenty-one killed, and forty-seven wounded; at Nivelle, and Orthes, and Toulouse they added yet more to the glory they had won.

With the Peninsular War ended the career of the Second Battalion of the Royal Irish Rifles. They were disbanded in 1817, leaving to the remaining battalion a heritage of honour which has not diminished but increased in later years.

The 83rd served in Ceylon and in the operations against Candia; under Sir John Colborne they fought at St. Eustache and Prescott in the Canadian rebellion, and subsequently repaired to India, where they remained for many years. During the Mutiny they served in the Rajpootana Field Force, and gained great praise at the storming of Kotah, "a large town girt by massive walls and defended by bastions and deep ditches cut in the solid rock, a strong and stately place, standing on a wooded slope beneath which lies a vast lake, reflecting on its placid surface the domes and marble pinnacles of the splendid shrine of Jugmandul." Again they fought at Nusserabad, and the following year at Tonk, gaining "Central India" as the finishing touch to their achievements. Since that date, though continuously employed in various parts of the Empire, it has not fallen to their lot to participate in any wars of importance.

The Second Battalion of the Royal Irish Rifles is the old 86th Regiment, raised in 1793. Amongst the names of officers may be observed that of Rowland Hill, afterwards a "household word" wherever men talked of the Peninsular War, and told how, one fine December day, at St. Pierre, a certain "gallant old Shropshire gentleman, whose kind heart made him the idol of the troops," with less than 20,000 men, held at bay at least 40,000 of the veterans of Soult. The first duty on which the 86th were engaged was service as marines in some of the naval engagements which signalized the years 1795—96. In 1797 they were employed at the Cape of Good Hope, and a couple of years later sailed for India, whence in 1801 they proceeded under General Baird to Egypt. To us who have in recent recollection another campaign in the land of the Pharaohs, the accounts handed down of this war, which gained for the 86th the badge of the Sphinx, are full of interest. Three companies marched from Suez across the desert to join Hutchinson's army, and the accounts of their sufferings are wonderfully graphic in their intensity. They started with only three pints of water per man. The march was seventy-six miles through a country where "no vegetation, bird, or beast had been seen;" men and animals dropped fainting, exhausted, and dying from the ranks; the scanty supply of water was consumed ere half the distance had been done; they feared to eat lest their raging thirst should become unbearable. Yet through it all they struggled on, some, at least, surviving to join their comrades-in-arms, when they were assigned to Stuart's division.*

Returning to India the 86th won for themselves an honourable name in the Mahratta warfare which raged between 1802 and 1806, particularly distinguishing themselves at Baroda and Baroach. At the latter place the official records relate that, having learnt by experience that the bayonets were frequently seized and pulled out by their dauntless foes, the Royal Irish fixed them "by the introduction of a piece of cotton cloth." The forlorn hope at Baroach was led by Sergeant J. Moore with twelve men, followed at a short interval by Captain Richardson with a hundred more, the whole being under the command of Major Cuyler, a son of the first colonel of the regiment. Before long,

* On arriving at the end of their terrible journey, great caution had to be exercised in assuaging their thirst. Discipline and self-restraint saved the men from any evil effects; but a lurid light is thrown on the picture of what they had undergone by the fact that two horses, which broke loose, rushed to the river and drank till they fell dead.

though not without desperate fighting, the colours of the Royal Irish were waving on the walls, planted there by the gallant Moore. The dispatches of the General commanding speak in the highest terms of the distinguished courage evinced by the regiment on this occasion. At the siege of Bhurtpore in 1805, the 86th arrived after a forced march, eager, as British soldiers ever are, to "be in at the death." Their appearance was suggestive of the well-known aphorism of the melancholy Jacques— "Motley's the only wear!" As Colonel Archer puts it, their costumes might well have shocked a fashionable tailor; we read that "their worn-out uniforms were patched with various colours, or replaced by red cotton jackets; many of the men wore sandals in the place of shoes, and turbans instead of hats; but beneath this outward war-worn appearance the innate courage of Britons still glowed."* And good need was there for this innate courage, for Bhurtpore was no castle of cards manned by puppets, but "a maiden fortress amazingly strong both naturally and artificially, and garrisoned by a numerous and well-organized army. At last our cannon made a breach, and under Captain Grant a party of the Royal Leinsters—as the 86th were then styled—penetrated within the walls and captured eleven guns. But still the fortress held out, and, so far as material result went, the assault had failed, though so highly did Lord Lake think of the gallantry of the 86th, that he directed the captured guns to be placed outside their camp. Another assault was ordered under Brigadier Monson, in which the 86th again took a conspicuous part. Owing to the plan of the fortress only small parties of the besiegers could mount at a time, and these were met by "discharges of grape, logs of wood, and pots filled with combustible materials," which effectually prevented the top of the breach from being attained, and compelled Lord Lake to abandon the idea of carrying Bhurtpore by storm.† The blockade that followed was more effectual, and the Rajah sued for peace; on the establishment of which the 86th returned to their headquarters from which they had been absent five years, spent in the most arduous and eventful service, and had lost ten officers and over a thousand rank and file.

In 1806 the regiment formally received the territorial appellation of the Leinster Regiment of Foot. After a few years of comparatively quiet service in India—though the quietest times were stirring enough in those days—the 86th joined, in 1810, the expedition under Commodore Rowley and Colonel Keating against the Mauritius. Here—at

---

* Official Records.
† The various attempts cost the besiegers no less than 3,100 of all ranks.

the capture of St. Denis—they again obtained "particular praise" from their leader, not a little of which was due to a singularly gallant action performed by Corporal Hall. This brave fellow, at a time when the shot flew thickest and the fighting was most stubborn, "climbed the flag-post under an incessant fire of round shot and bullets, and fixed to the top the 'King's colours' of the Royal Leinster." When Horatius plunged, all with his harness on his back, into the foaming Tiber, Macaulay tells us that—

> "All Rome sent forth a rapturous cry,
> And even the ranks of Tuscany
> Could scarce forbear to cheer."

In this case the "ranks of Tuscany," or rather of "la belle France," had no thought of forbearing, but vied with their foes in cheering to the echo the brave soldier of the 86th who had held life so cheap and the fame of country and regiment so dear.*

In 1818 the "County Downs"—which title they received in 1812—were engaged in numerous petty skirmishes in the fatally unhealthy country of Candia, and the following year returned to England. They had been absent twenty-three years, and of all that left its shores in 1796 only two individuals now returned. Seven years later they went to the West Indies, dividing their time during the years preceding the Mutiny between this country and India. During the Mutiny they did most sterling service under Stuart in the Mhow Brigade; Poonah, Belgaum, Goa, Mundisore, and Guzerat being amongst the places where they fought. They stormed and captured Chandari; at the battle of the Betwa they crowned their previous record with a chaplet of glory. A company of the regiment was ordered to take a gun, which, at very short range, was playing upon them. Some, probably many, deaths must have occurred had not Adjutant Cochrane galloped up and single-handed dispersed the gunners. Later on, in an attack made by the regiment on the enemy's rear-guard, the same officer had three horses shot under him. A few days later three men of the 86th gained the Victoria Cross. Captain Jerome and Private James Byrne seeing Lieutenant Sewell— also of the 86th—lying in an exposed position dangerously wounded and helpless, rushed out of cover and brought him back, Byrne receiving a wound on the arm while doing so. Subsequently Captain Jerome again distinguished himself at the storming of Jhansi and at the battle of Calpee, where he was severely wounded. On the same two occasions another private—James Pearson—gained the coveted decoration "for valour." At Jhansi he attacked, single-handed, a party of rebels, three of whom he put *hors de*

* Hall was immediately promoted to the rank of sergeant.

combat; at Calpee, Michael Binns was lying desperately wounded in the open, when Pearson, at imminent risk of his own life, brought him in under a heavy fire. The 86th shared in the victorious action at Gwalior, and in some of the remaining actions that completed the pacification of the country, and returned to England in 1859, since which date they have not participated in any important campaign.

THE BUFFS (EAST KENT REGIMENT),* consisting of the 3rd Foot, have, like one or two other regiments, a history considerably anterior to their appearance on the English establishment. As in all such cases, so especially with the Buffs, this history extends over the period in which were enacted some of the most dramatic scenes in history; in which individual and national fame sprang into being with the leap and the shout of a war-god; when in all parts of the known world the love of adventure, the dauntless courage and endurance, the lordly masterfulness of the Anglo-Saxon were proving with a logic keen as the swords and halberds with which it was enforced his right to domination and power. It is from the "spacious times of great Elizabeth," when

> "We sailed wherever ship could sail,
> We founded many a mighty state,"—

that the Buffs date their origin, though for many years before that the embryo of the gallant corps had existed in the train-bands of the City of London. In 1572 one Sir William Morgan, with a band of Englishmen, fought under Ludwig of Nassau against the hosts of Spain. Later on a namesake of his, Captain Thomas Morgan, raised, with the tacit approval of the cautious Elizabeth, a company of three hundred men out of the various London guilds. From one or both of these Morgan-led bands are the Buffs lineally descended. Years went by; the band of English warring in Holland waxed and waned in numerical strength, but waxed ever in fame and honour; the names of those who have made history—Essex, Vere, Sidney, William Russell, Leicester, and Stanley —are found amongst its leaders or warriors; and the deeds they did, with what valour they fought, with what courtesy they lived and moved, with what brave, old-fashioned piety they died, read like a chapter from some enchanting romance that the reader can scarce believe—and yet knows, and is the better and prouder for know-

---

* The Buffs have as badges the Green Dragon on cap and the White Horse of Kent on collar. The mottoes are "Invicta" and "Veteri frondescit honore." On its colours are the Dragon and the Rose and Crown, with the names of the following battles:—"Blenheim," "Ramillies," "Oudenarde," "Malplaquet," "Dettingen," "Douro," "Talavera," "Albuera," "Pyrenees," "Nivelle," "Nive," "Peninsula," "Punniar," "Sevastopol," "Taku Forts," "South Africa, 1879." The uniform is scarlet with facings of white.

ing—is all unvarnished historical truth. Doubtless the heritage of all this is the nation's, but doubtless, too, in an especial manner is it the possession of the Buffs.

A goodly-sized book might be filled with the record of the various battles in which these English soldiers of fortune taught the world anew how mighty was the nation that brought forth such sons, but anything beyond a passing reference to the warfare of the time would be foreign to our present purpose.

Before passing on to the period when "The Holland Regiment" became more intimately connected with purely British service, we are fain to record, in the words of an eloquent writer,* some details of the battle of Zutphen, in which the English fought so splendidly. Five hundred Englishmen, amongst whom were some of the flower of the nobles, found themselves "face to face with a compact body of more than three thousand men. There was but brief time for deliberation; notwithstanding the tremendous odds, there was no thought of retreat. Black Norris called to Sir William Stanley, with whom he had been lately at variance, 'There hath been ill blood between us; let us be friends together this day, and die side by side if need be for her Majesty's cause.' 'If you see me not serve my Prince with faithful courage now,' replied Stanley; 'account me for ever a coward. Living or dying, I will stand or lie by you in friendship.' As they were speaking these words the young Earl of Essex, General of the Horse, cried to his handful of troopers, 'Follow me, good fellows, for the honour of England and England's Queen.' As he spoke he dashed, lance in rest, upon the enemy's cavalry, overthrew the foremost man, horse and rider, shivered his own spear to splinters, and then, swinging his curtel axe, rode merrily forward. The whole little troop, compact as an arrow-head, flew with an irresistible shock against the opposing columns, pierced clean through them, and scattered them in all directions. . . . . The action lasted an hour and a half, and again and again the Spanish horsemen wavered and broke before the handful of English. Sir Philip Sidney in the last charge rode quite through the enemy's ranks, till he came upon their entrenchment, when a musket ball from the camp struck him upon the thigh, three inches above the knee. Although desperately wounded in a part which should have been protected by the cuisses which he had thrown aside, he was not inclined to leave the field; but his own horse had been shot under him at the beginning of the action, and the one upon which he was now mounted became too restive for him, thus crippled, to control. He turned reluctantly away, and rode a mile and a half back to the entrenchments, suffering extreme pain, for his leg was dreadfully shattered. As he passed along

* Mr. Motley, "History of the United Netherlands."

the edge of the battle-field his attendants brought him a bottle of water to quench his raging thirst. At that moment a wounded English soldier, 'who had eaten his last meal at the same feast,' looked up wistfully in his face, when Sidney instantly handed him the flask, exclaiming, 'Thy necessity is even greater than mine.' He then pledged his dying friend in a draught, and was soon afterwards met by his uncle. 'Oh, Philip,' cried Leicester in despair, 'I am truly grieved to see thee in this plight.' But Sidney comforted him with manful words, and assured him that death was sweet in the cause of his Queen and country. Sir William Russell, too, all blood-stained from the fight, threw his arms around his friend, wept like a child, and, kissing his hand, exclaimed, 'Oh, noble Sir Philip ! never did man attain hurt so honourably or serve so valiantly as you.'" Thus died Philip Sidney, leaving an example which other officers of the Buffs in after times have followed, not once or twice or with faltering purpose, but often and gladly as beseemed English gentlemen and soldiers.

After many other battles in which the Regiment of Holland took part, but which, as has been observed, it would be impossible in our present limits even to enumerate, the regiment came to England, after the Peace of Munster (1648), and were placed on the English establishment seven years later.* After their adventurous career for the past three-quarters of a century, the first years of service in England must have seemed singularly dull to the bold spirits of the Holland Regiment. Gradually that name sank into desuetude, as the veterans of the Holland service died out, and in 1689, when the incorporation of the 3rd Foot into the Guards advanced the Buffs to their present numerical rank, they received the title of "Prince George of Denmark's Regiment of Foot." † The custom of the historians of the day was, however, to designate a regiment by the name of its colonel, and the Buffs were accordingly known by the honourable title of Churchill's Regiment, the brother of the great captain himself being their commander. They soon went abroad to the neighbourhood of their early achievements, and at Walcourt showed that the years of peace had in no way lessened their martial aptitude. They fought at Steenkirke and at Landen, where they suffered so severely that active measures had to be taken to recruit them. While in the neighbourhood of Ghent, the official record relates that General Churchill, Colonel of the Buffs, had an alarming adventure. During an

---

* The official record of the Buffs thus commences its history :—"This distinguished regiment is the representative of that renowned body of British Troops who fought in the glorious cause of civil and religious liberty in the Netherlands during the reigns of Queen Elizabeth, King James I., and King Charles I."

† About this time the distinctive uniform of the regiment was "red lined with ash, with ash-coloured laced hose and stockings."

inspection, he, with two or three other officers and about a dozen men, halted for a short time at a roadside house. Almost directly afterwards it was surrounded by the French: half the guard were killed, and the other half kept up a gallant fire from the windows. Churchill trying to escape was taken prisoner, " and plundered of his money, watch, and other valuables. While the marauders were engaged in sharing the booty, he stole away under cover of a hedge and succeeded in safely reaching the allied army. The small band left in the house defended themselves for some time, but reinforcements for the enemy constantly coming up, abandoned the unequal struggle and surrendered." The Buffs took part in the expedition under the Duke of Ormond against Vigo, where the allies captured two men-of-war and eleven galleons, worth about 7,000,000 pieces of eight. Soon after occurred the famous battle of Blenheim, the first distinction the Buffs bear on their colours, followed, eighteen months later, by Ramillies. At the latter battle the Buffs, led by the son of their colonel, made a most brilliant charge. They were posted upon a rising ground; "beneath them raged the battle with varying fortune, until the genius of the British leader and the valour of his troops extorted a reluctant victory. The enemy were driven back and fell into terrible confusion. At this important crisis Lieutenant-Colonel Churchill proved himself worthy of his descent. Placing himself at the head of his Buffs, followed by Lord Mordaunt's regiment, and five squadrons of dashing sabres, he swept down the slope, crossed a morass which lay in his way, passed the Little Ghent, clambered up the steep hill beyond, and crashing with musket and bayonet into the enemy's left flank, drove three regiments into a miry hollow, where most of them were captured or slain." * At this period of their career, when by Royal order the colours of English regiments received the addition of St. Andrew's Cross, " Prince George of Denmark's Regiment," says the official record, " was permitted to display a dragon on its colours, as a regimental badge, as a reward for its gallant conduct on all occasions. The dragon, being one of the supporters to the Royal Arms in the time of Queen Elizabeth, also indicated the origin of the corps in Her Majesty's reign."

They fought at Oudenarde; at Malplaquet, "Marlborough's last great victory, and his most decisive as well as his most sanguinary," the Buffs were in the thick of the fighting, suffering so much that again they were forced into retirement to await the arrival of recruits. It is recorded that during the battle, when the retreating French were being pursued through the wood and fiercely disputing every step, the Duke of Argyll,

* Adams, " Famous Regiments."

then Colonel of the Buffs, "threw open his waistcoat to show his men that he was no better provided with armour than themselves." It was about this time that the regiment acquired the title of "Buffs," the facings being changed to that colour. They fought at Dettingen, at Fontenoy, and Falkirk—at the last-named battle almost turning defeat into victory, and when obliged to retire showing a marked difference from the confused stampede of many of the other troops. Lord Stanhope, quoted by Mr. Adams, thus speaks of the demeanour of the Buffs: "Theirs was a retreat, and not like their comrades, a flight; they marched in steady order, their drums beating and colours displayed, and protected the mingled mass of other fugitives." They fought at Laffeldt, at Guadaloupe, and Belle Isle. Then followed the American War of Independence in which they were actively engaged, and in which, especially at Ewtaw Springs, they were conspicuous for their valour. "The British Force," writes the historian before quoted, "was far inferior in numbers to the American army. . . . . About nine o'clock on the morning of September 8th, the attack commenced. It was delivered with valour; it was withstood with patience. A fierce swift fire of musketry ensued, and then the Buffs took to the bayonet, driving back the troops opposed to them for a considerable distance, until, advancing too far, they exposed their flanks to the enemy, suffered a sharp loss, and retired to their original position." Seven years afterwards they joined the British Army in the Peninsula. Some of the regiment were with Sir John Moore at Corunna; the first Peninsular name on their colours commemorates the passage of the Douro, of which it has been said that "no exploit in Spain was more brilliant, grand, and successful." When the able arrangements had been made, and Wellesley's laconic, "Well, let the men cross," had given the command, the officer and twenty-five soldiers, who, as Napier says, "were silently placed on the other side of the Douro in the midst of the French Army," were soldiers of the Buffs. The gallantry of the Buffs, who, at first unsupported, had borne the brunt of the enemy's attack, was rewarded by the Royal license to bear on their colours the word "Douro." At Talavera they lost a hundred and forty-two killed, wounded, and missing. At Albuera they were well-nigh annihilated. With three other regiments they charged up the hill in the face of a seathing fire. They were rushing onward, "confident in their prowess and cold steel," when they were charged by four regiments of cavalry, and fell in scores. Then occurred some of those instances of heroic valour which are good to chronicle. "Ensign Thomas was called upon to surrender the colour he held, but he declared he would give it up only with his life, and fell, pierced with many wounds, a victim to his gallantry. The staff of the colour borne by Ensign Walsh was broken by a cannon ball, and the Ensign fell severely wounded, but he tore the colour from the broken staff and concealed it in his bosom, where it was found when the battle was over." They were engaged, having received some reinforcements—badly needed—from England, in all the operations of Hill's division, and joined the main army in time to join in the battle of Vittoria. They fought at Nivelle, a battle at which seemed present all the material required for the epic of the poet or the masterpiece of the battle painter.

"A splendid spectacle was presented," writes one whose brilliant pen seems inspired with the genius of both. "On one hand the ships of war, sailing slowly to and fro, were exchanging shots with the fort of Socoa; while Hope, menacing all the French lines in the low ground, sent the sound of a hundred pieces of artillery bellowing up the rocks. He was answered by nearly as many from the tops of the mountains, amid the smoke of which the summit of the green Atchulia glittered to the rising sun, while fifty thousand men, rushing down its enormous slopes with ringing shouts, seemed to chase the receding shadows into the deep valley. The plains of France, so long overlooked from the towering crags of the Pyrenees were to be the prize of battle; and the half-famished soldiers in their fury were breaking through the iron barrier erected by Soult as if it were but a screen of reeds." With indomitable valour the Buffs acquitted themselves that day; they bear on their colours the record of their service at Nive; at St. Pierre they formed part of the right of the army, under Byng, where at an opportune moment they checked the French under d'Aurargnac. The word "Peninsula" commemorates, as the official announcement puts it, with a not ungraceful formalism, "the meritorious exertions of the regiment on the field of honour during the preceding seven years."

Service in America—where they fought at Plattsburg—and in Canada prevented the Buffs from sharing in the victory of Waterloo, but they arrived in France in time to form a portion of the army of occupation. Passing over the next few years, during which they were quartered in New South Wales, we next find the regiment actively engaged in India. At Punniar, the twin battle of Maharajpore, the Buffs were with the force under General Grey which, "despite the fatigue of a long and toilsome march," inflicted a crushing defeat upon a large body of the Mahrattas.

They joined the forces in the Crimea in the spring of 1855, and were not consequently present at either of the three great battles—Alma, Balaklava, Inkerman—whose names we recall involuntarily when the Crimea is mentioned. But there was another engagement, almost as familiar, in which the principal *dramatis personæ* were officers and men of the Buffs. We refer to the assault on the Redan. The French were to attack the Malakhoff, and as, unless that were first secured, the possession of the Redan would be useless, because untenable, we were to wait until an agreed rocket signal should inform us that our allies had performed their part of the allotted task. Not till seven in the evening did a universal exclamation announce that the signal was made—" four rockets almost borne back by the violence of the wind, and the silvery jets of sparks they threw out on exploding being scarcely visible against the raw grey sky." A hundred of the Buffs under Captain Lewes formed half the covering party, with the scaling ladders were a hundred and sixty men of the same regiment under Captain Maude, while others were in support. Soon the stormers advanced at a run, "while the round shot tore up the earth beneath their feet, or swept men away by entire sections, strewing limbs and fragments of humanity everywhere." The officers of the Buffs were amongst the very few that survived that terrible approach unwounded. Even when our men streamed in it was impossible to retain possession. The Russians were being constantly reinforced; by some oversight our stormers were left unsupported. In vain did the Buffs and their companions fight desperately, stubbornly; they were driven out, and on the slopes and in the embrasures lay heaps of those who had given their lives in vain. But though the assault was a failure, it was a failure devoid of shame, and to many the opportunity for deeds of signal courage. Amongst these were Captain Maude, who has been mentioned as commanding the covering party, and Private John Connors. Twelve years previously Maude had fought with his regiment at Punniar, and while in the Crimea had shown himself a most able officer. On this occasion, with only nine or ten men, he had gained an important position within the works, "and though dangerously wounded, did not retire until all hope of support was at an end." For this he won the Victoria Cross. Connors won his by displaying no less intrepidity. "Fighting furiously hand to hand with the Russians, he sought to save the life of an officer of the 30th by shooting one and bayoneting another of the latter's assailants. As the body of this officer was found the farthest in the Redan of any, it is a proof that Connors was one of the foremost of the stormers."

After the Crimea the Buffs repaired to India, though not in time to participate in the suppression of the Mutiny, and their next active service was in the China war of 1860. Here they were in the Third Brigade, which formed part of the Second Division under Sir Robert Napier, and in the engagement at Sinho were the first to come into actual contact with the enemy. It was decided that the Second Division should take the chief part in the capture of the Taku Forts, and when Tangkoo had been taken, the Buffs were posted at the gates leading to the forts. About this time the Chinese began to consider the advisability of coming to terms, and, as an earnest, returned a couple of prisoners who had fallen into their hands. One of these was a sergeant of the Buffs "who had suffered such barbarous treatment at their hands as to be incapable of standing," and whose sufferings had driven him quite mad. After the fall of the forts and the capture of Pekin, the Buffs enjoyed another spell of leisure till the war in Zululand of 1879. Here they were in the first column commanded by Colonel C. Pearson, of the regiment, their immediate chief being Lieutenant-Colonel H. Parnell. They speedily tried the metal of the enemy at Inyezane, where both the officers above named had their horses shot under them. Before long Colonel Pearson was practically blockaded at Etschowe, and during the weary time of waiting the Buffs had to deplore the death from fever of Captain J. Williams. Throughout the campaign the regiment behaved in a way worthy of its traditions; and when it is remembered what the traditions of the Buffs are it would be difficult to utter greater praise.* Since 1879 the services of the Buffs have been in China, Egypt, and in England; Zululand being the last important campaign in which they have been engaged.

THE QUEEN'S OWN (ROYAL WEST KENT REGIMENT †), Regimental District No 50, is comprised of the old 50th and 97th Regiments. The former were raised in 1756, being at first numbered the 52nd, and in 1760 joined the British forces in Germany, where they took part in the battle of Corbach. A few years after that we find them serving

---

* Amongst the sobriquets of the Buffs were "The Buff Howards," from the name of the Colonel from 1737 to 1749; as a secondary source of the name it is stated that the accoutrements were made of Buffalo leather. Another name was the "Nutcrackers," the origin of which is lost; and the "Resurrectionists," from their unexpected reappearance at Albuera after the charge of the Lancers. Occasionally the regiment was known as the "Old Buffs," after King George's mistake at Dettingen had given the 31st Regiment the nickname of "Young Buffs." For this and much other information on the subject of the nicknames in the Army, the writer is indebted to the very interesting and exhaustive list compiled by Miss Pattie Osler, which, though unpublished, has been kindly placed at his service. The right of marching through the City of London with bands playing and colours flying, which the Buffs share with the Royal Marines, is probably a surviving recognition of their civic origin.

† The Queen's Own bear as badges the White Horse of Kent on the cap and the Royal Crest on the collar. The mottoes are "Invicta" and "Quo Fas et Gloria ducunt." On the colours are the Sphinx and Egypt, and the names of the following battles:—"Egypt," "Vimiera," "Corunna," "Almaraz," "Vittoria," "Pyrenees," "Nive," "Orthes," "Peninsula," "Punniar," "Moodkee," "Ferozeshah," "Aliwal," "Sobraon," "Alma," "Inkerman," "Sevastopol," "Lucknow," "New Zealand," "Egypt, 1882," "Nile, 1884–85." The uniform is scarlet, with facings of blue.

as marines during the numerous naval engagements that then occupied our sea forces, and the next land service in which they took part was the campaign in Corsica in 1794. In this it is recorded that they achieved considerable distinction, notably at the storming of the Convention Redoubt, which was taken by the bayonet alone, not a shot being fired. Bastia and Calvi also fell to their arms, and for a very short period the style of his Majesty George III. was "King of Great Britain, Ireland, and Corsica." After a few years of varied duties, the Queen's Own were ordered to Egypt, where their services at Aboukir, Cairo, and Alexandria gained the distinction of the Sphinx. Another interlude, and then followed the Peninsular war, where the 50th were to reap so rich a harvest of honours. At Vimiera the 50th *—"The Black Half Hundred" as they were called from the colour of their facings—inflicted a crushing repulse upon the French. The latter were rushing on with seemingly resistless force, having driven in the skirmishers, when they found themselves face to face with the Queen's Own—"a regiment which had won renown in Egypt by its unflinching coolness. The volley of the 50th at close quarters broke the head of the column; and then leaping with their bayonets upon front and flank, the regiment forced the shattered ranks over the edge of the parapet" (Clinton). The odds against the Queen's Own in this battle were more than five to one, the figures given by Archer being five thousand French against nine hundred of the 50th. At Corunna they, with the 42nd, bore the brunt of the battle. At Elvina, "Well done, the 50th! well done, my majors!" exclaimed Moore with elation, as he saw Napier and Stanhope at the head of their regiments force back the foe into the village. "Entering the streets of Elvina with the routed and disordered masses of the French, without giving them a moment of respite, the two victorious regiments drove them out, still fighting, on the other side." Then owing to some misunderstanding, the bulk of the 42nd halted, and with only the grenadier company of the latter regiment, the gallant 50th pressed on—*quo fas et gloria ducunt*. Of the two majors apostrophised by Moore, one—Stanhope—fell mortally wounded; the other—Napier—"surrounded by a hundred bayonets, was denied quarter, yet he fought like a lion till five pierced him, and he was rescued at last by a gallant French drummer." When the fleet stood out to sea with the British army, saved from annihilation by the genius

---

* Also called the "Blind Half Hundred" from the number of their ranks that suffered from ophthalmia in Egypt; the "Dirty Half Hundred" from the marks made when the men wiped their streaming faces with their black facings; and, in recognition of their courage at this battle, subsequently called "The gallant Fiftieth."

of its commander, a hundred and eighty-five of the Queen's Own remained in solemn companionship with the leader who, in the deserted citadel—

"lay like a warrior taking his rest."

The 50th fought at Fuentes d'Onor; at Almaraz they shared with the 71st the honours of the day. "The grey dawn was just stealing in .... and the garrison of Fort Napoleon, crowding on the ramparts, were gazing on the portentous signs of war, when quick and loud a British shout broke on their ears, and the 50th Regiment with a wing of the 71st came bounding over the low hills." The forlorn hope commenced its attack, and straightway Captain Candler of the 50th paid with his life the toll of that fearful passage. The stormers would not be denied. A berme jutting out proved to them no obstacle: "they leaped on the berme itself, and drawing up the ladders planted them anew." They fought gallantly at Vittoria, Bayonne, and Nivelle; at Orthes they charged to the rescue of a body of Portuguese troops, and "by the vehemence of their assault," the Queen's Own and another regiment* "hurled back the French upon their reserves."

They were not at Waterloo, and in 1819 were ordered to Jamaica. There was no actual warfare to be engaged in, yet during that year the 50th lost eleven officers and two hundred and fifty-six men, and a few months later again nearly half that number from illness.† After a sojourn in New Zealand they were ordered, in 1842, to India, and distinguished themselves at the battle of Punniar. It is recorded, as exemplifying the courage and *morale* of the regiment, that a corps under Lieutenant Crosse, which had been left invalided at Cawnpore, "marched fifty-three miles in twenty-four hours in their endeavour to be in line with the regiment on going into action." They fought at Moodkee in 1845, and at Ferozeshah, where they captured two standards. At Aliwal they suffered severely, being the only British regiment in Wheeler's irresistible brigade, which swept on "like a scarlet flood, charging with the bayonet through fire and smoke, carrying guns and everything before it." At Sobraon their gallant charge was spoken of with enthusiastic praise. Passing over the next few years, the Queen's Own found a field for their prowess in the Crimea. They arrived early, and were fully engaged in all the arduous work in which the Third Division, to which they belonged, was employed. They were not actually engaged at the Alma; at Inkerman, where they were the only regiment of their Division present, they lost eleven killed and sixteen wounded. After the

* The 92nd.   † Archer.

Crimea the next important service for which they were detailed was the campaign in New Zealand. Here they acquired great distinction by their gallant conduct in a style of warfare which calls forth and keeps in tension all the faculties of endurance, resource, and individual courage. Particularly were these qualities exhibited at an engagement at Rangiawhia, where the 50th, under Colonel Weare, were at the head of the column. "The word being given, the 50th, ably led by Colonel Weare, dashed, under a heavy fire, at the enemy's position, in a manner worthy of the reputation of that distinguished corps." The construction of the enemy's works, however, prevented their being captured by this form of attack, and " Colonel Weare accordingly ordered a small storming party of twenty men, under Lieutenant White, of the 50th Regiment, to break cover, in the first instance, to endeavour to draw out the first fire of the enemy. This party was almost simultaneously followed by the stormers, consisting of Nos. 1 and 10 companies of the same regiment, under command of Captain Johnston and Captain Thompson respectively, and these officers entered the enemy's work at the head of their men, at the same time closely followed by the remainder of the regiment." After this action the Queen's Own were specially thanked "for the brilliant manner in which they had assaulted the enemy's position." Later on, the 50th were moved to Wanganui, during the march to which they had some sharp encounters. Lieutenant Johnston was killed, Lieutenants Wilson and Grant very severely wounded, and there fell of the rank and file fifteen killed and thirty wounded.* Though they were frequently engaged ere peace was restored, the 50th did not meet with many more casualties, the total during the campaign being nineteen killed and thirty-three wounded.

Space forbids our dwelling on the details of their subsequent services; we must pass on to a period within the memory of all, when the campaign in Egypt afforded another opportunity for the troops engaged to confirm the reputation in which they were held. The Queen's Own were in Sir Gerald Graham's brigade of the First Division, and took part in the second action of Kasassin, a detachment under Lieutenant Maunsell being present at Tel-el-Kebir. They shared in the Nile Expedition of 1884, furnishing their quota to the mounted infantry force. In this capacity they were represented at Abu Klea and Metemneh. Of the many names of officers and men of the West Kent which occur frequently through the reports of the campaign we can mention but those of Major Smith; Captain Morse, who was wounded at Metemneh; Captain Maunsell, who

* At this time Colonel Waddy of the 50th had been appointed Brigadier-General; Colonel Weare, Major Locke, and Captain Leach, were mentioned as having distinguished themselves.

commanded the English Camel Corps in the Nile Expedition of 1884—85; and Captain Alderson, who served all through the campaign, embellishing the record of the last few months by gallantly saving from drowning a private of the regiment, for which action he was awarded the medal of the Royal Humane Society.

The Second Battalion of the Queen's Own West Kent Regiment is the 97th, formerly the "Earl of Ulster's." The present 97th only dates from 1824, though there have been no fewer than five regiments which have borne that number, some of which had served in Egypt, in the Peninsula, and in the famous defence of Gibraltar. The first years of existence were uneventful for the 97th, but at the Crimea they had opportunities for showing that they were no whit behind the veterans of Abercromby, or Elliott, or Wellington. On the occasion of a sortie, on the 22nd of March, 1855, three columns of Russians "came suddenly upon the men in our advanced trenches, and rushed in upon them on the right with the bayonet before we were quite prepared to receive them. When they were first discovered they were close at hand, and on being challenged, replied with their usual shibboleth, 'Bono Franciz.' In another moment they were bayoneting our men, who had barely time to snatch their arms and defend themselves. Taken at a great disadvantage, many of them roused suddenly out of sleep, and pressed by superior numbers, the 17th and 97th, guarding the trenches, made a vigorous resistance, met the assault with undaunted courage, and drove the Russians out at the point of the bayonet, but not until they had inflicted on us serious loss, not the least being the death of the good and gallant Captain Vicars of the 97th" (Russell). It was on this occasion that John Coleman, a sergeant of the 97th, gained the Victoria Cross. When the Russians made their first onslaught, the suddenness of the attack drove the working party, with whom Coleman was, back. He, however, remained till "all around him were killed or wounded," and when at last he did retreat he bore back with him one of his officers who had received his death wound. On the occasion of the attack on the Redan, the 97th were again singularly distinguished. Colonel Handcock, who led them, fell dead, but they pressed on, accompanied by a few men of the 90th Regiment, "but they were too weak to force the breastwork, and had to retire behind the traverses." They suffered heavily, though perhaps not more than might have been anticipated, having in view the desperate character of the assault; the loss being four officers and one man killed, and three officers and forty-eight men wounded. "Among the severely wounded was Captain Charles Lumley. He was one of the first inside the Redan, and immediately on entering found himself engaged with three Russians loading a field-piece.

He shot two of them with his revolver, but was then knocked down by a stone. Stunned for the moment, he soon recovered himself, drew his sword, and was in the act of cheering on his men, when he was severely wounded by a ball in the mouth. For his conduct on the occasion he received the Victoria Cross and a brevet majority" (Knollys). After the Crimea the 97th were dispatched to India, where the Mutiny was raging, and where they gained the distinction of "Lucknow." Amongst the more important actions in which they participated were the relief of Lucknow, and the fierce assault on the Kaiser Bagh. In 1881 they were engaged in the campaign in South Africa, forming part of the Natal Field Force, and in common with other regiments contributed their quota to the mounted infantry corps which did such good service in Egypt at the battles of Abu Klea and Metemneh.*

THE KING'S OWN SCOTTISH BORDERERS †—Regimental District No. 25—is composed of the 25th Foot. Until quite recently the title of the regiment was "The King's Own Borderers," the localising epithet being added in 1887, and being a return to the distinctively Scottish element in its nomenclature. "The regiment," says Murray, "was raised in the City of Edinburgh by the Earl of Leven, in 1688, from amongst the noblemen and gentlemen who had come over from the continent as the adherents of William, Prince of Orange." This account would seem to give a somewhat unduly aristocratic character to the corps, which (another writer says) was raised out of a number of Cameronians. Tradition, as Archer designates it—which, however, is followed by most historians of the regiment—declares that it was raised to its full strength of a thousand men in *four* hours! Their first employment was the blockade of the Castle of Edinburgh, their next the battle of Killiecrankie. Here, according to Mackay, who was in command of King William's army, they, with Hastings' troop (afterwards the 13th Regiment), acquitted themselves like Milton's Abdiel—

"Faithful found
Amongst the faithless, faithful only they."

"There was no regiment or troop with me," writes the indignant General, "but behaved

* The nickname of the 97th was "The Celestials," from the colour of their facings—sky blue; they being the only regiment which had that colour.

† The King's Own Scottish Borderers bear as badges the Castle of Edinburgh on a St. Andrew's Cross within a thistle wreath, with the Royal Crest on the cap; and the Castle of Edinburgh on the collar. The mottoes are "Nisi Dominus frustra," "In Veritate Religionis confido," and the Guelphic motto, "Nec aspera terrent." On the colours are the White Horse, and the Sphinx with "Egypt," and the names of the following battles: "Minden," "Egmont-op-Zee," "Martinique," "Afghanistan, 1878—80."

like the vilest cowards in nature, except Hastings' and Lord Leven's, whom I must praise at such a degree as I cannot but blame others." They then served in Ireland —at Galway, Athlone, Aughrim, and other places—and then exchanged, what was at best but civil war, for service on the continent. At Steenkirke they behaved with great gallantry, but were nearly annihilated. At Landen they again acquitted themselves with brilliant courage; at Namur the explosion of a mine still further reduced their shattered ranks, no fewer than twenty officers and five hundred men being killed.

The mention of "Namur" recalls "my Uncle Toby" and the unfortunate wound which he received during the siege, and it may be of interest to note that both Uncle Toby and Corporal Trim were real characters, having their originals in Captain Sterne (the author's uncle), and Corporal Butler, both of the Edinburgh Regiment. An incident which throws a light on the comparative simplicity of warlike tactics in those days is quoted by Murray from Grose's "Military Antiquities," and as it refers to an occurrence which befell the 25th it may not be out of place to reproduce it here. "In an engagement, during one of the campaigns of King William III. in Flanders, there were three French regiments whose bayonets were made to fix after the present fashion, a contrivance then unknown in the British Army; one of them advanced with fixed bayonets against Leven's regiment, when Lieutenant-Colonel Maxwell, who commanded it, thinking the enemy meant to decide the affair point to point, ordered his men to 'screw bayonets;' but to his great surprise, when they came within a proper distance, the French threw in a heavy fire, which for a moment staggered his men, who, nevertheless, recovered themselves, charged, and drove the enemy out of the line." At Sheriffmuir, which was the next engagement of importance in which the Edinburgh Regiment took part, the Hon. Captain Elphinstone went over to the Jacobite forces, a defection, however, which did not in any way influence the fortune of the day.* They took part in Lord Cobham's expedition against Vigo in 1719, and fought at Fontenoy and Culloden, at the latter place particularly distinguishing themselves. The chronicler before quoted describes how a body of three hundred men of the 25th occupied the Castle of Blair. The men were immediately posted in the way most favourable for defence, with strict orders not to fire unless actually attacked—a somewhat necessary precaution seeing they only had nineteen rounds of ammunition per man. "For the protection of a new, unfinished building, to which the only communication from the castle was by ten or twelve steps of a ladder from a door in the east end, a platform of loose

* Thirty years later the Hon. Arthur Elphinstone, then Lord Balmerino, was executed on Tower Hill.

boards was hastily laid on the joists, and Ensign Robert Melville (afterwards General Melville), of the 25th Regiment, with twenty-five men, was posted on it, who was not relieved during the whole of the blockade, which ended 1st April," having commenced on the 17th of March. Major Murray goes on to quote, from the biography of the General Melville above mentioned, that Lord George Murray, General in the Stuart Army, " wrote a summons of surrender to Sir Andrew Agnew, which he could not find a Highlander to deliver, on account of the well-known outrageousness of Sir Andrew's temper, but a pretty girl, who was acquainted with the garrison, undertook the task, but could scarcely find an officer to receive it, for the reason before mentioned ; however, after much entreaty, one was bold enough to carry the summons, when Sir Andrew, in so loud a voice that he was heard distinctly by the girl outside the castle, desired him to be gone, and tell Lord George that the ground would before long be too hot for him to stand upon, and any future messenger would be hanged or shot if sent upon such an errand." Red-hot shot were fired upon the devoted garrison, which " were lifted off the floors by an iron ladle, and deposited in the cellars in tubs of wine, as water could not be spared ! " Eventually the garrison was relieved and the detachment of the 25th " thanked in public orders for their steady and gallant defence."* Returning to the Netherlands they were in time to share in the charge which prevented the defeat at Roncoux from degenerating into a rout; at Laffeldt, or Val, they " bore a prominent part with equal credit," capturing two French standards, which, Archer says, " used to adorn Whitehall, but have long since disappeared."

Passing over the few following years, during which the Edinburgh Regiment were employed in the skirmishing descents then in vogue upon the coast of France, we come to 1759, in which year the 25th, despite their more than usually arduous services, won their first distinction at Minden. Here, under Waldegrave and Kingsley, they were with the brigade which attacked the left wing of the French Army, where its most renowned troops and generals—the black and grey Mousquetaires, the Carabineers, and other *corps d'élite* under Prince Xavier of Saxony—were stationed. " The guns of the enemy opened a tremendous fire, which rent terrible chasms in the brigades of Waldegrave and Kingsley," the cavalry charged with their accustomed fury, but were met by such a storm of hurtling lead from the impenetrable British regiments that they

---

* The biographer of the gallant general is responsible for the following assertion :—" A Highland pony which had been seventeen days (without food) in a dungeon of the castle, being still alive, was recovered by care and proper treatment, and became in excellent condition."

retired in confusion. The 25th suffered very severely during this campaign, "their loss at the battle of Campen alone amounting to two-thirds of their number." When peace was restored the regiment enjoyed *otium cum dignitate* for many years.

In 1782 occurred what one Scottish writer terms a "petty quarrel" with the Lord Provost of Edinburgh, the result of which was that they ceased being known as the Edinburgh Regiment. In recognition of the circumstances of their incorporation, the regiment had always claimed and enjoyed the privilege of recruiting in the streets of the city at any time "without asking leave of the Lord Provost." In 1781, however, the Provost for the time being refused this privilege, and, according to Murray, the Duke of Richmond, whose brother, Lord George Lennox, was the colonel of the 25th, applied that the regiment should be called the Sussex Regiment. Archer adds that the regiment was at that time stationed at Goodwood, and that the change of title being very unpopular, Lord George Lennox strongly opposed it, and retained the distinctive national customs.* The territorial title of Sussex Regiment accordingly died out, and the title of the King's Own Borderers was bestowed by George III. himself, at the same time that his Majesty "conferred on it the Badge of the King's Crest, with an accompanying motto chosen by himself." The 25th shared in the latter part of the famous defence of Gibraltar, and afterwards did most excellent service as marines—in which capacity they on one occasion assisted in the capture of a treasure-ship "containing about one million sterling"—and gloriously terminated their marine career by the famous fight of the glorious 1st of June, off Ushant. The year following, the 25th were ordered to the West Indies, and at Granada evoked universal praise for their heroic conduct. The particular combat in which they so distinguished themselves has been described as "one full of the most gallant actions to be found in the records of our army." They had ample ground for fighting well and fiercely. It was not long before the defence of Pilot Hill that the Governor of Granada, a former officer of the 25th, had been "shot in cold blood in the presence of his wife and daughter, together with forty-seven other white inhabitants, by the brigand chief." The regiment under Major Wright had been "reduced by disease and the sword to about a hundred and thirty officers and privates, yet refused to yield, well knowing the ferocious character of the enemy with whom they had to deal. At length exhausted, and without the means to sustain life or longer maintain the post, they determined to break through the enemy, which they successfully accomplished, joining the few British that yet remained in St. George's, the capital, where they were

* The privilege has been subsequently revived and confirmed.

THE 68th—DURHAM LIGHT INFANTRY

hailed by the inhabitants as the saviours of the island, the ladies, in token of their appreciation of such valour, wearing ribands round their wrists inscribed, "Wright for ever!"

The 25th joined the British army in Egypt towards the close of the campaign of 1801, and six years later went to the West Indies. The name Martinique recalls their share in the capture of the island of that name, where they remained on garrison duty for some few years. An incident which is related of Colonel Light, then in command of the regiment, may be recommended to the notice of those who register annals of "hairbreadth 'scapes." One night the Colonel was riding home when he was caught in a terrific thunderstorm, which raged with all the violence peculiar to the locality. His horse took fright at a flash of lightning, and sprang over "a precipice fifty-four feet deep into a river considerably swelled by the rain. The horse was killed by the fall, but Lieutenant-Colonel Light swam on shore with very little injury, and walked home to his barracks, a quarter of a mile distant from the place." Their duty at Martinique prevented the King's Own Borderers from sharing in the triumphs of the Peninsular campaign, though a second battalion (which was disbanded in 1816) "was in garrison at Antwerp during the Waterloo campaign." The 1st battalion returned to England the year after that decisive battle, and for the ensuing ten years or so were engaged in various home duties in the United Kingdom. They again served in the West Indies during the years from 1826 to 1834, and found plenty of work provided by the ferment and excitement consequent on the freeing of the slaves. For the next thirty years no very important fighting fell to their share. From Colonel Archer's *résumé* we learn, however, that their duties were diverse and often arduous, at one time imposing upon them the care of convicts in New South Wales, at another a skirmish with the Boers at the Cape, at another obedience to perpetual letters of route, orders and counter-orders, which kept them in a state of transition between Madras, Hongkong, Singapore, and Ceylon. In the year 1864 they were engaged in crushing the waspish Fenian raid into Canada, and fourteen years later earned the latest distinction on their colours by sharing in the Afghanistan campaign of 1878—80.* Here they were with the division under General Bright—the Khyber Line Force—and that under General Maude—the Peshawur Valley Field Force. Since that time the King's Own Borderers have not been engaged in any warlike service.†

* The 1st battalion.
† The only sobriquet which seems to be known for the 25th is "the K. O. B.'s"—from the initial letters of their title.

The KING's ROYAL RIFLE CORPS,* consisting of the famous 60th Foot, and having four line battalions, dates from 1755, when it was raised in America, and known as the "62nd Loyal American Provincials."

The first strength of the regiment was four battalions, but this number was very speedily augmented as the value of the corps became recognised. A very considerable minority of the strength was composed of Swiss and German Protestants, who, it was considered, were naturally hostile to the French; but none of the foreign officers were allowed to attain a higher rank than that of lieutenant-colonel. The first Colonel-in-Chief was the Earl of Loudoun, and it is worthy of note that the King's Royal Rifle Corps, and the Rifle Brigade, are the only infantry regiments the chief officers of which are denominated Colonel-in-Chief and Colonel-Commandant.† The "Loyal Americans" were not long numbered 62, as the following year the disbanding of two regiments raised them to their present numerical position. Their first active employment was in 1757, during which they were engaged at Charlestown, on the Canadian frontier, and at the serious "affair" of Port William Henry. The following year gained for them their first "distinction," which commemorates the share they had in the second expedition against Louisbourg. Nor was Louisbourg the only scene of their prowess in 1758. Six companies were with the British force that met with so severe a repulse at Ticonderoga; they are the only regiment now in existence which was represented at the siege of Fort Duquesne; they fought at Kingston and Prince Edward's Island. In 1759 they fought under General Prideaux at Fort Niagara; some of the regiment were with Sir Jeffery Amherst; others again were with Wolfe, when on the heights of Abraham he gained Canada for the British Crown and died in the gaining. Here they so distinguished themselves that, according to tradition, the gallant Wolfe himself bestowed on them their motto, *Celer et Audax*. It does not seem that there exists any positive record of this fact, but the wording of the Order which in 1824 gave special permission for its resumption bears out the theory. Apparently the motto had fallen into desuetude for some time, and representations were made to the authorities

* The King's Royal Rifle Corps have as a badge a bugle on the glengarry. On the helmet plate is a bugle with strings on a Maltese Cross with the motto "Celer et Audax." On the cross are the names of the following battles:— "Louisbourg," "Quebec, 1759," "Roleia," "Vimiera," "Martinique," "Talavera," "Busaco," "Fuentes d'Onor," "Albuera," "Ciudad Rodrigo," "Badajoz," "Salamanca," "Vittoria," "Pyrenees," "Nivelle," "Nive," "Orthes," "Toulouse," "Peninsula," "Punjaub," "Mooltan," "Goojerat," "South Africa, 1851—53," "Delhi," "Taku Forts," "Pekin," "South Africa, 1879," "Ahmad Khel," "Kandahar, 1880," "Afghanistan, 1878—80," "Egypt, 1882—84," "Tel-el-Kebir." The uniform is green with scarlet facings.

† The Household Cavalry have the former officer, and the Royal Artillery the latter. Another distinctive feature of the King's Royal Rifle Corps is that no fewer than six Acts of Parliament have been passed concerning it.

with a view to obtaining official recognition for it. This was duly given by the order referred to, which ran as follows : " Sir,—I have the honour to acquaint you, by direction of the Commander-in-Chief, that His Majesty has been pleased to permit the 60th Regiment, 'the Duke of York's Own Rifle Corps,' to resume the motto *Celer et Audax*, which was formerly worn by the regiment in commemoration of its distinguished bravery whilst employed with the British army in North America, under Major-General Wolfe, in the year 1759." While on the subject of Quebec the following fact, described by Captain Wallace as a "curious and noteworthy coincidence," may be noted. "The 2nd and 3rd battalions of the 60th, as part of the *first* English garrison of Quebec, were present in September, 1759, when the British ensign was hoisted over the citadel by an officer of the Royal Artillery; and in November, 1871, one hundred and twelve years afterwards, a detachment of the 1st battalion of the 60th, the remnant of the *last* English garrison of Quebec, consigned the imperial flag to the keeping of another artillery officer, while the flag of the Dominion of Canada was hoisted in its stead."

They fought at Martinique under Monkton ; under Albemarle they shared in the conquest of Havannah ; in Florida, St. Vincent, and throughout the troublous American quarrels they were always to the fore. Again, in 1794, were the 60th represented at the capture of Martinique by the force under Sir C. Grey ; they fought at St. Lucia and Guadaloupe ; with their old leader, General Abercromby, they performed good and arduous service in the West Indies ; and in 1798, forty-three years after their institution, performed their first duty within the United Kingdom, sharing in the stern repression of the Irish rebellion in that year. The following year they took part in the unsatisfactory invasion of Holland, and not long after joined Sir Charles Green's expedition against Surinam. Captain Drummond, of the regiment, with a naval officer, was directed to demand submission from the governor, which, though then refused, was tendered very shortly after. Then followed the long struggle of the Peninsular War, from the blood-red battle-fields of which the 60th reaped a rich harvest of renown. It is to the 5th battalion, raised in 1797 and disbanded in 1817, that the King's Royal Rifle Corps of to-day owe their Peninsular distinctions. It was a glorious twenty years of existence that that 5th battalion—drawn from the foreign corps of Hompesch and Lowenstein—enjoyed. They were not novices in the art of war, these new recruits, and required little preparatory training for the career which was opening before them. At the skirmish at Obidos, which preceded the battle of

Roleia, the 60th gave earnest of the fierce enthusiasm which they showed throughout the war, their eager pursuit, indeed, on this occasion, exposing them to some danger. At Roleia they were with the centre column; at Vimiera they and the 95th fought side by side. In the course of these battles of 1808, one of the corporals, named John Schwalbach, particularly distinguished himself, and by order of Sir Arthur Wellesley was transferred to one of the Caçadore regiments. His subsequent career may be cited as another proof that promotion is not closed to the rank and file, for he rose to be a general officer in the Portuguese service, and to be ranked amongst the nobility of the land. At this time, too, general officers were directed to "pay particular care and attention to the companies of the 5th battalion, 60th Rifles, serving under them; they will find them to be most useful, active, and brave troops in the field." Though the name does not appear amongst their distinctions they were specially thanked for their conduct at the passage of the Douro; they fought at Salmunda, leading the attack in conjunction with the Household Brigade; at Talavera "the steadiness and discipline of the 60th (and the 45th) were conspicuous," and were undoubtedly the salvation of Wellesley and his staff, whom the collapse of some troops which had not been under fire before placed in considerable danger. At Busaco the headquarters were with Picton, and they greatly distinguished themselves, though, by an unfortunate oversight, no mention was made of them in despatches. Great was the chagrin, for if any troops had deserved eulogistic mention undoubtedly the 60th had, and Colonel Williams brought the matter to the notice of General Picton. In reply he received the following letter, which, coming from such a man as the writer, went far to make amends for the disappointment:

"*October* 10*th*, 1810.

"MY DEAR SIR,

"On reading over the *Gazette* account of the action of the 27th ultimo at Busaco, I was much disappointed and concerned not to find your name among those of the commanding officers of corps in the Third Division who were particularly noticed on that occasion.

"You cannot have any doubt of my sentiments, as they were expressed in the Division Orders of that day; yet I must take the blame to myself for the omission, having neglected to make a written report of the circumstances of the day to his Excellency, the Commander of the Forces, who, being present on a commanding situation, and immediately contiguous to that part of the position defended by the Third Division, I conceived to be fully acquainted with the merits and services of each particular corps; but on reflection I find the position you defended (with the Light Corps of the Division) with so much gallantry for so many hours, was so situated that he could not, probably, have seen your situation or witnessed your exertions; but you may be assured that I will take an early opportunity of mentioning to his Lordship that no commanding officer of any corps had more claim to public notice on that occasion than yourself.

"I am, dear Sir,

"Your faithful servant,

"THOS. PICTON."

At Fuentes d'Onor the General commanding spoke highly of the 60th, their position being "defended in the most gallant manner by Lieutenant-Colonel Williams of the 5th battalion." Valiantly did the three companies present at the sanguinary conflict of Albuera acquit themselves; at Arroyo dos Molinos a company was in each of the columns commanded by Colonel Stewart and General Howard respectively, and Captain Blassiere of the regiment earned the distinguished approbation of General Hill. The 60th was in the leading brigade at Ciudad Rodrigo, though they fortunately escaped with small loss; at the terrible assault of Badajoz Colonel Williams was again pre-eminent for his courage, even amongst the crowd of heroes that fought and died in that awful "space of less than a hundred yards square," and Lieutenant-Colonel Fitzgerald was killed at the head of his men. At Salamanca some of the 6th battalion were in the Third Division under Pakenham, and shared in that memorable charge which has been described as "one of the most perfect movements made in battle." The French General, Marmont, "with sanguine expectation still looked for victory, until Pakenham shot with the Third Division, like a meteor, across Thomière's path; then pride and hope alike died within him." Others of the regiment were with "Hulse's noble brigade," which forced the French dragoons to give place to the infantry of Britain. Heavy was their loss at Salamanca, and heavy again at Vittoria, but immeasurably great the meed of glory the British troops won ere the close of that day, which saw, effected by their prowess, "the wreck of a nation." At the passage of the Adour we read that "the 60th Rifles and the Light Infantry of the Guards began to fight; all were deliberate and cool. . . . . Three different times had they turned the head of the attack, and at last the enemy retired." Amongst their distinctions is the word "Pyrenees," telling of the continuous fighting which occupied the British Army during the latter part of July, 1813.

They fought at Nivelle, the Nive, and Orthes, and shared in the final conflicts of Toulouse and Bayonne. "In a blaze of useless bloodshed died out the Peninsular War, and the 60th Rifles, who with the 95th had opened the war in 1808 at Obidos, saw it fairly (or rather unfairly) completed at Bayonne." And thus, too, ended the connection of the 5th battalion of the 60th Rifles with the Peninsular War, in which the British army "had won nineteen pitched battles and innumerable combats; had made or sustained ten sieges and taken four great fortresses; had twice expelled the French from Portugal, once from Spain; had penetrated France, and killed, wounded, or captured two hundred thousand enemies, leaving of their own number forty thousand dead, whose bones whiten the plains and mountains of the Peninsula." In 1817 the 5th battalion was disbanded, leaving the heritage of their Peninsular honours to the regiment.

In 1826 the 60th were represented in the expedition to Portugal under General Blakeney, and from that time till 1846 their career was a comparatively uneventful one. In the latter year the 1st battalion went to India, and were subsequently engaged in the Punjaub and at the battles of Mooltan and Goojerat, at the latter place being under Colonel Bradshaw. Then they were engaged against the Euzuffzie tribes, and in 1850 found themselves, under the leadership of the gallant Colin Campbell, warring against the turbulent Affreedees. In another part of the world—namely, in Kaffirland—the 2nd battalion, under Generals Sir H. Smith and G. W. Cathcart, were meeting other savage foes no less brave and cruel than the wild mountaineers of India. In the attack on the Waterkloof the 60th were in the centre column, commanded by Colonel Mitchell, and under Captain the Hon. A. Hope and Major Bedford signally distinguished themselves, with fixed swords driving the enemy "right over the krantzes with terrible loss, taking 560 cattle and 75 horses." They were not at the Crimea, but, fortunately for the Empire, were in India during the Mutiny, and perhaps none of the gallant regiments, to whom our countrymen and women owed so much for their conduct in that awful struggle, are held in more affectionate and grateful remembrance than are the "gallant 60th." On the outbreak of the Mutiny they were at Meerut, and by their gallant behaviour effectually overawed the mutineers, of whom there were three regiments present. Subsequently they shared with the Carabineers the honour of dispersing some mutinous sappers and miners who, happily for us, fell to disputing between themselves. "The dispute waxed so hot," we read, "that at last it required the intervention of Captain Frazer, the officer commanding them, but he had barely spoken when he fell mortally wounded by a musket ball. On this the whole company broke and dispersed or fled towards Delhi, but were overtaken by parties of the 6th Dragoon Guards and 60th Rifles, who cut down or shot most of them. The scenes in Delhi and elsewhere had hardened the hearts of our men, and daily they were becoming less and less inclined to encumber the stations with prisoners." During the siege of Delhi they gained immortal credit. Under Brigadier Wilson they advanced from Meerut, and two companies were ordered to keep possession of an important bridge. On these companies the mutineers, "every man of whom knew that he fought with a halter round his neck," poured a devastating artillery fire, so two more companies of "the gallant 60th" were sent forward. "Led by Colonel Jones, the Rifles charged with unexampled fury and captured the guns, bayoneting the 'pandies,' as they named them, beside the limbers and wheels; but at that moment an ammunition waggon blew up and killed four privates and Captain Francis Andrews, an officer who had served with the 60th at Moultan, Goojerat, and the expulsion of the Afghans beyond the Khyber Pass." Yet their ardour was irresistible. The words of one present at the time give a graphic picture of the sentiments which actuated our soldiers. "Our blood is fairly roused! We have seen friends, relations, mothers, wives, and children brutally murdered, and their bodies mutilated frightfully. This alone . . . . would enable us, with God's assistance, to be victorious. As the Riflemen charge, *ten to a hundred*, the word is passed, 'Remember the ladies! Remember the babies!' Then everything flies before them, and hundreds are shot down or bayoneted. The Sepoys, it is true, fight like demons; but we are British and they are natives." During the siege a hundred or so of the rebels ensconced themselves in a serai, where they imagined they would be in security. But they calculated without the 60th, a party of whom dashed in and bayoneted every man. "So fierce was the fury of our men that in many instances the sword bayonets on their short Enfield rifles were twisted and bent by pinning the enemy against the stone walls."

Space will not allow of our following in any detail the events of the siege; but as illustrating the brilliant share borne in it by the 60th, it may be mentioned that no fewer than seven Victoria Crosses were won by them. Sergeant Stephen Garvin volunteered with a small party to dislodge a force of the enemy from a position whence they were seriously annoying our batteries. "He accomplished his purpose, but only after a severe contest." Private Thompson won his cross in one of the fierce skirmishes that took place under the walls. A party of fanatics surrounded Captain Wilton of Thompson's company. "Several men rushed to their officer's assistance, but Thompson was first on the spot and slew two of the enemy before his comrades came up." "Bugler

William Sutton behaved with conspicuous gallantry throughout the siege of Delhi. On the 2nd of August he particularly distinguished himself. The enemy made a formidable attack on our position, and Sutton, who was in the advanced trenches, saw one of the rebel buglers in the act of sounding. Fired, perhaps, with professional jealousy, Sutton rushed to the front and killed the bugler before he could produce a note. The action, however, which specially earned him the cross took place on the night before the assault. It was considered desirable to ascertain the state of the breach. The service was one of desperate peril, but Sutton volunteered to perform it, and, providentially, returned unwounded. He was elected by the privates of his regiment."* Lieutenant Heathcote, Sergeant Waller, and Privates Divane and Turner, also won the coveted decoration by their splendid courage in the face of overwhelming danger. The following year, during the Rohilcund campaign, the 60th further distinguished themselves. Baga-Wallah, Nuguna, Bareilly, Shahjehanpore, Shahabad witnessed their prowess; † and again with the Oude Field Force they performed most sterling service. At Bareilly, we may remark *en passant*, Private Bambrick of the 60th gained a Victoria Cross. Being attacked by three mutineers at once, he disabled one and kept the others at bay, receiving, however, two wounds. After the termination of the Mutiny proper the disturbed state of the country found them plenty of employment, and, under Generals Seaton and Troup, and Colonel Dennis of the regiment, they added to the renown already achieved.

General Seaton, in his interesting reminiscences, gives the following account of an action which took place near Bunkagong in October, 1858, and which reflects not a little to the credit of the 60th:—"The moment our artillery commenced firing the enemy's cavalry moved forward on both flanks; and as soon as they got within seven hundred yards, I made the 60th and the 82nd try the power of their Enfield rifles on them. I was watching the cavalry on the left, for it was the largest body by far. They were coming round the end of the morass, to get into our rear, by the road on our left. As soon as they got clear of some intervening trees, the light company of the 82nd began to fire on them, and we could see the men's heads and shoulders, and here and there a horse's head, above the cultivation in the fields. The effect of this fire was curious. The impetuous horsemen suddenly pulled up and looked about, astonished and alarmed at the storm of bullets raining upon them, they knew not whence, and hitting them with such force. The noise, confusion and jumble in their ranks, horses rearing and

---

* "Victoria Cross in India." Knollys. Dean & Son, Fleet Street.
† Some of the 2nd battalion shared in these exploits.

stumbling, and men falling, presented such a scene as is rarely witnessed, and in almost as short a time as I have taken to describe it, the whole mass turned and fled.

"Our guns had silenced their opponents, the cavalry on the right had been dispersed by the 60th, and the Sepoys disappeared through the village, their artillery going off to the left after the main body of their cavalry. I now advanced into the village, but with great caution at first, and in the middle of it came upon an old fort that looked as if it had been recently repaired. As the morning sun was at the moment shining in our eyes, we could not see whether this stronghold was manned or not, but as we advanced within shot, and it did not open fire, I concluded that it was deserted, which, on entering it, I found was the case. I now sent the 60th with their guns to sweep round the village to the right, and ordered the Europeans, the whole of the cavalry, and the remaining three guns, in pursuit of the rebels, following with the 82nd and the 12th Punjaub Infantry in the same direction, but sweeping round to the left. We soon joined the 60th Rifles, who had dispersed everything before them in the shape of parties of rebels."

The North China campaign of 1860 next engaged their services, the 2nd battalion forming part of the second brigade of the First Division. In the attack on Taku the 60th were on the right of the advance, the direction of which lay across a deep moat, forty or fifty feet wide. "In plunged the brigade and sank as deep as their waist-belts in the most vile and odious of slush, but boldly they struggled onwards, dragging and assisting each other till all reached the road." At the storming of Tangku the 60th vied with the French who first should be in, a contest which, according to Swinhoe, resulted in favour of our men, though our allies claimed the distinction for themselves. The regiment served with its customary valour throughout the rest of the campaign, and at the seizure of Pekin, on the conclusion of peace, they remained for a time to garrison the Taku Forts.

Omitting the less important services of the next few years, we find the 1st battalion taking part in the Red River Expedition in 1870, under Sir Garnet Wolseley. The fact that this expedition involved no actual fighting must not in any way detract from the very high praise due to the troops engaged. The distance to be traversed was some six hundred miles, only forty-eight of which partook at all of the nature of a road. The march is described as being "through a trackless wilderness, without any transport animals, but only manual labour, and across lakes and rivers with rapids not less difficult than those of the Nile and requiring equal skill for their passage. There were no less than forty-seven 'portages,' across which everything had to be 'portaged' on men's backs, and the latter part of the route, that by the Winnipeg River, was known to be so difficult and dangerous that none but experienced guides could attempt it." Add to these circumstances the fact that for half of the fourteen weeks occupied in the march rain fell in torrents, with the result that, as Sir Garnet Wolseley put it in his General Order—" on many occasions every man had been wet through for days together," and enough has been said to show how arduous and desperate was the task in which the 60th shared. The next important service on which they were engaged was the Afghan War, when the 2nd battalion, under Colonel Algar, were with the field force commanded by Sir Donald Stewart, and took part in the battles of Ahmed Kheyl, Ghuzni, and Kandahar. The 3rd battalion meanwhile was engaged in South Africa, and fought at Guighlovo, Etschowe, Ulundi, and the Ingogo River. In the relieving column which was despatched by Lord Chelmsford to the relief of Etschowe, the 60th were in the Second Division, commanded by Lieutenant-Colonel W. C. Pemberton, of the regiment. On arriving at Guighlovo, the Rifles were in the front of the lager, and by their example stimulated the other troops to bold resistance. Lying down behind a low breastwork, they were unseen by the enemy, who came on, ten thousand strong, in all the pride of their savage war bravery. A terrible fire greeted them when they came within 300 yards, yet they rushed on over the prostrate and falling bodies of their fellows. "Beaten back twenty times, these brave fellows rushed forward twenty times with greater fury than ever." Yet "their attack on the face held by the 60th was completely and signally repulsed, and Lord Chelmsford rode along the line complimenting the Rifles on their behaviour." So complete was the repulse, so cool and valiant the demeanour of the regiment, that when the other sides of the lager were in their turn furiously attacked, "even the youngest soldiers," writes Major Ashe, in his account of the campaign, "seemed to gain skill and inspiration from what they had seen performed by the 60th." Amongst the losses incurred that day by the British was that of Colonel Vernon Northey, of the King's Royal Rifle Corps, who, despite a severe wound, never left his men till he fell fainting from loss of blood. "At the close of the action, however, and when he was roused from his state of insensibility by the ringing cheers of the British, which proclaimed the flight of the enemy, he suddenly raised himself on one hand and joined in the shouts of the men, thus bursting the bandaged wound and causing violent hæmorrhage to recommence." This brave enthusiasm sealed his doom; in four days the brave soldier, who had shared in the regiment's struggles and glories in the Oude campaign, died, to the great grief of officers and men alike.

On the reorganization of the troops effected by Lord—then Sir Garnet—Wolseley, the 60th, under Major Tuffnell, were attached to Colonel Clarke's column, which was ordered to re-occupy Ulundi, and on the conclusion of the war were quartered in Natal. In the Boer campaign they were also engaged and were with Sir George Colley's force at the unfortunate affair on the Ingogo River, where—or, rather, in retreating from which—Lieutenant Wilkinson, a most popular officer, lost his life by drowning in the swollen river, "which he was supposed to have re-crossed with a view to succour the wounded." Besides Lieutenant Wilkinson, the Rifles lost Lieutenants Garrett and O'Connell, "who fell in the gallant performance of their duties." In the Order issued the day following the battle, Sir George Colley speaks with high admiration of the conduct of the 3rd battalion, 60th Rifles, whose unflinching steadiness and discipline under fire, and perfect order, coolness, and spirit with which the night march was carried out, were worthy of any veterans. He also specially recognised the distinguished conduct of "Sergeant-Major Wilkins, 3rd battalion, 60th Rifles, who was to be seen wherever the fire was hottest, setting an example of cheerful gallantry, and cool, steady shooting." After the terrible disaster of Majuba Hill those of the Rifles present were fortunate enough to fight their way back to camp without losing a single officer. None of them were, however, actually engaged in defence of the hill, but two companies—those above mentioned—covered the retreat, and General Wood expressed himself as "perfectly satisfied with their behaviour."

When war broke out in Egypt the 60th were represented by the 3rd battalion in the divisional troops of the Second Division, commanded by General Hamley. At Kasassin Lieutenant C. B. Piggott, of the regiment, commanding the Mounted Infantry, was wounded; in the second engagement at the same place they captured a gun. At Tel-el-Kebir the Rifles were with General Ashburnham's brigade, in support of the guns under Colonel Goodenough, and before long were ordered to the support of the Highland Light Infantry, which was engaged in a fierce struggle at one of the redoubts. None of the 60th were killed in this action, but twenty non-commissioned officers and men were amongst the wounded. After the termination of the first phase of the war, the regiment remained to garrison Cairo, and so were on the spot when the subsequent operations became necessary. They then, under Colonel Ogilvie, joined the expeditionary force to relieve Tokar, and on the occasion of the battle of El-Teb were in the first brigade with the Irish Rifles and Gordon Highlanders. Amongst the killed at this battle was Quartermaster Wilkins, the same brave soldier who was mentioned in General Colley's Order for his gallantry at the Iugogo River. At Tamai, where they were hotly engaged, Lieutenant Scrope Marling, of the regiment, serving with the Mounted Infantry, gained the Victoria Cross for the heroic manner in which, at the imminent risk of his own life, he rescued a wounded private. They fought at Tamanieh and at Abu Klea; and with the Egyptian campaign closes the record of the more important events in the career of the King's Royal Rifle Corps.

THE LANCASHIRE FUSILIERS* consist of the two battalions of the famous 20th Regiment. Raised in 1688 by Sir John Peyton, the regiment served under the renowned Gustavus Hamilton at the battle of the Boyne and throughout the remainder of the Irish War. After that fratricidal quarrel they served in the West Indies† and Portugal, in the latter country winning golden opinions by the splendid stand they made at Caza. They served at Gibraltar and in Flanders, winning the first of their distinctions at Dettingen, where they fortunately incurred but small loss; which immunity, however, did not attend them at Fontenoy, where, amongst other officers and men, they lost a lieutenant-colonel. They were at Culloden, where one of their Majors was appointed aide-de-camp to General Hawley. This Major was James Wolfe, the hero of Quebec, and the mention of whose name invariably and rightly recalls the deeds of the famous 20th Regiment, with which he was so intimately connected. The colonel of the regiment at this time was Lord George Sackville, whose subsequent military career was in marked contrast with that of Wolfe. In 1757 they took part in the expedition against Rochefort, their commander there being Colonel Kingsley, by whose name—Kingsley's Regiment—the 20th were so long and honourably known. The splendid charge made by the brigades of which the 20th formed part lives in the history of the times.

"Pressing onward with a conquering violence the British brigades became exposed to the fire of the enemy's musketry, but nothing could stop them. Elevated by success and confident in their own prowess, they followed up the advantages they had already

---

* The Lancashire Fusiliers have as badges the Sphinx in a laurel wreath on a grenade, with the word "Egypt" on cap, and a grenade on the collar. The motto is that of the Garter. The uniform is scarlet, with facings of white and fusilier's cap. On their colours are the Sphinx, superscribed "Egypt," "Dettingen," "Minden," "Egmont-op-Zee," "Maida," "Vimiera," "Corunna," "Vittoria," "Pyrenees," "Orthes," "Toulouse," "Peninsula," "Alma," "Inkerman," "Sevastopol," "Lucknow."

† We learn from the regimental Record that one of the soldiers of Captain S. Clair's company proved to be a female.

gained and drove the French cavalry out of the field. Two brigades of French infantry endeavoured to stem the torrent of battle, but they were broken and dispersed. A body of Saxon troops made a show of coming down upon the British regiments, but they were soon put to flight. The enemy's line gave way, a general confusion among the French regiments followed, and the numerous legions of France were driven from the field, with the loss of forty-three pieces of cannon, ten pair of colours, seven standards, and many officers and soldiers."

The heavy loss—six officers and eighty men killed, eleven officers and two hundred and twenty-four men wounded—caused the Commander-in-Chief to direct in a General Order that "Kingsley's Regiment of the British line, from its severe loss, will cease to do duty." The 20th, however, were not the class of soldiers to care for this exemption, petitions against it poured in to Prince Ferdinand, and two days after, the Order just quoted was followed by another: "Kingsley's Regiment, at its own request, will resume its portion of duty in the line." They shared in the glories of the Seven Years' War, fought desperately at Warbourg, took part in the battles of Zierenberg, Kirchdenken, and Groebenstein, and in the capture of Wesel. Then, after a comparatively peaceful interlude, they were ordered to America, where they bore a full share in the checkered fortune of our troops. At Stillwater we read that the stress of the action lay upon the 20th, and that they incurred severe loss. At Saratoga they were commanded by Lieutenant-Colonel Lind, and with the rest of the British army capitulated on honourable terms, which, however, were basely broken by the American Congress. It was agreed that they should be permitted "a free passage from Boston to Europe, upon condition of their not serving again during the war." This part of the compact was evaded on "the meanest and most futile pretences," and "the brave soldiers who had fought so gallantly, and who did not submit till surrounded by five times their number, were detained in America" (*Regimental Records*). Their next service was in the West Indies, in the fierce guerilla kind of warfare against the Maroons; and during the two years that they spent there their numbers were reduced by the fatal climate to six officers and seventy men. In 1799 the 20th—then called the East Devonshire Regiment—joined the expedition despatched to the Helder under General Abercromby. At Crabbendam they particularly distinguished themselves. "Lieutenant-Colonel Smythe, who commanded, evinced something of Spartan firmness. Perceiving that the enemy were likely to carry his post, notwithstanding that the blood was flowing copiously from a wound in his leg, he desired some of the soldiers to support him, and in this situation he brandished his sword and cried, ' 20th, remember Minden!' The names of Wolfe and Kingsley and the memory of Minden were treasured then as now by the East Devonshire. Three hearty cheers were given, and both battalions rushing on with the bayonet scattered the foe like chaff before the wind." Well might the gallant Abercromby report of them, that "the two battalions of the 20th did great credit to the high reputation that regiment has always borne." Then followed the battle commemorated by "Egmont-op-Zee." The description of the scene of conflict reads almost like a prose paraphrase of the account of that "great battle in the West," where—

> "On the waste sand by the waste sea they closed.
> * * * *
> A death-white mist swept over sand and sea:
> Whereof the chill, to him who breathed it, drew
> Down with his blood, till all his heart was cold.
> * * * *
> For friend and foe were shadows in the mist.
> . . . . . and in the mist
> Was many a noble deed, many a base,
> And ever and anon with host to host
> Shocks, and the clash of brands, and shrieks
> After the Christ of those who falling down
> Look'd up for Heaven and only saw the mist."

The loss of the 20th who were in the brigade of General Don was very severe. A few months later, and we find the regiment in Egypt, where, at Alexandria, Lieutenant-Colonels Smith and Clepham with the regiment carried the enemy's outposts in most brilliant style. They then served for some time in Naples and Calabria, and gained the well-merited distinction of Maida. They only landed on the morning of the battle from Messina, and arrived on the field at a running pace when the fight was raging at its hottest. The French cavalry were making a gallant and formidable charge on our exhausted troops, when Colonel Ross with the 20th poured in such a destructive fire that the dragoons were almost annihilated. The loss to the regiment was only one man, Captain McLean, who was the only officer on the British side killed during the action. In 1808, under Lieutenant-Colonel Campbell, they joined the forces in Portugal, and at Vimiera formed part of Acland's Brigade, where they shared in the victory, which, if followed up, would have proved incalculably effective. Here, it has been well said, "Napoleon had found a people who hated without fearing him; and in the English his soldiers had encountered enemies who repelled their fiercest attacks, or assailed their strongest posts, with equal ardour and success." At Vimiera they fought in the full confidence of winning. The reply given by General Anstruther to the aide-de-camp who offered to send troops to his assistance was eminently representative of the feeling which actuated officers and men alike. "Sir," said the General, "I am not pressed; I want no assistance; I am beating the French, and am able to beat them wherever I find them." The next great battle in which the 20th were engaged was Corunna, the story of which has often been told, after which they returned to England, joining the army in the Peninsula again in 1812. Here they were brigaded with the 7th and 23rd Regiments and attached to the 4th brigade under General Lowry Cole. They fought at Vittoria, Pampeluna, and Roncesvalles, at the last-named place acquitting themselves with "great gallantry," and incurring heavy loss. At Roncesvalles, where Soult was exerting all his powers to frustrate the strategy of the British, Napier relates that "a wing of the 20th Regiment and a company of Brunswickers, forming the head of Ross's column, had gained the Lindouz, where suddenly they encountered Reille's advanced guard. The moment was critical, and Ross, an eager, hardy soldier, called aloud to charge, whereupon Captain Tovey of the 20th ran forward with a company, and full against the 6th French Light Infantry dashed with the bayonet. Brave men fell by that weapon on both sides, yet numbers prevailed and Tovey's soldiers were eventually pushed back. Ross gained his object, the remainder of his brigade had time to come up and the pass of Atalosti was secured, with a loss of one hundred and forty men of the 20th Regiment and forty-one of the Brunswickers." Two captains and about twenty men of the regiment were with the storming party at St. Sebastian; the 20th took part in the battle of Bidassoa, "by which the invasion of France was successfully inaugurated;" at Nivelle and Nive they added still further to their honours. At Orthes again we read of their "great gallantry," and how they captured two of the enemy's guns, and themselves lost heavily in the action; at the dubious battle of Toulouse they earned well their meed of the praise which lauded the "indomitable courage of the British soldier." With Toulouse ends the record of the Peninsular triumphs of the 20th; they returned to England where they remained for some five years. During the Waterloo Campaign they were in Ireland, being subsequently sent to St. Helena as part of the guard over the fallen potentate, the might of whose victorious armies they had so often assisted to crush. The following anecdote relating to their sojourn there is related by Barlow in his "Orders of the 20th Regiment":—

"Dr. Arnott, Surgeon of the regiment, was called in during Napoleon's last illness, and remained in constant attendance on him till his death; and on one occasion, when urging him to take some medicine, said, 'You must, sire!' Napoleon immediately replied—'Oh, doctor, that is the way, I suppose, you deal with the sick men in the Hospital; you should be kind to them, for there are no better soldiers in the world. Now I am on the subject I will make a present to your regiment, and I don't think I can send one more acceptable than the life of one of your greatest generals." When at last the restless spirit of the great Napoleon passed away, his body was carried to its temporary resting-place by twelve grenadiers of the 20th Regiment.

The regiment next spent some years in India, returning home in 1837. At the coronation of Her Majesty they were the senior regiment then in England, and as such had the honour of being stationed at the Abbey during the ceremony. Their next notable service was at the Crimea, when they were attached to Cathcart's—the Fourth Division. The names of Alma, Inkerman, and Sevastopol tell of their service there. At Inkerman they suffered severely. In the charge led by Sir George Cathcart in the valley of the Tchernaya, Lieutenant Dowling of the regiment met his death. When the Guards retired from the Sandbag Battery, where they had fought so gallantly, they were reinforced by a wing of the 20th under Major Crofton. "Another gallant effort to regain the redoubt was made by the 20th and 47th. Of the former slender corps 200 men had just come in from the trenches, after twenty-four hours of exposure and rain; but the bugle called all to the front—500 strong. Their orders were to support the Guards, who were heavily pressed by the enemy, many of whom crouched among the brushwood but were driven down the hill. 'We killed numbers of them,' says an officer of the 20th, 'and as we had no orders to halt, we continued keeping along the hillside, about half-way down, and firing at the retreating enemy. I then heard the bugle sound to retire, and set about trying to get the men back, no easy matter, as by this time, from several regiments being sent after each other, they were all mixed up.'"

"The Fourth Division lost at Inkerman all its generals—Cathcart, Goldie, and Torrens, and seven hundred, or more than one-quarter of its strength, put *hors de combat.*" The command of the Fourth Division then devolved upon Sir Frederick Horn, of the 20th, who had been in positions of command at Alma and Balaklava, and who, during the fierce fight at Inkerman, was twice wounded, and had his horse shot under him. When at last Sevastopol fell, it is recorded of the 20th that they were the only regiment which marched into the town with band playing and colours flying. They also formed part of the expedition against Kilburn, and then, the Crimean War being at an end, returned to England, only, however, to leave it again for a more distant scene of war in India. The 20th fought at the battles of Chanda and Sultanpore and at the final capture of Lucknow, subsequently taking part in the important operations in Oude. With the Indian Mutiny ends the "record of active service" of this famous regiment, their more recent employment not being of the nature to call forth the warlike prowess of which they have given so many and memorable proofs.*

THE EAST LANCASHIRE REGIMENT†—Regimental District 30—is composed of the 30th and 59th Regiments. The former of these (the 30th) was originally raised as a marine regiment in 1702. The first colonel was Colonel Thomas Sanderson, who had gained great renown in the Low Countries. The regiment served as marines till 1814, during which period "they appear to have been with Rooke, at the capture of Gibraltar in 1704, and in the subsequent great sea-fight off Malaga. They went with Sir Cloudesley Shovel and Lord Peterborough to Spain the year after, and served at the capture and at the following defence of Barcelona. Afterwards they were at Alicant and Tortosa, and signalised themselves by a gallant but unsuccessful defence of Lerida in 1707. They were with General Wills at Cagliari in 1708; and detachments of the regiment were employed in the expedition to Nova Scotia and at the occupation of Dunkirk. Detachments afloat saw much service in the Channel, the West Indies, and elsewhere."—*Archer*.

After the peace of Utrecht they became a regiment in the regular army, being placed on the Irish establishment. During the siege of Gibraltar in 1727—28 they were engaged as foot soldiers, but a few years later we find them again serving as marines in Lord Anson's fleet, and as such sharing in the glories of the naval victory off Finisterre. The regiment then served for a time in America, on returning from which they subsequently again did duty as marines in the operations at Minorca and Malta. In Egypt, under Abercromby, we find the 30th—then called the Cambridgeshire Regiment—figuring as a purely land force. They were brigaded with the Royal Irish, the 44th, and 89th Regiments, and earned with their comrades the eloquent distinction of "Egypt, with the Sphinx." Shortly after landing, in the brilliant affair of the 13th of March, they lost an officer, Ensign Rogers, while Captain Douglas was amongst those wounded. At the

* The 20th is also known as " The Two Tens," " The Double X.'s," and " The Minden Boys."
† The East Lancashire Regiment bear as badges the Rose of Lancaster, with the Sphinx and the word " Egypt" on the cap, and the Rose on the Collar. The motto is that of the Garter. The uniform is scarlet, with facings of white. On the colours are the names " Egypt," " Cape of Good Hope, 1806," " Corunna," " Java," " Badajoz," " Salamanca," " Vittoria," " St. Sebastian," " Nive," " Peninsula," " Waterloo," " Bhurtpore," " Alma," " Inkerman," " Sevastopol," " Canton," " Ahmad Khel," " Afghanistan, 1878—80."

R R

battle in which their gallant general received his death wound, the 30th had two officers and twenty-four men wounded and four men killed, and at the siege of Alexandria, on the 17th of August, they had twenty-seven of all ranks killed or wounded. A second battalion, which was raised a few years later, served in the Peninsular campaign, and in the famous battle of Waterloo, where they suffered severely. So heavy were the losses of the regiment after Salamanca that they were ordered away to recruit, their place in the Sixth Division being taken by the present 2nd battalion, the 59th. At Waterloo the 30th were brigaded with the 33rd, 69th, and 73rd Regiments, in Count Alten's Division. It is related—as showing the decimation which the gallant regiment suffered —that at one time "the Duke sent Colonel Gordon to Sir Colin Halkett to ask what square of his that was which was so far in advance? *It was simply a mass of the killed and wounded men of the 30th and 73rd Regiments*, which his Grace had mistaken for a square." The 1st battalion found scope for its energies in the Pindaree War which followed. At the siege of Asurghur they shared with the Royal Scots the chief honours of the day.* Then, after a long period of useful but uneventful service, they joined the British army in the Crimea, and won "Alma," "Inkerman," and "Sevastopol" for their colours. They were in the Second Division under the renowned Sir de Lacy Evans, and at the Alma were on the right of the British line.

At Inkerman a gallant act was performed by Lieutenant Mark Walker, 30th Regiment. "During a critical moment of the first period of the battle, Colonel Mauleverer, with two hundred and two men of the 30th Regiment, found himself about to be attacked by some fifteen hundred Russian infantry in two battalions—one broken up into company columns, the other in support in battalion columns. Mauleverer's men, formed in line, tried to open fire, but their rifles, having been during the night exposed to the damp, would not go off. On this the men seemed disposed to waver, but Mauleverer checked the impulse, and instead of retreating advanced to the barrier, a short wall of loose stones from three and a-half to four feet high. There they lay down for a few moments, when perceiving that the enemy were already within a few yards they resolved to charge. Springing on to the wall, Mauleverer, Walker (who was Adjutant), and all the other officers, jumped down on the farther side, regardless of the storm of shot by which they were received, and without looking back to see if they were supported dashed at the enemy. Their men followed them promptly, and with a joyful hurrah sprang forward with the bayonet. Many officers and men fell, but nothing could check the onset of the

* Major Dalrymple of the regiment was in command of the reserve.

brave little band; and the Russians recoiled in disorder, hotly pursued for some distance by the eager and shouting British soldiers. For the conspicuous bravery which he displayed on this occasion, Mauleverer recommended Walker for the Victoria Cross, which was duly bestowed on him."

At the Redan, under Brigadier Warren, they particularly distinguished themselves, and were terribly cut up. After the Crimea they were ordered to Canada, in which country and in India they have been since employed.

The 2nd battalion of the East Lancashire consists of the old 59th Regiment, which dates from 1755, when it was numbered the 61st. The first service of the regiment was in the American War, during which they were present at Bunker's Hill. They took part in the famous defence of Gibraltar, and after that in the continental battles of Nimeguen, Bremen, St. Vincent, and the rest of the desultory fighting in which our troops were engaged.* They shared in the expedition under Sir David Baird in 1806 against the Cape of Good Hope, and there gained the first distinction on their colours. Their next duty was in India during the troublous times of 1806—7, from whence they were despatched to join the troops charged with the capture of the Isle of France, and the following year won "Java" as an addition to their roll of honours by their participation in the capture of that island, which at the time was considered to be "a second India."

The 2nd battalion, which was raised in view of the threatened French hostilities, had a short and stormy though creditable career. Throughout the Peninsular campaign they were employed, though it did not fall to their fortune to share in all of the more memorable actions. Yet they "fought under Moore at Corunna, and at Vittoria, at the siege of San Sebastian, at the battles on the Nive and the investment of Bayonne." They were not actually at Waterloo, being, with three other regiments, stationed at Halle. After the capitulation of Cambray the 2nd battalion of the 59th remained for a few months in Paris, and, returning to England at the close of the year, came to a premature end, as a distinct regiment, by an untoward occurrence the following January. While proceeding to Dover the transport in which the bulk of the battalion were was wrecked, only four officers and twenty-five men escaping; these, with a few survivors from another ship, were "transferred to the 1st battalion, and thus the 2nd battalion came to an end." (*Archer.*) The 1st battalion was busily engaged in the

* Colonel Archer states that, at the time of the renewal of the long war with France, the 59th were engaged in the erection of the Martello Towers on the south coast, so familiar to the holiday makers of this more peaceful age.

Mahratta wars of 1817 to 1819, and a few years later added "Bhurtpore" to the list of the regiment's honours. The 59th was ordered to lead the assault, directly the tremendous mine which had been prepared had facilitated the operation. The result of the explosion was not altogether satisfactory, but the 59th carried out the glorious task perfectly, though considerable havoc was made in the ranks by the "volleys of round shot, grape, and musketry which were fired down upon them." They were stationed in China during the time of the Indian Mutiny, and performed most valuable service at the conquest of Canton and the subsequent operations, at which they were the chief representatives of the British Army under General Straubenzel. A period of unimportant service at home and in the colonies followed, till 1878, when the Afghan War furnished an opportunity for the regiment to again distinguish itself.

In October, 1879, the 59th found themselves in fierce combat with the fierce and warlike Ghilzais. The enemy had concentrated a force, which subsequent information has proved to have exceeded three thousand men, at a place near Shahjui. It was determined to take advantage of tidings brought by a friendly native and effect a surprise. The force to whom this was entrusted was placed under command of Colonel Kennedy, and consisted of a couple of guns, ninety men or thereabouts of the 59th, and a hundred Belooches. Under the guidance of the native they came within sight of the enemy's piquet fire.

"Colonel Kennedy then ordered up a party of the 59th and another of the Belooches in support. He pointed out the fire, and directed that, without the slightest noise, they should steal forward, surprise, and take or destroy the piquet.

"Captain Sartorius was in charge of the surprise party. He silently led the way down the hill and reached the bottom, and with ever-increasing caution gradually drew near the fire, always directing his party to take advantage of the cover of tree-trunk and brushwood to hide their advance. The distance of thirty yards or so from the blazing sticks which formed the fire was reached; Captain Sartorius looked around for a moment, and saw by the dim light of the fire that his men, having crept from bush to bush, were now well about them. Another step and the blaze would expose them all. A solitary Ghilzai was pacing slowly to and fro in front of the fire; his companions lay about, their arms by their side. With a loud cry the captain sprang forward. He was swiftly followed by his men.

"In a moment Captain Sartorius was seen. A bullet from the Afghan sentry's rifle whizzed by the Captain's ear. The report aroused the sleeping men, who sprang to their feet; but the British were amongst them."

The effect of this was to give the alarm, and before long the Ghilzais threatened the slender British force in formidable numbers. A sharp cavalry combat ensued, and then once more came work, desperate, but therefore congenial, for the brave 59th.

"Colonel Kennedy directed Captain Sartorius, with his company of the 59th British Regiment, to assault and take the earthwork at the foot of the steep mound. A loud English 'hurrah!' and direct at the place this officer led his men. Within a few moments they were over the work, and the Ghilzais were streaming out of it around the back of the hill and over the country side towards the nearest villages.

"But there still remained the men who had taken possession of the castellated work at the extreme top of the mound. These were, by the slow nature of their rifle fire, not many—at most seven or eight. They could not, however, be left there to shoot upon and kill as they chose the soldiers who had taken the earthwork below.

"Again, therefore, Captain Sartorius was requested by Colonel Kennedy to capture an enemy's post, and this time the tower above him. The gallant officer cheerfully undertook the task; yet, as he did so, he knew that he had taken upon himself a desperate duty, for the party in the building were now surrounded and would die fighting to the death. He was almost certain that his own life, and perhaps nearly the whole of those who would accompany him, would be sacrificed in the attempt; still he never shrank from his order, neither did the men selected to help him. He took with him fifteen men, and then coolly commenced his serious service.

"The rock up which he began to toil was almost perpendicular on all its sides. So difficult of access was the building at the top, that three rough zigzag narrow paths had been cut out of the surface of the mound towards it. Up, therefore, the path nearest to the earthwork, Captain Sartorius, with the skill and sure-footedness of a practised mountaineer, climbed his perilous way. His men in the earthwork below tried to keep down the fire of the desperate Ghilzais at the top, by a rapid discharge from their Martini rifles.

"The slow progress of the Captain and his men was watched by the whole force beneath, who now looked on in admiration at the example of cool courage, never to be outdone, which was displayed before their eyes.

"Captain Sartorius, under a rapid fire from above, and a yard or two in front of the nearest man of the 59th, at last gained the final turn of the zig-zag path. His men were toiling up in his footsteps. He had scarcely rounded the corner of the path close to the building when seven Ghilzais, with cries like wild beasts, rushed furiously down upon him and those who followed. Swords, sharp as razors, were instantly slashing right and left amongst the English soldiers. For a few minutes, what appeared to be an indiscriminate melée took place upon the narrow path; then, to the astonishment of all the onlookers, there came rolling over and over, like huge stones shot down the sides of the precipitous rock, the bodies of the whole of its defenders, dead! but accompanied by another having on a red uniform. This was the body of a fine young English soldier, a private of the 59th, whose skull had been cleft through by the sword of his adversary, almost at the same moment as the Afghan himself had received his death-wound by the soldier's bayonet thrust.

"Captain Sartorius was severely wounded by having both his hands slashed across, and two of his brave followers of the 59th were also seriously injured by cuts from swords wielded by the desperate Ghilzais.

"But the silent bayonet had done its deadly work; not a shot had been aimed by Captain Sartorius or his gallant party, for they had not time to fire.

"Captain Sartorius recovered from his wounds, and regained the use of his hands. He was recommended—and justly so—for the Victoria Cross. He received it, and he deserved it, for an act of valour which was a fine example to the men who witnessed it."*

At Ahmad Khel, under Sir Donald Stewart, the 59th were again hotly engaged. The ferocious Ghazni Horse charged full at the infantry, to be received by the regiments (of which the 59th were the only British) with a fire so withering as to entirely demoralize the enemies' cavalry. "Most fearful was the effect of this sudden and concentrated fire. In the wildest confusion—rising, sinking, kicking, plunging, and rolling over each other went the Afghan cavalry," and amongst the wounded of that invincible phalanx of infantry were Lieutenant-Colonel Lawson and Lieutenant Watson of the 59th. It will be conceded that no regiment that bears "Afghanistan, 1879—80" on its colours, more gallantly earned the distinction than did the 59th, whose latest active service of importance it commemorates.†

THE LOYAL NORTH LANCASHIRE REGIMENT ‡—Regimental District No. 47—the

* "Victoria Cross in Afghanistan." Major Elliott. Dean and Sons.
† The 59th were occasionally known as "Lily Whites."
‡ The Loyal North Lancashire Regiment bear as badges the Royal Crest (crowned lion) with the Rose of Lancaster on cap, the arms of the city of Lincoln (a fleur de lys on a cross of St. George) on the collar. The uniform

only regiment which boasts that distinguished prefix, consists of the 47th and 81st Regiments of Foot. The former was raised in 1740, and passed the first years of its career in Scotland and America, and in 1758 took part in the capture of Louisbourg. The following year they served under Wolfe at Quebec, and, under Lascelles, formed the reserve. They soon, however, came to the front, and were one of the three regiments on whom devolved the hottest of the fighting. An officer, writing at the time, said: "Our regiments that sustained the brunt of the action were Bragg's, Lascelles', and the Highlanders; the two former had not a bayonet, or the latter a broadsword, untinged with blood." They served throughout the operations in Canada, and were subsequently stationed at Martinique, which place they quitted for service in America on the breaking out of the war, during which they fought at Bunker's Hill, Lexington, and Saratoga. A few years later they took part in the capture of Monte Video (at which they were brigaded under General Lumley), and in the unfortunate affair at Buenos Ayres. A second brigade which had been formed shared in the struggles and victories of the Peninsular War, during which they gained "Tarifa," "Vittoria," and "St. Sebastian" on their colours. Like many other "2nd battalions" raised at the same time, they were disbanded on the termination of the war. The 1st battalion meanwhile served in the Pindaree War, and subsequently in the first Burmese War, where, in that campaign in which "pestilence slew more than the bullet," they earned the high praise of the Governor-General of India, and the distinction of "Ava" to their colours. During the period that elapsed between the close of the Burmese War and the campaign in the Crimea, the 47th were detailed for duty in various places throughout our Colonial Empire. In the Crimea they were in the Second Division, under Sir de Lacy Evans. They fought at the Alma; at Inkerman they joined in the splendid charge mentioned in the account of the 20th Regiment. Colonel Haly, who commanded, was severely wounded, and would have been killed by the pitiless foe who surrounded him had it not been for a gallant rescue organized by Captain V. Rowlands, of the 41st, who, with some of his own regiment and a few of the 47th, charged at and dispersed the Russians. None played a more prominent part in this rescue than Private John M'Dermond, who, seeing a Russian about to bayonet his prostrate officer, sprang forward and slew the savage ruffian. For this brave act he received and well

is scarlet, with facings of white. The officers have a black line bordering each side of the gold lace on the tunics. On their colours are the names "Louisbourg," "Quebec, 1759," "Maida," "Corunna," "Tarifa," "Vittoria," "St. Sebastian," "Peninsula," "Ava," "Alma," "Inkerman," "Sevastopol," "Ali Musjid," "Afghanistan, 1878—79."

merited the Victoria Cross. Since the Crimean War the record of the 47th has been uneventful, garrison and colonial duty having chiefly occupied their time.

The 2nd battalion of the Loyal North Lancashire is the old 81st, the Loyal Lincoln Volunteers of famous memory, and dates from 1793, when General Albemarle Bertie, afterwards Earl of Lindsey, was commissioned to raise a regiment of foot at Lincoln. The fact of this alacrity to serve, coupled with the coincidence of the motto of their Colonel—*Loyauté m'oblige*—caused the newly raised regiment to be known as the Loyal Lincoln Volunteers. Their first foreign service was in the West Indies, where they suffered severely from yellow fever; in 1799 they were engaged at the Cape and had some sharp fighting with the Kaffirs. On returning to England the exigencies of the time necessitated the formation of a 2nd battalion, which proceeded to the Continent and served with great distinction. "At the destruction of the Bridge of Batarizos, the gallantry of Private Thomas Savage was very conspicuous. At the battle of Corunna, the conduct of the 81st was equal to the crisis; the loss of the corps in that action and the previous retreat was three hundred and twenty-six, including thirteen officers." The subsequent career of the 2nd battalion embraced the disastrous Walcheren Expedition, and the campaign in Holland in 1814—15, not including Waterloo, during which battle they were quartered in Brussels. The following year they were disbanded. In 1806 the 1st battalion, who were then with the force under Sir John Stuart in Calabria, participated in the battle of Maida, in which they particularly distinguished themselves. On this occasion, Colonel Kempt, perceiving that the 81st were encumbered with the blankets they carried, made them halt and disburthen themselves of the latter. The enemy, mistaking the pause for hesitation, came on to the charge, but, discovering their mistake, recoiled at the impact, but too late, for the bodies of seven hundred Frenchmen paid the penalty of their over-confidence.* Here, too, in conjunction with the 78th, they made the charge which did so much to decide the fortune of the day. Shoulder to shoulder the Englishmen and Highlanders pressed on, "in aspect strangely cool, compact, and resolute; their advance through the smoke and over heaps of dead and dying so utterly discomfited the enemy that their whole left wing gave way and fled in confusion." The 81st remained in Sicily for some years, and took part in the numerous small but, collectively, important actions which resulted in the evacuation by the French of Catalonia. About the time when Waterloo was fought they were in Canada, but

* Colonel Archer says that "the 81st still preserve, as a spoil of the field, a curious silver-mounted snuff-box."

returned in time to join the Army of Occupation. For many years after that their history is a peaceful one; fortunately, however, for themselves and for the empire, they were in India at the outbreak of the Mutiny. Fortunately for themselves, because of the honour and glory that they won; fortunately for the empire, because, to quote a recent summary of their history, "the admirable conduct of the 81st, then stationed at the cantonment of Lahore, was the turning point in the destiny of India." It was on the 11th of May that the awful tidings reached Lahore of the mutiny at Meerut. The consternation excited was terrible. "This vast city, with its ninety thousand inhabitants, could at a word give forth hundreds who would only be too ready to emulate the atrocities of the Meerut and Delhi monsters. Nor was it from the city alone that danger was to be apprehended. At the military cantonment of Mean Meer, six miles off, were quartered four native regiments, three of infantry and one of cavalry, with comparatively but a small force of Europeans, consisting of the Queen's 81st, with two troops of horse artillery and four reserve companies of foot artillery." To add to the danger already threatening, information reached the authorities which changed surmise into certainty. A plot was on foot at Mean Meer to overpower the garrison, seize the guns, set free the two thousand prisoners confined in the gaol, and a promiscuous massacre of the Europeans was to crown the devilish triumph. That all this did not happen, and that another ghastly chapter was not added to the black record of the Mutiny, we may thank Mr. Montgomery and Brigadier Corbett, and the gallant 81st and artillery which enabled them to carry out their bold and prudent resolve.

"It happened that that night there was to have been a ball at Mean Meer. It might have been thought that, in the midst of such a crisis as that which now hung over the empire, the dancers would postpone their amusement. But it was wisely decided that such a step would needlessly excite suspicion, and the guests came as though nothing had occurred to disturb their security. Hardly one of those present knew the object of the parade which was to take place on the morrow, but a few who were in the secret must have thought of that famous ball at Brussels from which Wellington started for the field of Quatre Bras.

"Early in the morning the troops were drawn up on the parade ground. The Europeans were on the right, the native infantry in the centre, and the native cavalry on the left. The natives outnumbered the Europeans by eight to one. First of all the order of Government for the disbandment of the 34th at Barrackpore was read to each regiment. Then the native regiments were ordered to change front to the rear. While they were executing this manœuvre the 81st changed front also and faced them, and the gunners, hidden behind their European comrades, moved round likewise, loading their guns as they went. The Sepoys were told that, as so many other regiments had begun to display a mutinous spirit, it had been thought right to shield them from temptation by disarming them. The order was given to 'Pile arms.' The Sepoys, momentarily hesitating, heard a strong and resolute voice—Colonel Renny's—pronounce the words, ' Eighty-first, load !' and, looking up as their ears caught the clang of the ramrods, saw the English gunners in front of them standing by their guns, port-fires in hand. Perceiving the hopelessness of resistance, they sullenly laid down their arms. Meanwhile three companies of the 81st had marched to Lahore. On their arrival they disarmed the native portion of the garrison, and took possession of the fort. Never was a more decisive victory gained. By that morning's work Montgomery and Corbett had not only saved the capital of the Punjaub—they had saved the empire."

For some years after the Mutiny and the subsequent operations under General Cotton in the neighbourhood of Peshawur, in which they took part, had become things of the past, the 81st remained in India. Returning to England in 1865, seven years later they returned to the familiar scene, and in 1878 took part in the Afghan War. At the siege of Ali Musjid the 81st were with the force under General Sir S. Browne, the officer in command of the regiment being Colonel Chichester; at the assault of the Citadel they were in reserve, and though under fire escaped without any casualties. The subsequent service of the regiment has been uneventful.

THE PRINCE OF WALES'S VOLUNTEERS (South Lancashire Regiment)*—Regimental District No. 40—consists of the 40th and 82nd Foot. The former dates from 1717, and boasts the distinction of being the first Foot Regiment added to the army after the accession of the House of Hanover to the throne of England. Archer sums up the history of the origin of the regiment as follows :—"Certain independent companies of foot which for many years had served in the West Indies and America were formed into a regiment at Annapolis Royal under command of Colonel, afterwards General, R. Philips, Governor of Nova Scotia." Their first warlike service was at the capture of Louisbourg, and some of

* The Prince of Wales's Volunteers have as badges the Prince of Wales's Plume with the Sphinx and "Egypt" on the cap, and the Prince of Wales's Plume and Motto on collar. The motto of the regiment is "Ich Dien." The uniform is scarlet with facings of white. On their colours are the names "Louisbourg," "Egypt," "Monte Video," "Roleia," "Vimiera," "Talavera," "Badajoz," "Salamanca," "Vittoria," "Pyrenees," "Nivelle," "Orthes," "Toulouse," "Peninsula," "Niagara," "Waterloo," "Kandahar," "Ghuznee," "Kabul, 1842," "Maharajpore," "Sevastopol." "Lucknow," "New Zealand."

their number were included in the ranks of the Louisbourg Grenadiers who did such great things under Wolfe at Quebec. Subsequently they served at Guadeloupe and the Havannah, and were amongst the royal troops in America at the time of the War of Independence. They fought at Long Island, Brooklyn, and others of the battles, and two years later repaired to the West Indies. In various duties in this neighbourhood they found employment for several years, some of the regiment being with the British troops in Holland and sharing the hardships of the Bremen retreat. Then they served in Jamaica during the Maroon disturbances, and in 1799 were again in Holland, where they fought at Egmont-op-Zee and elsewhere. The regiment was represented in the famous campaign in Egypt of 1801, and at Aboukir, Alexandria, and Rosetta earned great distinction. At Aboukir they were aligned with the Welsh Fusiliers, and "rushed up the heights with almost preternatural energy, never firing a shot, but charging with the bayonet the two battalions that crowned them, breaking and pursuing them, till they carried the two hills which commanded the plain to the left, taking at the same time three pieces of cannon." At Alexandria they were on the right of the British line, encamped in the midst of ruins whose builders had perchance themselves fought in fierce battles on that very spot. The battle commenced by an attack by the French on this position. They came on with "incredible fury," but the other regiments of the division—especially the gallant Welsh Fusiliers—met the onslaught with more than equal determination, "and the 40th coming up rendered more complete the victory on the right by a steady and well-directed fire, which cut down whole sections of the now disordered enemy." A few years later the 40th earned another distinction for the colours* which were destined to boast such a glorious list. They formed part of the expedition of Sir Samuel Auchmuty against Monte Video.

Shortly after landing, a force of some six thousand of the enemy attacked our line and pressed our left so hard that "Colonel Browne, who commanded on the left, ordered three companies of the 40th, under Major Campbell, up in support." The three companies dashed forward with the greatest gallantry; severe fighting followed, but the enemy at last gave way, leaving one gun and fifteen hundred men dead, wounded, or prisoners as testimony to our victory. When the assault was ordered the 40th, under Major Dalrymple, were detailed to support the stormers. "At the appointed hour the troops marched in silence to the assault, and approached the breach before they were dis-

* "At the time of the recent change of title the 40th Foot displayed more battle honours than any other corps possessing colours, with the exception of the 1st Foot, the 23rd Fusiliers following next."

covered, when a destructive fire from every gun that would bear and from the musketry of the garrison opened upon them. Severe though our loss, it might have been comparatively trifling had the breach been, as our troops expected, open; but during the night the enemy, unseen, had closely and densely barricaded it with rolled hides, so as to render it nearly impracticable. The morning was extremely dark; hence the head of the column missed the breach, and, when it was reached, it was so built up as to be mistaken for the untouched wall. In this situation the troops remained helplessly under a heavy fire for more than a quarter of an hour, till the actual spot was discovered by Captain Rennie of the 40th Light Company, who pointed it out with joy and ardour, and fell gloriously as he mounted to the assault. Difficult though the access, our soldiers rushed gallantly on; the dense, though slippery barricades, were surmounted; grenadiers, light infantry, 40th and 87th, swarmed over it, and with the bayonet fought their way into the town." As an example of the darkness and consequent confusion that prevailed, it is recorded that the 40th *twice* missed the breach, and had twice undergone the heavy fire of the batteries. Besides Captain Rennie, the regiment had to deplore the loss of Major Dalrymple, who was also killed during the assault. They were subsequently engaged at Buenos Ayres, the sad narrative of which has been before touched on. Then came the era of the Peninsular War, during which few regiments more distinguished themselves than did the 40th. They fought at Roleia, "the beautiful vale which witnessed the first of the Peninsular battles in which the British were concerned, and the first victory of Wellesley—'the General of Sepoys,' as Napoleon called him—in an independent command in Europe." (*Clinton.*) At Vimiera they shared with the 36th and 71st the glory of that memorable charge which followed "discharges of musketry exchanged at a distance which hardly allowed a bullet to miss its mark."* They fought at Talavera; took part in the storming of Badajoz; at Salamanca the historian of the war records that "a wing of the 40th, wheeling about with a rough charge, cleared the rear," threatened by the regiments of Maucune. The 40th—the 2nd Somersetshire, as their official title had for some time been—were, too, with the British hosts which on that eventful morning of the 21st of June moved forward to give battle to the French under the *fainéant* King Joseph.

"The mists had now disappeared from the mountain sides, to which the puffs of smoke were slowly ascending; the summer sun was shining brightly in a cloudless sky on the brilliant scene—on the hillsides the gleaming bayonets, the waving silken stan-

* Marquis of Londonderry.

dards of many a hue, the scarlet tunics of the British, and the blue uniforms of the Portuguese, relieved by the sombre brown of the Spaniards and the dark dress of the riflemen, and on the Vittoria heights the blue-coated masses of the French line and light infantry regiments and horse artillery, the green uniforms and brass helmets of the heavy cavalry, the gay dresses of the lancers and hussars, and the buff belts and cocked hats of the gendarmerie-à-cheval; and around Vittoria itself the parti-coloured mob which collected to witness the struggle which had now begun along the whole line."

Gallantly did the 40th acquit themselves on that day, which closed on the spectacle of an army fleeing in the very madness of panic, leaving untold treasure and countless trophies behind them, and carrying off only *two* pieces of artillery of all the guns which were expected to work such destruction on the stubborn Britons. The "Pyrenees" testifies to the share the regiment bore in the numerous battles included in that term—a series of battles not less remarkable for their strategical importance than for the respect which by that time the opposing forces had learned to feel each for the other. Before Roncesvalles—where, we may remark, the 40th were particularly distinguished—Soult issued the following Order to his army:—"Let us not defraud the enemy of the praise that is due to him. The dispositions of the General have been prompt, skilful, and consecutive; the valour and steadiness of his troops have been praiseworthy." With no less chivalry, though with a commanding consciousness of superiority, Wellington, at Zabaldica, referred to his opponent. The British Commander had ridden forward to an eminence where his presence could be discerned by both armies. "A Portuguese regiment on the left, first recognising him, raised a joyful cry, and soon the joyful clamour was taken up by the next regiments, swelling as it ran along the line into that stern and appalling shout which the British soldier is wont to give upon the edge of battle, and which no enemy ever heard unmoved. A spy who was present pointed out Soult, then so near that his features could be plainly distinguished. Fixing his eyes attentively upon that formidable man, Wellington thus spoke:—'Yonder is a great commander, but he is a cautious one, and will delay his attack to ascertain the cause of those shouts; that will give time for the Sixth Division to arrive, and I shall beat him.'"

The 40th fought at Nivelle, at Orthes, and Toulouse. At Waterloo—which they reached on the eve of the battle—they were attached to the Sixth Division, under General Sir James Lambert, and were in reserve with Picton's force. It is impossible to do more than mention the effect of their presence; in the case of such a regiment as the

40th such mention is equivalent to the assertion that they acquitted themselves gallantly and valiantly as beseemed their traditions.

After Waterloo they served abroad, enjoying a cessation of fighting till 1829, when they were ordered to India, and, after a sojourn of some eleven years there, shared in the first Afghan War. They won the distinctions of "Kandahar" and "Ghuznee," and, a few years later, fought brilliantly at Maharajpore. Here Colonel Valiant of the regiment held the local rank of General, and matters looked serious for the British force, till, by one grand rush, his brigade charged the brave enemy, seized twenty-eight pieces of cannon, and finally forced the Mahrattas to retire. The 40th "lost in succession two commanding officers, who fell under the very muzzles of the Mahratta guns—namely, Major James Stopford and Captain Fitzherbert Codrington. Four standards were taken that day by the regiment." Again followed a period of comparative quiet, and the next campaign in which the 40th were engaged was the Maori War in New Zealand in 1860-61. Here they won fresh honours, the more brilliant, perhaps, as the warfare was of an unfamiliar kind. On the Waitara some gallant deeds were done by the regiment, and Sergeant Lucas earned for himself a Victoria Cross, and the admiration of all whose hearts respond to the tale of gallant courage under adverse circumstances.

It was at Taranaki that Sergeant-Major Lucas won his laurels on the 18th of March, 1861. "A party, consisting of about thirty men of the 40th Regiment, was sent out in front of a redoubt situated on the river Waitara, in search of the enemy. Between the redoubt and the bush there intervened an open space of some eight hundred or nine hundred yards in breadth, over which our men were allowed to advance without resistance; but no sooner had they entered a narrow defile, surrounded on either side by bush and fern, than a heavy fire was opened on them by an invisible foe. Captain Richards, who was in command of the party, threw out his men in skirmishing order, and ordered them to fire in the direction whence the smoke proceeded. The enemy being concealed in the bush had the advantage of being able to take deliberate aim, and several of our men were killed or wounded. Lieutenant Rees, who was next in command to Captain Richards, seized a rifle a wounded soldier had dropped, and encouraged the men by his example to keep up a steady fire. At the same time he requested Colour-Sergeant Lucas to send two men to remove two of the wounded who were badly hit. As the men were preparing to execute this order, a fresh volley from the enemy placed one of them *hors de combat,* and a bullet hit Lieutenant Rees in the right groin. He staggered and fell, when Colour-Sergeant Lucas, with great presence of mind, ran up to his assistance and sent him to the rear, under the charge of the soldier who remained unhurt. Three wounded men and four stand of arms still remained on the field, and the gallant Sergeant resolved to present a bold front to the enemy till he was relieved. Sheltering himself behind a tree he opened a brisk fire on the enemy, and kept them at bay. So long as he remained behind the tree he was safe, but whenever he left this shelter to take aim he was exposed to the fire of the enemy, who, deterred from advancing by his gallant resistance, endeavoured to shoot him down. Two soldiers had the courage to stand by him, and for a quarter of an hour they kept the enemy at bay without being hit, though they were exposed to a constant fire from a distance of only thirty yards. Several of the Maoris were wounded, and carried off by their companions; the brave little band, anxious, but not discouraged, still continued to hold out. The tree behind which he found shelter had several creepers suspended from its top; a bullet from the bush hit one of these creepers and cut it in two at a distance of a few inches from his head. If the Maoris had been better marksmen the whole of the little party must have perished, and the wounded men have fallen into the hands of a relentless foe; but in moments of excitement the natives fire wildly, without taking aim at any particular object. It was to this fortunate circumstance that Sergeant Lucas and his two followers owed their lives. If the enemy had been more skilful in the use of the rifle none of the party could have escaped; as it was, they were enabled not only to continue their resistance, but to inflict considerable loss on the enemy. For a quarter of an hour the unequal combat was kept up, till a party under Lieutenants Gibson and Whelan came up to their assistance, on which the enemy retired. Only one of the three wounded men recovered, and Lieutenant Rees, in consequence of the severity of his wounds, was obliged to return to England. It would be difficult to over-estimate the importance of Sergeant Lucas's gallant conduct on this trying occasion; he prevented the bodies of his wounded comrades from falling into the hands of the enemy, and saved four stand of arms. Nor was this all; the moral consequences of his heroic resistance were soon evident. The next morning the white flag was hoisted by the natives, and this was the last engagement in the Taranaki War."

On another occasion, on the Wakaito river, "the General had the satisfaction of seeing the 40th regiment landing from the *Pioneer* and *Avon*, not far from the spot which had been selected. Colonel Leslie, with Irish spirit—without waiting for companies to form—directed Captain Clarke to take the first fifty men that were landed and attack the ridge in the rear of the enemy's position, whilst he moved with one hundred men round its base for the purpose of intercepting the enemy. The ridge, honeycombed with rifle-pits, was carried at once, and a great number of the enemy were killed or drowned in endeavouring to escape across the swamp of Lake Waikare." The official report gave out that "the rapid and spirited manner in which the 40th Regiment, under Colonel Leslie, attacked and carried the ridge in rear of the position reflected great credit on the corps."

At Wairi they again performed most valuable service. "The leading men of the 40th, under Captain Fisher, were supported on the left and rear by Captain the Hon. F. Le Poer Trench of the same regiment. A party under Major Bowdler, of the 40th, assisted to hem in the Maoris. After much hot firing the troops were able to dash across the Mahgapiho into the old entrenchment, over a bridge formed by a single plank. The banks of the river here were forty or fifty feet high, and densely wooded."

Since the New Zealand War the regiment, deservedly holding a high place in the "roll of the brave," have not been engaged in any campaign.

The 2nd battalion of the Prince of Wales's Volunteers (South Lancashire Regiment) is composed of the 82nd* Regiment, which was raised in 1793. It is from this battalion that the title of "Prince of Wales'" and the badge of his plume comes, their first Colonel having been a gentleman in the Prince's household. It was not long before they were engaged in active work, the year 1795 seeing them with the forces at St. Domingo, where they performed "much gallant service," during part of the time being brigaded with their present first battalion. On the 82nd, as on a terrible number of other British regiments, the climate wrought fearful havoc, twenty-two officers and over a thousand men falling victims to its deadly influence. When they returned to England there landed only one officer and twenty-two men of the strong corps that had left this country for the West Indies! In 1807, after having recruited, the Prince of Wales' joined the force under Lord Cathcart despatched to storm Copenhagen. The position of affairs on the Continent was ominous indeed! Everywhere "the tempest of revolution had extended its ravages and changed the political aspect of Europe. Bonaparte had arrived at the summit of his grandeur, and the ruin of one nation only was wanted to place him at the head of a Western Empire. To this nation, strong in its imperial power, majestic and self-reliant from a knowledge of its prowess, all eyes were turned; and oppressed nations cried aloud to the unconquered mistress of the seas, "Come over and help us!" Stern measures were necessary—measures seemingly harsh and cruel—but in reality needful, as

---

* The present is the third regiment which has borne this number.

the sharp pain of the surgeon's knife to restore health to the diseased body. The fleet of Denmark might be used against us; time would not allow of protracted negotiations; if it were not delivered up, it must be taken by force. And this was the object that the armament, of which the 82nd formed part, had in view. On the left of the trenches dug before the city was a windmill, which it was deemed necessary to hold; and this duty was consigned to the 82nd, under Colonel Smith. Throughout the whole of the blockade they held this position, exposed to the fire of the Danish gunboats and to sorties from the garrison." After this, the 82nd found themselves in the thick of the Peninsular War. They fought at Roleia and Vimiera, at the latter battle sharing with the 71st the credit of the charge which drove back the columns of Brennier and made the General himself a prisoner. (As related in the account of the 71st Regiment, the latter corps and the 82nd were lying on the grass to rest when the French fell upon them. If for a moment they seemed to be thrown into disorder, it was *only* seemed, and only for a moment. They fell back to recover, and then executed the charge above described.) "Talavera" and "Badajoz" are on their colours; during the defence of Tarifa, Lieutenant Welstead of the 82nd made a brilliant sally, penetrating into the enemy's very camp and capturing a field-piece. Meanwhile a portion of the regiment took part in the Walcheren expedition, under the Earl of Chatham. At Barossa the 82nd, under Major Browne, almost outdid in gallantry even their foregoing deeds. The dastardly conduct of La Peña had placed the British troops under General Graham in a most dangerous position. His army had been "under arms nearly twenty-four hours without refreshments, and they had, contrary to the Spanish General's promise, been brought up by forced marches, though the roads were bad and imperfectly known to the guides." Yet, with great temper, Graham obeyed the "discourteous order" of the Spaniard to march forward, and left the light companies of the 9th and 82nd Regiments under Major Browne to guard the luggage. Against this slender force Marshal Victor directed an overwhelming attack, and Browne retreated in good order. Then "he sent for orders to Graham, who was then near Bermeja. 'Fight,' was the laconic answer; and Graham, facing about himself, regained the open plain, expecting to find La Peña and the cavalry on the Barossa hill. But when the view opened, he beheld Ruffin's brigade, flanked by the two grenadier battalions, near the summit on the one side, the Spanish rearguard and the baggage flying towards the sea on the other, the French cavalry following the fugitives in good order, Laval close upon his own left flank, and La Peña nowhere! . . . . Meanwhile Graham's Spartan order had sent Browne headlong upon Ruffin, and though nearly half his detachment went down under the first fire, he maintained the fight. . . . . A dreadful, and for some time doubtful, combat raged; but soon Ruffin and Chaudron Rousseau, who commanded the chosen grenadiers, fell, both mortally wounded; the English bore strongly onward, and their incessant slaughtering fire forced the French from the hill with the loss of three guns and many brave soldiers."

At Vittoria the 82nd were in the Seventh Division, on the left of the British line, which before the close of the day completely routed the French right opposed to them. In the battles of the Pyrenees and at Pampeluna they displayed "great valour," notably at the battle of the Pass of Maya, the most desperate of all the Pyrenees battles. Called from their station on the summit of the Atchiola to succour the sorely-tried 71st, they held the position assigned to them with unflinching valour, though they were reduced at last to defending "with stones the rocks whereon they were posted," all their ammunition being exhausted. At Nivelle, and Orthes, and Toulouse they fought, and thus ended their record of the Peninsular campaign, which was for the 82nd a continuous narrative of gallantry and success. After the termination of their services in the Peninsular War, the 82nd were engaged with the forces in America and Canada, in the campaign which is commemorated by the distinction of "Niagara;" and after that, until the Crimean War, were employed in colonial garrison duty. They only participated in a small part of the Crimean campaign, joining the army a few days before the fall of Sevastopol. The following year they went to India, and were on their way to China when the outbreak of the Mutiny caused their journey to be arrested at Singapore. On the invaluable services rendered by the regiment to the empire during this time space forbids us to dwell in detail. They were with the force under Sir Colin Campbell which effected in November the relief of Lucknow, and shared to the full in the stern retribution dealt out to the inhuman fiends whose hands were red with the blood of women and children. Subsequently, under Wyndham, they had a sharp and discouraging encounter with Nana Sahib's troops at Pandoo Nuddee; and at Rohilcund, and many other places, assisted in quelling the terrible Indian Mutiny. A small party of the 82nd, with some other troops, under Colonel Hall, of the regiment, were left by Sir Colin Campbell to garrison Shahjehanpur, and the defence of this position in the face of overwhelming numbers constitutes what a History of the Mutiny well characterizes as a "very remarkable episode." Colonel Hall "formed the gaol into a small intrenched position with four guns, and as large a supply of provisions as he could procure. All this was done in one day . . . and, indeed, not an hour was to be lost, for a spy appeared on the following morning to announce that a large body of rebels had arrived within four miles of the place. The announcement proved to be correct. . . . Colonel Hall and Lieutenant de Kautzow retired into the gaol with their handful of troops, and prepared for a resolute defence. . . . It was computed that the rebels were little less than 8,000 strong, with twelve guns. Against this strong force Hall held his position for eight days and nights, sustaining a continuous bombardment, without thinking for a moment of yielding." Directly Sir Colin heard of the sore straits in which the gallant wing of the 82nd and their comrades were placed, he sent a relieving force under Brigadier Jones, in whose rescue of their comrades another wing of the regiment had the satisfaction of sharing. Subsequently, while with the force under Colonel Seaton, the 82nd again distinguished themselves, at a place called Kankur. No fighting of any great importance has since that time fallen to the lot of the gallant Prince of Wales's Volunteers, whose subsequent stations have been in South Africa and the Straits Settlements.

The King's Own, The Royal Lancaster Regiment* (Regimental District No. 4), may lay claim to rank amongst the most distinguished of British regiments. It consists of two battalions of the 4th Regiment of Foot, and dates from 1680, when it was formed, partly from recruits in the neighbourhood of London, partly from the neighbourhood of Plymouth, and numbered a thousand and forty strong, being divided into sixteen companies of sixty-five men each. Amongst the recruits were many officers and men of Monmouth's Regiment, which had served with such rare distinction in Germany and the Netherlands, under the most famous of the French commanders. With as much speed as possible, the 2nd Tangier Regiment (as it was then called) embarked for Tangier, to be met on landing by two pieces of unwelcome news—first, their brave Colonel, the Earl of Plymouth, had recently died of disease; and, secondly, a six months' truce had been agreed on. Lieutenant-Colonel Kirke, whose name was so familiar in military circles of the period, was appointed Colonel, to be succeeded by Lieutenant-Colonel Charles Trelawney, whose patronymic gave welcome evidence of his connection with the fair "west countrie" which so many of his officers and men claimed

---

* The King's Own (Royal Lancaster Regiment) have as badges the Red Rose of Lancaster with Lion above it on cap, and on collar a Golden Lion (crowned). The motto is that of the Garter. The uniform is scarlet, with facings of blue. On their colours are the Royal Cypher in a Garter, and the names "Corunna," "Badajoz," "Salamanca," "Vittoria," "St. Sebastian," "Nive," "Peninsula," "Bladensburg," "Waterloo," "Alma," "Inkerman," "Sevastopol," "Abyssinia," "South Africa, 1879."

as home. The sojourn of the regiment in Tangier was undisturbed by any serious fighting, and in 1684 they returned home, receiving, a few months later, the name of "Her Royal Highness the Duchess of York and Albany's Regiment"—a title which, on the accession of the Duchess to the position of Queen Consort, was changed into that of "The Queen's Regiment of Foot." Troubles soon began, and in July of the following year the Queen's found themselves opposed to the raw levies of the unfortunate Duke of Monmouth. Passing over the stormy domestic history of the next few years, we find the Queen's amongst the regiments which most warmly welcomed the Prince of Orange.* After his accession to the throne they fought at the Boyne, and at the sieges of Cork, Kinsale, and Limerick, exchanging this fratricidal warfare in Ireland for the continental campaign of 1692. They were at Steenkirke, where, however, only a detachment was actually engaged; and in 1693 fought in the severely contested battle of Landen, where the list of killed, wounded, and prisoners included five officers of the Queen's. At the siege of Namur they greatly distinguished themselves, taking part in many of the assaults, and losing in killed and wounded many gallant officers and men. In the early part of the following reign the 4th were despatched to Spain, where they formed part of the force under the Duke of Ormond, and shared in the useless sieges and engagements—at Rota, Port St. Mary, Fort St. Catherine, and Matagarda—which made up the campaign. In 1703 the Queen's was transformed for a time into a regiment of Marines, their commander, Colonel Seymour, being "appointed to the care and command of H.M. Marine Forces;" and it was while serving in this capacity that "they had the proud distinction of taking part in the capture of the stupendous fortress of Gibraltar." It is worthy of note that "on taking possession of the fortress the seamen and marines were astonished at their own success; and they viewed, with a mixed feeling of wonder and delight, fortifications which a comparatively small body of men might have defended against a numerous army." Soon the Queen's, when in garrison on the Rock, were in a position to prove the accuracy of this opinion. The French were not willing quietly to acquiesce in the loss of so important a possession, and a strong force, under the Marquis of Villadarias, commenced to besiege it. There was no lack of courage in the enemy, and our Marines found the defence no sinecure. "During the night of the 11th of November five hundred of the enemy contrived, by means of rope ladders and other inventions, to ascend the

* "It is said that a scheme was laid and measures taken by Churchill (Lieutenant-Colonel of the Queen's) and Major-General Kirke to deliver up the King to the Prince of Orange, but accident frustrated the design."—*Memoirs of the Duke of Berwick.* The Official Record adds: "Brigadier-General Trelawney is also charged with participating in this design, but no direct proof on the subject has been adduced by any historian."

mountain by a way which was deemed impracticable, and were supported by another body of three thousand men. The men engaged in this daring enterprise were, however, soon discovered, and were charged by five hundred of the Marines in garrison with such resolution that two hundred of the enemy were killed on the spot, upwards of two hundred were taken prisoners, and the remainder, endeavouring to escape, fell down the rock and were dashed to pieces." (*Official Record*.) Throughout the siege the Queen's behaved in such wise as to elicit the assertion that "the English Marines gained immortal honour." When the siege was raised, representatives of the corps found scope for their energies at the capture and defence of Barcelona, the battle of Almanza, and the capture of Minorca. In 1710 their seven years' connection with the fleet terminated, and they resumed their position among the regular regiments of infantry. In July, 1710, the Queen's were detailed to join the proposed expedition under General Hill against Quebec, but a sad mishap occurred to thwart this arrangement. "As the fleet was proceeding up the river St. Lawrence, it became enveloped in a thick fog and encountered a severe gale of wind; and the veterans who had fought the battles of their country found themselves in the dangerous navigation of this immense river, in a dark and stormy night, with inexperienced men collected on a sudden to serve as pilots. Eight transports crowded with men were dashed upon the rocks, and a number of officers and soldiers, who but a few hours before had meditated scenes of conquest, victory, and glory, were entombed in the deep." Amongst these were "eleven officers, ten sergeants, eighteen corporals, thirteen drummers, and a hundred and sixty-seven private soldiers" of the Queen's Regiment. After this the regiment spent some years in England, recruiting; and being stationed at Windsor in the autumn of 1715, received from George I. the title by which they have won so widespread and fair a fame—"The King's Own." Not till 1744 did occasion arise for the 4th to engage in hostilities; in that year, however, they joined the allied armies encamped on the Scheldt to do battle for the rights of Maria Teresa. Only unimportant operations, however, fell to their lot; and in 1745 they returned to England, to take part in opposing the Stuart rising. They fought at Falkirk and at Culloden, at the latter of which a report made at the time declares them to have "gained the greatest reputation imaginable. After the battle there was not a bayonet of this regiment but was either bloody or bent. There was not an officer or soldier of Barrett's (the King's Own) . . . . who did not kill one or two men each with their bayonets." As may be gathered from the above contemporary account, the conflict was a singularly fierce one, and the King's Own lost one officer and seventeen men killed, five officers and a hundred and eight men wounded. In 1754 they were ordered to Minorca, and were serving there when the unfortunate Admiral Byng committed the inexplicable error—for which he lost his life—of failing to relieve the garrison. In 1759 the regiment, nine hundred strong, embarked under Colonel Crump for Martinique, where, and at Guadeloupe and adjacent fortresses, they greatly distinguished themselves. Colonel Crump was appointed Governor of the Island, and the regiment was stationed there for some years; in 1761, under Lord Rollo, capturing Dominique. In 1762 another attack was made on Martinique, in which the King's Own participated, and the submission of the island was followed by the capture of Grenada, St. Lucia, and St. Vincent. A detachment of two hundred and twenty-five men, under Captain Kennedy, shared in the capture of the Havannah. Returning to England in 1764, the King's Own, ten years later, were ordered to America, where the first symptoms of revolt had then appeared. The flank companies were with Colonel K. Smith when the first blood was shed at Lexington, and during the retreat from Concord experienced somewhat heavy loss; an officer and seven privates being killed, an officer and twenty-five men wounded, and eight or ten men being returned as missing. At Bunker's Hill, which Cannon describes as "one of the most sanguinary battles on record," the King's Own, "by their undaunted resolution and steady perseverance, eventually triumphed over thrice their own numbers and carried the heights at the point of the bayonet." At Long Island, White Plains, and Washington, at Ridgefield, Campo, and Brandywine, they fought in the same manner; at the last-named place, under Colonel Ogilvie, "overpowering all opposition and capturing three brass field-pieces and a howitzer." The prowess of the regiment during the whole of the American War might well fill a volume, but we must perforce pass on and take up the record with the capture and defence of St. Lucia, in 1788, shortly after which they returned to England. The next twenty-eight years passed comparatively uneventfully for the King's Own, though wars and rumours of wars made the inaction the more irksome. Nor was even this period one of absolute quiet, for in 1793 they captured the islands of Iniquelon and St. Pierre; and in 1797 experienced—that is, the officers, sergeants, and drummers—the unpleasant mischance of being pursued and taken prisoners by a French privateer.* For a few months, too, the King's Own fought in Holland, distinguishing themselves at Egmont-op-Zee, and in a marked manner at Beverwyck, where they had two officers and twenty-five men killed, eight

---

* The rank and file of the King's Own, then in Canada, had been transferred bodily to the 26th Regiment, the nucleus, constituted as above, returning to England.

officers and a hundred and twelve men wounded, and no fewer than eighteen officers and five hundred and fifteen men prisoners and missing!

At the time when Napoleon's threat to invade England was deemed daily likely to be carried out, the King's Own were stationed on the south coast, under command of General Moore. In 1807 they took part in the bombardment of Copenhagen, and the following year proceeded to the Peninsula, where they joined the forces under Moore, being brigaded with the 28th and 42nd, commanded by General Lord W. Bentinck. At Corunna they were on the right of the line and bore the brunt of the battle. "The enemy's attempt to turn the right flank by the valley occasioned the right wing of the 4th to be thrown back, and the regiment opening a heavy flanking fire with terrible effect, it forced its opponents back in confusion. Sir John Moore, watching this manœuvre with care, saw the noble exhibition of valour made by the King's Own and the repulse of the enemy by the flanking fire with feelings of exultation, and called out, "That is exactly what I wanted to be done. I am glad to see a regiment there in which I have such confidence." That action of the King's Own may be regarded as the turning point of the glorious day. "Then the English General knew that his adversary's whole force and order of battle was unfolded;" the splendid charge of the 50th and 42nd followed; "everywhere the signs of coming victory were bright, when the gallant man, the consummate commander who had brought the battle to this crisis, was dashed from his horse to the earth. A cannon shot from the rock battery had torn away all the flesh from his left breast and shoulder, and broken the ribs over a heart undaunted even by this terrible, this ghastly mortal hurt; for, with incredible energy, he rose to a sitting position, and with fixed look and unchanged countenance continued to regard the fight until the Frenchman's backward steps assured him the British were victorious; then, sinking down, he accepted succour." After Corunna the King's Own took part in the disastrous Walcheren expedition before referred to, where the British army suffered terrible privations and distress, which cost the country, it is said, over twenty million pounds, and where the incompetency of the commanders was entirely responsible for the failure. "A powerful naval and military force accomplished nothing, and all that its leaders could point to were the bones of brave British soldiers rotting among the swamps of Walcheren, and the immortal ignominy of a celebrated epigram:—

'Sir Richard, longing to be at 'em,
Stands waiting for the Earl of Chatham;
The Earl of Chatham, with sword drawn,
Stands waiting for Sir Richard Strachan.'"

But more glorious times were in store for the gallant 4th, times of which it might well be said that—

> "Every morning brought a noble chance,
> And every chance brought out a noble knight,"

for the storm of the Peninsular War was now raging in full fury, and the King's Own were ordered to join Wellington's army. They joined in October, and remained encamped in the lines of Torres Vedras, till the retreat of Massena gave the signal for Wellington to pursue. The 4th were attached to the Fifth Division under General Leith, and after some months spent in manœuvring, joined the force besieging Badajoz. The final assault was to be made on the 6th of April, when "eighteen thousand soldiers, second to none in the world," were to attempt the capture of a fortress so strongly fortified as to seem impregnable. "It was known that the enterprise was a desperate one; that the defences of the town had been strengthened with the utmost art; that extraordinary precautions had been made to repel an assault. Powder barrels and grenades were laid along the trenches, and at the foot of the breach were placed sixty 14-inch shells, communicating with boxes embedded in earth, and all ready for explosion. Across the rampart extended a chevaux-de-frise, and the slopes of the breaches were covered with planks that tilted any who touched them upon a timber work studded with iron spikes, bayonets, and sword blades. Every species of combustible was got together; several loaded muskets lay by each man's hand; and wooden cylinders, filled with brick shot and slugs, which scattered terribly when fired, had been prepared in quantities. Yet, calmly confident of success were the soldiers who advanced in the shadow of the night against this formidable stronghold." (*Davenport Adams.*) The Fifth Division, in which were the King's Own, were directed to make two false attacks, one on the Pardilleras and another on the bastion of St. Vincent; and right well did they perform their task. We will quote again from Mr. Adams' eloquent description of their share in this memorable assault :—" Gaining the bank of the Guardiana, the Fifth Division advanced along the margin of the river, and the hum of their footfalls being lost in the roll of the waters, reached the outposts of the French undiscovered. At that moment an explosion in the breach, and the sudden emergence of the moon, revealed them to their enemy. Forward sped the British, and under a sharp fire struck sturdy blows upon the timber that defended the covered way. The Portuguese in a panic flung down their scaling ladders, but the men of the 4th snatched them up, forced the barrier, and leapt into the ditch. Perdition! The ladders were too short! A mine was sprung at this juncture, and added to the horrors of the scene, but the British never quailed. Three ladders at length were reared against a corner of the bastion, and one man, climbing an embrasure which had no gun, but was only stopped by a gabion,* gained the summit, and drew many of his comrades after him. The numbers increased, and the enemy could not drive them back. Half the King's Own pushed into the town, to dislodge the French from the houses: the others fought their way along the ramparts, and won three bastions. The portion of the 4th which worked its way along the ramparts had a terrible time of it after their gallant courage had won the bastions. 'In the last, General Walker, leaping forwards sword in hand, just as a French cannonier discharged a gun, fell with so many wounds that it was wonderful how he survived; and his soldiers, seeing a lighted match on the ground, cried out "A mine!" At that word, such is the power of imagination, those troops whom neither the strong barrier, nor the deep ditch, nor the high walls, nor the deadly fire of the enemy could stop, staggered back, appalled by a chimera of their own raising,' † and in this condition were roughly handled by the French under General Veillande. The other detachment of the regiment found themselves in a strange position, for the 'streets, though empty, were brilliantly illuminated, no person was seen, yet a low buzz and whisper were heard around, lattices were now and then gently opened, and from time to time shots were fired from underneath the doors of the houses by the Spaniards; while the regiment, with bugles sounding, advanced towards the great square of the town. . . . A terrible enchantment seemed to prevail, nothing to be seen but light, and only low whispers heard, while the tumult at the breaches was like crashing thunder.'" We will not dwell here upon the scene that followed the surrender of the citadel; before that took place the King's Own fought many fierce street combats, wherein fell many a gallant soldier; and the roll-call showed that in killed and wounded of all ranks Badajoz had cost them two hundred and thirty.‡ At Salamanca the Fourth Division was being seriously pressed when the King's Own, with the rest of the Fifth Division, advanced steadily against the columns of the foe, "and from that moment our victory was never doubtful." "No advance in line at a review," writes an historian of the campaign, "was ever more perfectly executed." The loss to the regiment was small at Salamanca, considering the fierce

* Gabions are cylindrical wicker-baskets, without any top or bottom, and are used for many purposes in engineering.
† Napier.
‡ Private Yeo Hatton distinguished himself on this occasion by capturing the colours of the Hesse-Darmstadt Regiment, in the French service, having bayoneted the officer who carried them.

resistance made by the enemy; but at Vittoria there was a heavier "butcher's bill"—seven officers and seventy-five non-commissioned officers and men being either killed or wounded. Their service that day consisted in the capture and holding of the village of Gamara Mayor.

A still more desperate service was demanded of this splendid regiment at the storming of St. Sebastian. The assault was entrusted to Robinson's brigade of the Fifth Division, in which the 4th were strongly represented. "The morning of the assault broke heavily, and as a thick fog hid every object, the batteries could not open until eight o'clock, but from that hour a constant shower of heavy missiles poured upon the besieged until eleven; then Robinson's brigade got out of the trenches, passed through the opening in the sea wall, and was launched against the breaches. While this column was gathering on the strand, near the salient angle of the horn work, twelve men under a sergeant, whose heroic death has not sufficed to preserve his name, running violently forward, leaped on the covered way to cut the sausage of the enemy's mines, and the French fired the train prematurely; the sergeant and his brave followers were destroyed, and the high sea wall was thrown with a dreadful crash upon the head of the advancing column, but not more than forty men were crushed, and the rush was scarcely checked. The forlorn hope had previously passed beyond the play of the mine, speeding along the strand amidst a shower of grape and shells, the leader, Lieutenant Macguire, of the 4th Regiment—conspicuous from his long white plume, his fine figure, and his swiftness—bounding far ahead of his men in all the pride of youthful strength and courage, but at the foot of the great breach he fell dead, and the stormers swept like a dark surge over his body. Many died with him, and the trickling of wounded men to the rear was incessant." Lieutenant Le Blanc, of the King's Own, was the only man of the advance who survived; and the regiment, out of three hundred or three hundred and fifty men, had no fewer than two hundred and sixty-one killed or wounded. At the battles of Bidassoa, Nivelle, and the Nive, the 4th were engaged; and the termination of hostilities in the following April brought to them no respite from fighting, for in the ensuing June they were ordered to North America, where war had broken out. Under Major Alured Clarke, some eight hundred bayonets of the King's Own were mustered, the other British regiments comprising the force being the 44th and 85th, with some artillery and engineers. Subsequent reinforcements somewhat strengthened "the troops, whose strength does not permit them to be called an army," but they were throughout infinitely inferior to the Americans in point of numbers. At the village of Bladensburg the English force came upon a body of above eight thousand American infantry, with artillery and a body of dragoons. The first brigade of the British pressed boldly on, but by sheer weight of numbers were forced back; by this time, however, "the second brigade had crossed . . . . the 4th went full at the enemy's front with levelled steel, and a general panic swept through the whole line. The reserve fled with a *sauve qui peut* alacrity, and the cavalry, riding hastily away, left the British in full possession of the field and of ten pieces of artillery." In this action the King's Own lost eighty-seven killed and wounded. After destroying all the public buildings at Washington, the British troops set out for Baltimore, and at Godly Wood fought a sharp and successful action. An eye-witness has given a graphic account of the occurrence. The 4th, under Majors Jones and Faunce, moved to the right of the English line, under cover of a wood, and gained a concealed position on the enemy's left. Directly they had reached this spot the signal was given for the whole army to charge. "A dreadful discharge of grape and cannister shot, of old locks, pieces of broken muskets, and everything which they could cram into their guns, was now sent forth from the whole of the enemy's artillery. Regardless of this, our men went on without either quickening or retarding their pace, till they came within a hundred yards of the American line. As yet not a musket had been fired, nor a word spoken on either side; but the enemy, now raising a shout, fired a volley from right to left, and then kept up a rapid and ceaseless discharge of musketry. Nor were our people backward in replying to these salutes; for, giving them back both their shout and their volley, we pushed on at double quick with the intention of bringing them to the charge. The bayonet is a weapon peculiarly British—at least, it is a weapon which in the hands of a British soldier is irresistible. . . . The Americans would not hazard a charge . . . they were broken, and fled just as the 4th Regiment began to show itself on the brink of the water which covered their flank, . . . nor do I recollect on any occasion to have witnessed a more complete rout." *

Shortly after this an attempt was made, under General Keane, to capture New Orleans. Here the King's Own, with two other British regiments, were surprised at night. A dropping fire which had caused some uneasiness stopped; then a fearful yell arose, "and the heavens were illuminated on all sides by a semicircular blaze of musketry. It was now evident that we were surrounded, and that by a very superior force." "And now," writes Mr. Adams, "began a desperate struggle. Sixteen hundred British were

* Gleig: "Campaigns of the British Army at Washington and New Orleans."

surrounded by five thousand Americans, but they neither faltered nor wavered. They rushed upon their enemy with vehement courage. Bayonet crossed bayonet; sword clashed against sword. Backwards and forwards rolled the eddying fight; the din was terrible; the carnage awful. At length the Americans were repulsed on every side, with the loss of many men killed, wounded, and taken prisoners. Nor was the success purchased without a severe reckoning; the British had to mourn two hundred and fifty killed and wounded." Despite further reinforcements from England, the enterprise had to be abandoned, unfortunately not before the King's Own, in a desperate encounter on the 8th of January, 1815, lost upwards of four hundred of all ranks, killed and wounded. Scarcely had they returned to England before they were summoned to the crowning battle of Waterloo. Here they were brigaded with the 27th and 40th, under General Lambert, and were placed in reserve of Picton's Division. Throughout that eventful day they stood unmoved, though shot tore through their ranks and cavalry hurled itself against their solid squares, and at the last decisive charge the King's Own were with the conquering line of British that changed the destinies of Europe and hurled a despot from his throne.

To the 4th Waterloo brought at last a period of rest, which was not disturbed till the Crimean War. Here they were in Sir Richard England's—the Third Division—and at the Alma, Inkerman, and throughout the siege of Sevastopol, fully maintained their splendid fame. They were ordered subsequently to India, where they arrived towards the close of the Mutiny, and gave by their presence additional reassurance to the English, whose sense of security in that portion of our empire the recent terrible events had so rudely shaken. Their next employment of importance was in the Abyssinian War, where they were placed in the First Brigade, under Brigadier-General Schneider. At the fording of the Bachelo river, which skirted Magdala, the 4th were in advance, and were the first to meet the impetuous sortie made by Theodore from his citadel. "Rapidly the King's Own continued to advance, driving the enemy before them," and were soon engaged in a spirited shooting match with the sharpshooters whom the King had stationed along the path, and in pits and ambuscades. Meanwhile a party of the regiment, under Captain Roberts and Lieutenants Irving, Sweeney, and Durrant, who had been told off to guard the luggage, were attacked by a large body of the enemy that had been repulsed higher up the ascent. But great though the disproportion in numbers were, the savage foe stood no chance against the rifles of the British, especially when handled by such men as the King's Own. They turned and fled in confusion, while on our side no one was killed and only thirty wounded. Amongst these was Captain Roberts of the 4th, who received a most severe wound in the elbow. At the storming of Magdala they were in reserve, and consequently did not participate to any great extent even in such fighting as there was. After the close of the war they were quartered in the West Indies, later on returning to England. The last distinction on their colours, that of South Africa, 1879, was won by the 2nd battalion, which had been raised in 1858.

THE LEICESTERSHIRE REGIMENT*—Regimental District 17—consisting of the old 17th Foot, dates from the year of the Revolution, which saw the line of the Stuarts displaced in favour of William of Orange. The first active service of the regiment after the accession of the new Sovereign was intended to be in Ireland. On arriving at Londonderry, however, the Governor, whose sympathies lay with the cause of King James, and who had arranged to yield to him the fortress, represented to Colonel Richards, of the 17th, that the services of the regiment would be useless, and the latter officer returned to England—to be rewarded for the too great facility with which he had allowed himself to be persuaded by the loss of his commission. In 1694 the 17th went to the theatre of war in the Netherlands, and the following year were for the first time engaged in action. At the siege of Namur they greatly distinguished themselves, following "with drums beating and colours flying" the storming party of grenadiers. They "advanced in gallant style, but were assailed by a storm of bullets which nearly annihilated the regiment," killing the Colonel, severely wounding the next in command, and putting *hors de combat* two hundred and fifty officers and soldiers. The 17th were engaged in all the following operations of the campaign till the conclusion of peace enabled them to return to England. Two years later war again broke out, and the 17th repaired to the Continent, and took part in the sieges of Venloo, Ruremonde, Huy, and other operations. It may be of interest to note that their Colonel at this period was one Holcroft Blood, son of the notorious Colonel Blood. The Colonel of the 17th, however, is described as being a most valuable and efficient officer, and one who gained considerable credit for his conduct during the campaign. A few years later the 17th took part in the operations of the army which, under Lord Gallway, supported the claims of Charles of Austria to the throne of Spain; and fought in various places—Badajoz,

---

* The Leicestershire Regiment bear as badges the Royal Tiger with the Irish Harp and "Hindoostan" on a scroll, on the cap, and on the collar the Royal Tiger within a laurel wreath. The motto is that of the Garter. On their colours are the names of the following battles : "Louisbourg," "Afghanistan," "Ghuznee," "Khelat," "Sevastopol," "Ali Musjid," "Afghanistan, 1878-79." The uniform is scarlet, with facings of white.

Ciudad Rodrigo, and others—which, a century later, saw British troops again gaining honour and victory in contention with the armies of France. Returning to England in 1709, the regiment enjoyed a period of rest till the rising in Scotland of the adherents of the Stuarts in 1715, which afforded to the 17th an occasion for distinction at Sheriffmuir. After a further sojourn of ten years at home, the regiment was despatched to Minorca, and in 1727 sent a detachment of men to assist in the defence of Gibraltar. Despite their active service at home and abroad, it was not till 1758 that the 17th gained their first distinction, that of Louisbourg. The capture of the fortress, followed as it was by the surrender of the whole island, was an agreeable variation from the usual tenor of our achievements in America—"a part of the world from which" (according to a contemporary record) "we had long been strangers to anything but delays, misfortunes, disappointments, and disgraces." The loss to the 17th included that of the Earl of Dundonald, a captain in the regiment, who was killed, and Captain Rycant and Lieutenant Tew, who were wounded. Though naturally well-nigh forgotten now, the capture of Louisbourg was a military success of the greatest importance. An historical summary written at the time thus describes it:—"The taking of Louisbourg was an event the most desired by all our Colonies; that harbour had always been a receptacle convenient to the enemy's privateers who infested the English trade in North America. It was the most effectual blow which France had received from the commencement of the war. By the taking of Louisbourg she lost the only place she had in a convenient situation for the reinforcements that were sent to support the war in the other parts of America; and with Louisbourg fell the island of St. John's. . . . It is incredible how much this success in America, joined to the spirit of our other measures, operated to raise our military reputation in Europe and to sink that of France." Well might the Chevalier Drucour, the French Governor of Louisbourg, commence a letter to a friend with the trite but apposite quotation, "*Infandum, regina, jubes*," followed by the melancholy wail—"I wish I could erase from my memory the four years I passed at Louisbourg. . . . We had three hundred and fifty killed and wounded during the course of the siege. . . . Of fifty-two pieces of cannon which were opposed to the batteries of the besiegers, forty were dismounted, broken, or rendered unserviceable."

The 17th served with distinction in many of the further operations—not including Quebec—which resulted in the conquest of Canada, and shortly afterwards were ordered to the West Indies. At the capture of Martinique, in which they participated, "their loss was limited to a few private soldiers killed and wounded." Then, commanded by

Colonel Campbell, they joined the forces under the Earl of Albemarle which were despatched to the Havannah. Here they were in the brigade under General Grant, and "took part in the service connected with the siege and capture of Moro Fort, which was the key position of the extensive works which covered the town." The labour was terribly arduous, and combined with the climate proved fatal to many of our soldiers. "Incredible were the hardships sustained by the troops during these operations. The earth was everywhere so thin that it was with the greatest difficulty that they could make their approaches under cover; and the want of water, together with the heat, proved most distressing. Fatigue parties had to convey it from a vast distance, and so scanty and precarious was the quantity that the troops had frequently to be supplied from the casks of the shipping. Through the thick, dense woods, that grew in all the rank luxuriance peculiar to the torrid zone, roads of communication had to be cut, and the artillery had to be dragged by pathless ways from a rough and rocky shore. In these painful efforts, under a burning West Indian sun, many of the soldiers and seamen, worn with toil, drenched with perspiration, and maddened by thirst, dropped down dead in the drag-ropes, in the trenches, and at their posts, slain by sheer heat and fatigue."

After an interval of a few years, passed in North America and England, in 1775 the 17th were ordered again to America, where the War of Independence had broken out. They fought at Long Island with conspicuous valour, losing an officer and two men killed, and about twenty of all ranks wounded. In the subsequent operations they also shared, and in the early part of 1777 were engaged in an "affair" which, very justly, was considered to have owed its successful result to the gallant conduct of the 17th. The succinct account given in the Official Record is worth repeating. "Early in the morning of the 4th of January, 1777, the three regiments (the 17th, 40th, and 5th), commenced their march. The 17th Regiment, commanded by Lieutenant-Colonel Charles Mawhood, being in advance, encountered the van of the American army, General Washington having suddenly quitted Trenton (where he had taken up his position during the winter), with his whole force, to surprise the three regiments. The morning being foggy, Lieutenant-Colonel Mawhood could not discern the numbers of the force he had met; but supposing it to be only a detachment he instantly attacked his opponents, and the 17th speedily drove back a force of very superior numbers with great gallantry. The regiment was soon environed in front and on both flanks by a numerous force; and Lieutenant-Colonel Mawhood, discovering that he was engaged with the American army, resolved to make a desperate effort to extricate himself.

Having confidence in the valour and resolution of the regiment, he directed a charge with bayonets to the front, to break through the American army. Undismayed by the multitudes of opponents which environed them, the 17th rushed upon the ranks of the enemy, broke through all opposition, and continued their march to Maidenhead. Their conduct excited great admiration, and the Americans acknowledged the superior gallantry of the regiment. A serious loss was, however, sustained; thirteen officers and soldiers being killed, fifty-three wounded, and thirty-five missing." The expression "missing," which one often meets with in accounts of battles in America, had a terrible significance to those who know the fate of such as fell into the hands of the Indians. The following incident is full of a grim suggestiveness as to its actual meaning, though it is to be feared that the stern presence of mind of its chief actor was wanting in many similar cases. In one of the skirmishes of 1760, Allan Macpherson, a private in one of the Scotch regiments, fell into the hands of the enemy. "Anxious to escape from the cruel torture that awaited him, he signified that he had something of importance to communicate. An interpreter was introduced, and the Indians stood by in solemn silence. He informed them that he was a medicine-man, and knew of certain herbs which, if applied to the skin, would enable it to resist the sword or the tomahawk, though wielded by the strongest arm; if they would conduct him to the woods, and allow him to collect these herbs, their bravest warrior might strike at his neck without injuring him. Such an assertion found ready credence with superstitious Indians, and they complied with his request. Macpherson was as cool and confident in his bearing as if he had nothing to dread; he rubbed his neck with the juice of the first herbs he had picked up, laid his head calmly on a block of wood, and invited the ordeal. An Indian raised his tomahawk and struck at his neck, with such force that his head flew several yards from his body."

The regiment fought at Brandywine and Germantown; at Freehold the captain of their grenadier company was severely wounded; at Stoney Point, under Colonel Johnson, after gallantly resisting for some time an attack made by *four thousand* Americans, under a general officer, a number of all ranks were killed, and the rest taken prisoners. They were exchanged, however, in time to take part in the action known as that of Guildford Court House, and to be again made prisoners of war after a gallant resistance at York Town. During their sojourn in America their territorial title was given to the 17th, who in 1786 returned to England. Ten years later they were sent to St. Domingo, where, in common with the rest of the British troops, they suffered severely from the climate. They fought—as a two-battalion regiment—in the Helder campaign, in one of the engagements losing eight killed, and nine officers and fifty-eight rank and file wounded or missing. They fought again at Bergen, where they were in the third column, and again suffered loss, though not so severe as on the last-named occasion. After some five years' home duty, the 17th were ordered to India, and in many fierce battles maintained their high renown as a "fighting corps." Chumar, Comona, and Gonoivie— forgotten battles now—witnessed the prowess of the regiment, and quiet homes in faraway England were filled at once with pride and sorrow when the tardy reports made public how Captains Radcliff and Kirk, Lieutenants McGregor, Harvey, and Harrison, and sergeants and privates whose names, though not their deeds, have passed from memory, had died in showing the savage foe what British soldiers could dare and do; how Sergeant Suttle had fallen at the top of the deadly breach; and how Colonel Hardyman, Lieutenants Wilson, Campbell, and Dadingstone—all wounded—had been complimented by the Governor-General for the courage they had shown. For many years they fought against the fierce Indian tribes, losing many a gallant officer and soldier, and earning repeated praise from generals and commanders. It was not till 1822 that the 17th returned to England, only sixty-five officers and men being with the regiment of those who had sailed from England nineteen years before. Peaceful home duties occupied the next thirteen years, at the expiration of which period they again repaired to India, and in 1839 gained further honours by their participation in the Afghan War. At the siege of Ghuznee, under Colonel Croker, they "took a conspicuous share; they led the assault on the citadel, and at five o'clock in the morning (of the 23rd of July, 1839) their colours were waving triumphantly on the fortress." A contemporary account thus describes the fighting at Ghuznee and the following siege of Khelat, at each of which places the 17th captured a standard:—"The storming party poured into Ghuznee. As at Herat, so here, the Afghans still disputed the ground inch by inch, hand to hand, with pistol, dagger, and sabre. The darkness was more favourable to the assailants than the besieged, every street was strewn with the slain; out of the garrison of three thousand five hundred persons not fewer than five hundred were killed within the walls, and fifty men fell in the defence of a single fortified house. Before sunrise the standard of England was planted on the citadel of Ghisneh. Nor was the treachery of the Khan of Khelat forgotten; General Wiltshire led a strong detachment against that formidable fortress." It was undoubtedly formidable. There were six guns admirably placed to defend the walls; the garrison was composed of the flower of the Beloochee warriors.

x x

The 17th, under Colonel Croker, were with the besieging party, which "succeeded in blowing open the gate and made their way into the town, the enemy disputing every foot of ground up to the walls of the inner citadel. The troops, however, succeeded in forcing an entrance into the last stronghold of the capital of Beloochistan. There a desperate resistance was made by Mehrat in person, and the Khan himself, with many of his chiefs, fell fighting sword in hand." Though the 17th only lost six privates killed, there were thirty-three of all ranks wounded. "Lieutenant-Colonel Croker caused the names of Colour-Sergeants J. Dunn and Mills to be entered in the records of the regiment on account of their bravery at Khelat." Other honours were no less freely though deservedly bestowed on the gallant regiment. Colonel Croker and Major Pennycuick were made C.B.'s; the same two officers and Major Derbon received a distinguished Order from the Shah; and Majors Pennycuick and Derbon and Captain Darley each received promotion. In 1841 the regiment was quartered at Aden, and for the next six years found occasional employment in field service against the Mahrattas, returning in 1847 to England, where they enjoyed a period of quiet till the outbreak of the Crimean War.

The 17th bear on their colours the word "Sevastopol," which tells of the share they bore in our last great war, our victories in which, it has been well said, "have added an imperishable lustre to the annals of the nineteenth century." After the fall of Sevastopol, the 17th took part in the capture of Kinburn. They were in the first division, and were the first regiment which landed, meeting—to the general surprise of all—no opposition from the Russians. A graphic account of the terrible bombardment which resulted in the capitulation of the fort describes how "bravely did the Russians handle the only guns that remained to them; heavier grew the broadsides, and death and carnage, wounds and suffering were increasing fast in Kinburn." At last, on the ramparts, swept by the fire from our fleet and battery, appeared a solitary figure, in whose hand was discerned the white symbol of surrender. The stern old commandant advanced, in one hand a pistol, in the other a sword. He discharged the pistol into the ground; on the ground he flung the sword he had so bravely wielded, and with the "great and exceeding bitter cry,"—"Oh! Kinburn, Kinburn! glory of Suvaroff and my shame!" surrendered to the allies.

After the close of the Crimean campaign, the 17th passed some time in Canada and America, and in 1878 formed a portion of the force engaged in the Afghan War. They took part in the capture of Ali Musjid, and the following day surprised a large body of the retreating enemy under Hyder Khan, whom they surrounded and took prisoner; and in the famous Kurram column, the command of the first infantry brigade was given to Colonel A. H. Cobbe, of the regiment, who was severely wounded at Peiwar Khotal. The 17th passed a considerable time in Jellalabad, and suffered in common with the rest of the force from the savage predatory raids made by the natives.* Under Brigadier Gough, they fought at Futtehabad, where they greatly distinguished themselves, and amongst the "moving incidents" of the day, none is more eloquent in its sadness and in its triumph than the death of Lieutenant Wiseman, of the regiment. Private Clarke, of the 17th, "says that they were in skirmishing order, and only about three hundred yards from the *sungahs* (breastworks). The Afghans, seeing them all on the ground, thought they were killed or wounded, and this tempted them to come out. The 17th— or, at least, the company Wiseman belonged to—fixed bayonets, and made a charge. Wiseman was twenty yards in front of his company, and thus got close to the Afghan bearing the flag. He ran forward, and seizing it in his left hand, sent his sword through the bearer's head in the lower part of his cheek. The Afghan fell, leaving Wiseman in possession of the flag. Clarke shot another man whom he saw coming to attack Wiseman, but he could not say who it was that cut the Lieutenant down, as he himself was knocked over by a severe blow from a stone, and it was while down that he shot the man coming up and flourishing his knife." "Clarke adds," continues a narrator of the occurrence, "that he was knocked down a second time by another stone, and avoided the knives of the Afghans by rolling over; and that there were only three or four men with Wiseman at that time, as the call had been sounded to retire, but being so far in advance these men had not heard it, and so were left to struggle against great odds. In a minute after the order was given to advance again, and during the brief interval the Afghans had found time to gash Wiseman's body with their *charahs* and strip it of everything valuable." Throughout the remainder of the campaign the 17th earned the highest praise. The names of Brigadier Cobbe, Colonel Tompson, and Captain Brind, with others of the 17th, were particularly mentioned for their gallant service; and the report of Sir Samuel Browne endorses all that has been said of the exceptional merit of the regiment. "Her Majesty's 17th Regiment," writes the General, "has been one of the most useful in the Division. Its good discipline, and the heartiness with which it entered into any work it had to do, reflect the greatest credit on Lieutenant-Colonel W. D. Tompson, who commanded it to my entire satisfaction, and on Lieutenant (now

---

* At Dakha, two men of the 17th Regiment were killed while on guard.

Captain) F. S. Anderson, the Adjutant." Altogether, it will be admitted that her Majesty's Leicestershire Regiment fully deserve the *dignitas* which has accompanied the *otium* that has fallen to their lot since that date.*

The next regiment in alphabetical order is the PRINCE OF WALES'S LEINSTER REGIMENT (ROYAL CANADIANS)†—Regimental District No. 100. The Prince of Wales's Leinster Regiment consists of the 100th and 109th Foot, and is one of the most recently formed of her Majesty's Foot regiments. The 100th Regiment was raised in 1858, and was the sixth to bear that numerical rank. The name "Niagara" on its colours was granted in commemoration of the notable services of the fourth "Hundredth Regiment" in America. Few wars in which the British army has been engaged present more numerous instances of heroism than this unsatisfactory struggle, and few regiments showed a nobler record than the old "City of Dublin Regiment," as the Hundredth of that date were called, but any enumeration of their services would be outside the scope of the present work, which is concerned with regiments in actual existence. The 109th Regiment is one of those formerly in the service of the Hon. East India Company, whose services were transferred to the Imperial Crown in 1861. As the Third Bombay European Regiment, raised in 1854, the 109th did sterling service in Central India at the time of the Mutiny, serving with the Central India force, and at Rashghur, Baroda, Betwa, Jhansi, and Gwalior.‡

The next regiment is the LINCOLNSHIRE REGIMENT§—Regimental District No. 10—consisting of the famous 10th Foot. The origin of the regiment must be sought for in the earliest years of Charles II., when, the Commonwealth army having been disbanded, certain of the more important towns and districts had "guards" or "garrisons" appointed to them. Amongst these nebulous commands was one at Plymouth, held by John, Earl

* The sobriquets of the 17th are "Bengal Tigers" and "Lily-Whites."
† The Prince of Wales's Leinster Regiment bear as badges the Prince of Wales's plume and coronet surrounded by the Garter, on the cap and collar. The mottoes are those of the Prince of Wales and the Order of the Garter. On the helmet plate and glengarry are two maple leaves. On their colours are "Niagara" and "Central India." The uniform is scarlet with facings of blue.
‡ Amongst the "folk lore," so to speak, of the Regiment, may be mentioned the fact recorded by Archer, that on the occasion of the Prince of Wales's visit to India, the sergeants of the 109th publicly presented to his Royal Highness a panther called Jumbo, which had been reared in the regiment.
§ The Lincolnshire Regiment bear as badge the Sphinx with "Egypt" on cap and collar. The motto is that of the Garter. On their colours are "Blenheim," "Ramillies," "Oudenarde," "Malplaquet," "Egypt," "Peninsula," "Sobraon," "Punjaub," "Mooltan," "Goojerat," "Lucknow." The uniform is scarlet with facings of white.

of Bath. Early in the following reign the ill-fated James II. made the Plymouth contingent the nucleus of a regiment, and from that time to the present, whenever and wherever fighting was to the fore, honour to be gained, and fealty and service done to sovereign and country, then and there, *primi inter pares*, loyal and brave amongst the loyal and brave, were sure to be found the gallant regiment known to us of to-day as Her Majesty's "Lincolnshire Regiment, the 10th Foot." From the "quaint and curious volumes of forgotten lore," which tell us of the mien and deeds of those famous soldiers of two centuries ago, we learn that the 10th Regiment was the only infantry regiment which wore blue coats, their uniform being blue coats lined with red, red waistcoats, breeches, and stockings, and round broad-brimmed hats, turned up on one side and ornamented with red ribbons. When William of Orange felt that the position of his consort and himself on the throne of England was either sufficiently well established to warrant, or so precarious as to render necessary, his active intervention in foreign politics, the 10th Regiment—then known as the Earl of Bath's—was ordered to Flanders, where the first gilding of their bold emblazonment was effected with no uncertain touch. At Steinkirke, where the British arms got undeniably the worst of it, the Baron of Pibrack, one of our allies, owed his rescue to two sergeants of the Earl of Bath's regiment; Fiennes and Dixmunde saw the prowess of the 10th. When the signal was given to force the French lines at D'Olignies it is recorded of the regiment that they "raised a loud shout and ran forward." The Grenadier Company being anxious to signalise themselves, dashed into the River Espiers, which was so deep that many were up to the chin in water; but they gained the shore without serious loss, sprang forward with astonishing rapidity, forded the ditch, pulled down the palisadoes, and ascended the lines sword in hand, and so were the first that entered the works. The French fled and the lines were carried with little loss." As a recognition of their bravery the Duke of Wirtemberg gave a ducat to each man, a form of guerdon not uncommon in those days. In 1695 the 10th were employed in marching and countermarching in pursuance of the military tactics then in vogue, and in protecting the maritime and other towns of Flanders, besides covering the army besieging Namur.

For the next few years no great battle fell to their lot, though they were engaged somewhat actively at the siege of Liege, where the grenadiers of the regiment again "behaved with great gallantry." After taking part in the sieges of Huy and Limburg, the following year the 10th proceeded to the Danube to join the Imperial army; and there —after fighting in the fierce combat at Schellenberg—gained at the battle of Blenheim their first distinction. At Neer-Hespen the regiment formed part of the leading brigade of infantry, and shared in the operations of the main army during the remainder of the campaign. Again at Ramillies did the regiment give good earnest of that stern courage and brilliant daring which have ever characterized it. At Oudenarde—that battle "fought with muskets, bayonets, and sabres," to the almost entire exclusion of artillery—the 10th again distinguished themselves; at Malplaquet, where the courage of victors and vanquished alike was splendid, the 10th were with the stubborn regiments of foot before whose withering fire "the gay, the vain, yet truly valiant cavalry of France was forced to fly." From that time till 1767 the annals of the regiment tell of comparatively peaceful times, during which they were on duty in England, Ireland, and Gibraltar. In the latter year, however, they were ordered to America, and were in Boston at the outbreak of the war. They fought at Bunker's Hill, of which it has been said, that "in the whole history of the British army there is no record of a more gallant feat than the capture of Bunker's Hill." And the drama was acted before a remarkable audience. The colonists who, despite concessions and proofs of amity, had determined to cast off the yoke of British supremacy, thronged from far and near to witness the destruction of the King's troops. "Far on the left, across the waters of the Charles, the American camp had poured forth its thousands to the hills, and the whole population of the country inland for many miles had gathered to a point to witness a struggle charged with the fate of their nation. Beacon Hill rose from out the appalling silence of the town of Boston like a pyramid of living faces, with every eye fixed on the fatal point, and men hung along the yards of the shipping, or were suspended on cornices, cupolas, and steeples, in thoughtless security, while every other sense was lost in the absorbing interest of the sight." At Long Island, where the Americans lost 3,300 killed, wounded, and prisoners, as against 367 of the King's troops, the 10th were actively engaged; at Brandywine, and Germantown, and the other minor engagements during the campaign of 1776–8, they fought, always with honour if not with victory. After a short sojourn at home for the purposes of recruiting, the regiment went to Jamaica in 1786, and remained there nine years, suffering severely during that time from the climate. In 1795 some detachments went to the West Indies—a shipwreck having prevented the whole regiment going, according to the original intention—and here they were employed against the insurgents in Grenada until 1798. In that year they returned home, and the whole regiment proceeded to India. In 1801 they were sent from thence to Egypt with the force under General Baird. The terrible march across the desert, and the sufferings from heat and thirst which the Indian contingent endured, have been before referred to; and it must have been terribly galling to the brave soldiers who had made such heroic efforts to find that all the fighting was practically over. As, however, a writer has remarked: "Our men and faithful soldiers from India, and our troops from the Cape, had not the opportunity of pulling a trigger in battle, but their approach took out of the enemy all the little heart that was left in them after Abercromby's victories." The 10th remained in Alexandria after the rest of the troops were withdrawn, when the plague breaking out compelled their removal to Malta in April, 1803.

In 1807, three years prior to which date a Second Battalion had been raised, the First Battalion went to Sicily, and took part in the expedition to Naples and the Ionian Isles, and the various engagements which occupied our army in that locality.

The Second Battalion went to Messina in 1811, and while in Sicily captured the island of Ponza, a brilliant exploit which they were fortunate enough to achieve without the loss of a man. The First Battalion left Sicily in June, 1812, and joined the expedition which sailed for Spain, taking part in the battle of Castalla, the siege of Tarragona, and the blockade of Barcelona, and subsequently returned to Palermo, May 19, 1814. It did not fall to the fortune of the regiment to be present at any of the most famous Peninsular battles, but they well merited the comprehensive distinction—Peninsula—that they bear. After a service of some years in England; in Portugal, where they formed part of the army of occupation; and in various pacific home duties, the regiment was ordered to India in 1842, and took part in the first Sikh War. At Sobraon the 10th greatly distinguished themselves. They were amongst the regiments which were to lead the attack under Brigadier Stacey. Early in the morning commenced a terrific artillery fire from a half circle having for its centre the Sikh works. "Nothing," writes Dr. Macgregor in his "History of the Sikhs," could be conceived grander than the effect of the batteries when they opened, as the cannonade passed along from the Sutledge to Little Sobraon, in one continued roar of guns and mortars; while, ever and anon, the rocket, like a spirit of fire, winged its rapid flight high above the batteries in its progress towards the Sikh intrenchment. . . . . The Sikh guns responded with shot and shells, and it now became a grand artillery concert, while the infantry brigades and divisions looked on with a certain degree of interest, somewhat allied, however, to vexation, lest the artillery should have all the work to themselves." This, however, was not to be the case. "At nine o'clock Brigadier Stacey's brigade moved to the attack in admirable order. . . . . But notwithstanding the regularity and coolness, and the scientific character of this assault, so hot was the fire of cannon, musketry, and zumbooruks (guns on camels), kept up by the Khalsa troops, that it seemed for some moments impossible that the intrenchments could be won under it." But the gallant 10th and their comrades pushed on, works and intrenchments were carried, and "our matchless infantry stood erect and compact within the Sikh camp." In this fierce combat the 10th lost three officers and a hundred and thirty rank and file, Colonel Franks, in command of the regiment, being wounded early in the day. After the submission of Dhuleep Sing, the 10th was for some time in garrison at Lahore, and on the breaking out of the second Sikh War, almost exactly two years later, they were in the first brigade of the force which captured Mooltan. At Goojerat they again won high honour. "The loopholed village of Chowtah-Kabrah was carried by one rush of Harvey's brigade, led by Colonel Franks; our 10th Foot fought their way in with the loss of sixty killed and wounded, and the cannon on the field were in some instances worked by the soldiers of this fine old regiment." During the Mutiny the 10th did most sterling service. Some of them were in garrison at Benares when Niell's splendid courage and presence of mind stemmed the wild torrent of mutiny which threatened the lives of Europeans in the "Holy City." At Dinapore the 10th overawed the regiments of mutineers; they were with the avenging army that captured Lucknow; they shared in the relief of Azimghur, and in the subsequent operations in Oude. At Arrah, under Captain Dunbar, they experienced severe loss in July, 1857, a fact which boded ill for the foe at their next encounter. This was at Narainpore in the following month, and an account of the engagement thus describes the doings of the Lincolnshire:— "The detachment of the 10th (about two hundred men), eager to emulate the heroism of their comrades of the 5th Fusiliers, and exasperated by their previous loss under Captain Dunbar, asked to be permitted to charge the enemy at once. Eyre consented; Captain Patterson led them on; they rushed with a shout and a cheer, and the enemy gave way before a charge which they found irresistible." They returned to England in 1859, and since that date, though the incidents of service have called them to numerous and distant regions of the empire, they have not been engaged in any important operations excepting the Malay and Perak operations of 1874—6, in which they worthily maintained their high reputation.*

* It is said that a nickname of the 10th was "The Springers."

THE KING'S (LIVERPOOL REGIMENT).† –Regimental District No. 8—consists of the 8th Foot, one of the most distinguished regiments of the Army. Like many other regiments, the 8th Foot date their origin from the time of Monmouth's rebellion, when Charles, Lord Ferrars of Chartly, under authority dated June 19th, 1685, raised a regiment from the districts of Hertfordshire, Derbyshire, and London, consisting of ten companies, and composed partly of musketeers and partly of pikemen, according to the system of the day. The first title given to the new corps was "The Princess Anne of Denmark's Regiment." After the abdication of James II., the regiment fought under King William at the Battle of the Boyne, and throughout the Irish campaign, down to the fall of Limerick. Subsequently they were stationed in England until 1697, when they repaired to Flanders, and joined the troops under the Duke of Wirtemberg. In the following reign, the Queen's—as the regiment was then called—went to Holland, and played a prominent part in the important warfare of that time and place. At the siege of Liege in 1702, we find it recorded that the grenadier company were much distinguished; they fought at Blenheim and Ramillies, at Oudenarde and Malplaquet. While the siege of the town of Tournay was in progress the Queen's Regiment formed part of the covering army, and when the attack on the citadel was commenced, the regiment left the covering army to engage in this service. In carrying out this operation the troops had to encounter dangers of a character to which they were not accustomed, from the multiplicity of the subterraneous works, which were more numerous than those above ground. "The approaches were effected by sinking pits several fathoms deep, and working from thence underground, until the soldiers came to the enemy's casemates and mines, which extended a great distance from the body of the citadel; several mines were discovered and the powder removed. The British and French soldiers frequently met underground, where they fought with sword, pistol, and bayonet. On several occasions the allies were suffocated with smoke in these dismal labyrinths, and the troops, mistaking friends for foes, sometimes killed their fellow-soldiers. The enemy sprang several mines, which blew up some of the besiegers' batteries, guns, and many men." The dangers attending this subterranean warfare were very serious. On one occasion a captain, lieutenant, and thirty men were blown

† The King's (Liverpool Regiment) bear as badges the White Horse in the Garter on the cap and the Red Rose of Lancaster on the collar. The mottoes are those of the Garter and "*Nec aspera terrent.*" On the colours are the Royal Cipher and Crown and the Sphinx, with the names of the following battles: "Blenheim," "Ramillies," "Oudenarde," "Malplaquet," "Dettingen," "Egypt," "Martinique," "Niagara," "Delhi," "Lucknow," "Peiwar Kotal," "Afghanistan, 1878-80." The uniform is scarlet with facings of blue.

up; on another a mine exploded, blowing to atoms four hundred officers and men, whose mangled limbs were hurled to a considerable distance. Nor were foe and powder the only adversaries they had to contend with. "The working parties underground, with the guards which attended them, were sometimes inundated with water; many men were buried alive in the cavities by explosions; and a number of veterans of the 8th, who had triumphed at Blenheim, Ramillies, and Oudenarde, lost their lives in these subterraneous attacks.

After the treaty of Utrecht the 8th, with the 18th, remained at Ghent until the barrier treaty was concluded, finding their next active employment in the suppression of the rising in Scotland of 1715. At the battle of Dunblane, it is recorded that they suffered severely, and the official record, after enumerating their deeds at some length, thus describes the close of that eventful day, so far as it concerned the 8th :—" In some places a veteran of the 8th was seen contending manfully against four or five mountaineers. The Earl of Forfar was at the head of the regiment; he evinced signal valour and intrepidity, and was wounded and taken prisoner.* Lieutenant-Colonel Hanmer was surrounded. He held several opponents at bay for a short time, but was overpowered and killed. Ensign Justin Holdman, a young officer of great promise, was conspicuous for personal bravery, and was mortally wounded and taken prisoner. The soldiers were unable to withstand the very superior number of their opponents; ten officers and a hundred men of the 8th had fallen, when the remainder, being favoured by a very gallant charge of the dragoons on the left of the line fell back to re-form their ranks."

After the suppression of the rebellion the regiment received its present title of "The King's" from George I., and at the same time the facings were changed from yellow to blue, and the "Horse of Hanover within the Garter" was directed to be borne as the regimental badge.

After a short time of home service the King's proceeded to Flanders, and fought at the famous battles of Dettingen and Fontenoy. One likes to linger in passing on the views of the former battle on which every fresh account throws a fresh light. We of to-day have much the same sort of tenderness for the plucky "dapper little George" who this day proved himself no unworthy scion of the mighty English monarchs whose blood ran in his viens, as had Thackeray. "Bravery," as the latter remarks, "never goes out of

* He is said to have received no less than sixteen sword wounds, besides a pistol shot in the knee. He died, after three weeks' suffering, at Stirling.

fashion," and it is no unpleasing picture to the patriotic Englishman that which the histories give us of the King, resolute to be where the danger was most threatening, dispensing with the charger whose unruly temper had well-nigh made the French the gift of a British monarch as prisoner, and placing himself at the head of " the unflinching infantry of England and the sturdy Hanoverian Foot, with whom the great merit of the victory remained. The victory was a splendid one, and the 'King's' contributed not a little to its gaining."*

Concerning Fontenoy, one of "the only two battles where the British infantry have been quite beaten and swept from the field by any enemy," it is well, while admitting the defeat, to recall the fact that "Marshal Saxe had 60,000 men, while the whole Confederate Army amounted only to 33,000. If we take off the Dutch, who so scandalously took themselves off, it will be found that the British and Hanoverians fought against more than triple their own numbers. The loss of such a battle certainly carried with it no disgrace to the pride of our army and long enduring, dauntless infantry." (*Low.*)

The King's were recalled to England on the occasion of the rising of '45, and joined the force assembled at Newcastle, being employed in several movements designed to cover Yorkshire, and taking part in the battles of Falkirk and Culloden. When the insurrection was quelled they returned to Flanders, and served at the battle of Val and in other engagements down to the peace, when they proceeded to Gibraltar, in which fortress they remained until 1751.

After a few years of rest, the outbreak of the Seven Years' War found fresh work for the regiment, which was augmented to two battalions, the second becoming, later on, the 63rd Foot. The King's served in Germany in 1760, and at Warbourg, Corbach, Wilhelmstal, Zierenburg, Campen, Kirch-denken, and Grafenstein greatly distinguished themselves. After five years of home service the 8th embarked, in May, 1768, for North America, to relieve the 15th. After passing several years at Quebec, Montreal, St. John's, Chambly, and other places in Canada, the regiment was removed up the country to the large lakes; and during their sojourn there Captain George Foster earned great praise by a most gallant enterprise against four hundred Americans who were stationed at Fort Cedars, on the St. Lawrence.

* It is recorded that "not long after, Voltaire met Lord Stair, the general of the allied forces on this occasion, and coolly asked his lordship what he thought of the battle of Dettingen. 'I think,' said the Scottish nobleman, 'that the French made one great mistake and the English two. Yours was not standing still ; our first, entangling ourselves in a most dangerous position, our second, failing to pursue our victory.'"

At the commencement of the French Revolutionary war the flank companies took part in the capture of Martinique and Guadeloupe, exploits which admittedly won the highest praise for officers and soldiers alike.* The rest of the regiment, meanwhile, served with the Duke of York in Flanders. While forming part of the garrison of Nimeguen, an opportunity occurred for winning fame, of which the gallant King's were not slow to avail themselves. On November 4th, 1794, a detachment of the regiment was engaged in attempting to destroy the enemy's works. "The attack was made with the most distinguished gallantry, and the French were driven from their works at the point of the bayonet" (*Official Record*). Subsequently the 8th took part in the terrible winter retreat to Bremen. The following few years were passed by the regiment in various services, including suppression of the rebellion in Grenada, garrison duty in Guernsey and in Minorca, and in the expedition against Cadiz. From thence they proceeded to Egypt and formed part of the force under Major-General Cradock that advanced to Ghizeh and Cairo, subsequently gaining great credit during the siege of Alexandria. The doings of the regiment for the next few years are thus summarized in the Official Records:—"At the conclusion of the treaty of peace in 1802 the 8th proceeded to Gibraltar, from which they were withdrawn in August, 1803, and sent to Portsmouth. The 1st battalion went to Hanover in 1805, to Copenhagen in 1807, to Nova Scotia in 1808, to the West Indies in 1809, where they took part in the capture of Martinique. Afterwards they returned to North America, and were present at nearly all the engagements on the Canadian frontier during the American War of 1812—14. the conduct of the regiment during this period being commended in the public despatches. In the winter of 1813—14 six companies of the 2nd battalion marched from New Brunswick to Quebec through the backwoods in snow shoes. This painful march through regions of snow and ice, exposed to violent storms and the most intense frost, was accomplished with little loss, and the condition of the troops on their arrival at Quebec in March—they started February 14th—was such as to call forth the approbation of the Commander-in-Chief in Canada. At Lundy's Lane the 8th highly distinguished themselves, and the marked gallantry displayed by the regiment while serving on the Niagara frontier was subsequently rewarded with the royal authority to bear on their colours the word 'Niagara.'" From this time

* The regiment landed at Portsmouth in August, when a tall grenadier, in full marching order, with a goatskin jack and a pair of mosquito trousers on, was met in High Street by a staff officer, and replied, on being asked who he was, " Please your honour, I'm the left wing of the 63rd regiment, and just arrived from Jamaica."

to the outbreak of the Indian Mutiny, the 8th were not engaged in any important warfare.

At the commencement of the Mutiny the King's were at Jallundur in the Punjab, and three days after the first outbreak at Meerut a detachment did important service in securing the fort and magazines at Phillour. In June, 1857, the regiment marched to Delhi and bore an active part in the siege, and, after the fall of the city, formed a flying column under Brigadier Greathead, which was sent to reopen communications with Agra and Cawnpore. They joined Sir Colin Campbell's force at the relief of Lucknow, and in the actions at Cawnpore and the operations in Oude more than fulfilled the conditions imposed upon them by their matchless traditions.

From that time till 1878 was a period of comparative inactivity; in the last-named year, however, they* joined the Kurram Line Force under General Roberts, and took part at the storming and capture of the Peiwar Kotal. The 8th were in the brigade commanded by General Cobbe, and on that officer being wounded the command devolved upon Colonel Barry Drew, of the regiment.

The guns that in the dim twilight of the 2nd of December moved out to engage the enemy's batteries were escorted by a party of the King's, and later on the whole regiment advanced into the valley. "The morning was beautiful," writes a graphic narrator of the events; "the warmth of the bright sun tempered the keenness of the air and lit up the landscape, the bold natural features of which were very striking, but as the enemy's riflemen crowded the pine-covered slopes of the Peiwar Kotal, few cared then to appreciate artistic effects." Soon our handful of troops had daringly, and in the face of mighty odds, worked their way upwards close to the summit of the Pass, but in front of them they found a deep and unforeseen chasm, which had to be dipped into; and it was now seen that, after ascending the opposite bank and traversing a mile and a half of the roadway, if such the rocky path could be called, the Kotal could only then be gained, and this under a fire of cannon and musketry! Desperate positions demand desperate endeavours. Seldom is there need for any commander of British troops to consider which of his soldiers is best fitted for such enterprises; had there been in the present instance, to none could the duty have more appropriately been assigned than to the regiment to which in fact it was, the gallant King's. "The fire from the heights seemed to fall harmlessly among them as they went plunging down to the road, and in less than ten minutes the Kotal was in their hands, while a ringing British cheer rang

---

* It was the 2nd battalion, raised in 1858, that shared in the Afghan War.

along the line." The Peiwar Kotal was gained, and in the gaining the King's regiment had won another distinction for their glorious colours.* The King's remained in garrison for some time at Peiwar Kotal, and the rest of their service during the campaign, though arduous, was not exciting. As an official account of the expedition says—"During the ensuing operations of the army of invasion the regiment was employed in the main in étappen duty, but, though no opportunities for distinguishing itself in the field again arose, it had its full share of the privations and hardships which fell to the lot of the division to which it was attached, and performed a considerable amount of hard and not unimportant work."

Subsequently the King's took part in the operations of the Burmah expeditionary force under General Prendergast, since which time no important service of note has fallen to their share. In his reference to the 8th, Colonel Archer points out that their badge of the Lancaster Rose differs from that of the other Lancashire regiments by having a very small detached gilt scroll, inscribed 'King's,' below it. Amongst other features peculiar to the regiment he instances the use of the old English letters in the badges, and that "the King's is the only regiment not specifically entitled 'Royal,' in which scarlet bands are worn to the round forage caps."

THE MANCHESTER REGIMENT† (Regimental District No. 63) consists of the 63rd and 96th Foot. The former was constituted, in 1758, from the Second Battalion of the 8th (the King's), the first colonel being Colonel David Watson. The first foreign service of the regiment was at Martinique, where they arrived in January, 1759. Before a week had passed they joined in the attack on Guadeloupe, where they incurred considerable loss, Lieutenant-Colonel Debresay and Captain Trollope being killed. In this neighbourhood—the descriptions of which recall vague reminiscences of "plantation scenes," as represented on stage and in fiction, with the "peaceful sugar plantations, the working of mills, the driving of bullock carts, the cutting of canes and boiling of sugar, while the negroes sang and chorused amidst green savannahs, long avenues of palms, and waving branches of cocoa-nut trees"—the 63rd remained for some time, being available conse-

---

* The cold was very severe, and many of the regiment were glad, writes Colonel Colquhoun, to annex the discarded postens of the fugitive enemy, which, despite their general dirty appearance, they were very glad to wear.

† The Manchester Regiment bear as badges the Sphinx and "Egypt" on cap and collar. On the glengarry cap and helmet plate are the arms and motto of the City of Manchester. The mottoes are those of the City and of the Order of the Garter, the former being "Concilio et labore." On the colours are "Egmont-op-Zee," "Egypt," "Martinique," "Guadeloupe," "Peninsula," "Alma," "Inkerman," "Sevastopol," "New Zealand," "Afghanistan, 1879—80," "Egypt, 1882." The uniform is scarlet with facings of white.

quently for the subsequent operations in 1762 against Martinique, Grenada, St. Lucia, and St. Vincent, returning home in 1764. The regiment proceeded to America in 1775, and took part in the conflict then raging. They fought with distinction at Bunker's Hill, at Brooklyn, at Brandywine, 1777, and at the storming and capture of Fort Clinton. They were with General Clinton's force during the operations in New Jersey and at the surrender of Charlestown, while a portion of the regiment acted as mounted infantry, and distinguished themselves at Sherar's Ferry in November, 1780. In 1782 the regiment went to Jamaica for a period, after which they enjoyed a few years' rest at home.

After sharing in the expedition to Holland, of 1794, where they suffered some loss at Nimeguen, the 63rd embarked for the West Indies in November, 1795, having the misfortune to lose two companies during the voyage by a tremendous storm. They saw considerable service under Abercromby, and in 1796 went to Jamaica, being represented a couple of years later at the brilliant defence of Honduras against a Spanish force of 2,600 men. On the return of the regiment to England, the attenuated ranks, numbering only 150 rank and file, bore grim witness to the severity of the service they had undergone. Under Abercromby the 63rd served in Holland; and at the landing at the Helder, at the action of Zuyp, the attack on Schagen-Burg, and all the other actions, including Bergen-op-Zoom, were conspicuous for their valour and endurance—Major McLeroth of the regiment being specially thanked by the Commander-in-Chief for his gallantry and brilliant conduct. Again at Egmont-op-Zee the gallant 63rd displayed signal gallantry and steadiness. The following year they took part in the Ferrol expedition, under Sir James Pulteney, where Sergeant-Major Nugent performed a gallant exploit, for which he was promoted. In 1801 the regiment went to Gibraltar, and to Malta in 1802. The next four years were passed in Ireland. They proceeded in "the expedition which resulted in the surrender of Madeira," and in 1808 joined the forces under Lieutenant-General Beckwith, which, the following year, took possession of Martinique. The articles of capitulation which, after the gallant defence made by General Villaret-Joyeuse, were at last enforced upon the enemy, were signed by Major O'Rourke of the 63rd on behalf of the King of England. When, six years later, the escape of Napoleon from Elba gave the signal for renewed hostilities, the 63rd joined an expedition again directed against Guadeloupe, which had been ceded to the French, and again distinguished themselves. "The eagles and standards of the French were here surrendered, and about this time the 63rd adopted a 'fleur-de-lis' badge." It was not till May, 1819, that they returned to England, and the following years till the Crimea, though full of change of scene to the 63rd, did not bring any important fighting.

On July 21, 1854, the 63rd embarked for the Crimea, and joined the Fourth Division under Sir George Cathcart. At the battle of the Alma, the Fourth Division was in reserve; at Inkerman it made the splendid charge, leading which the brave Cathcart fell dead. Throughout the war, the 63rd were to the fore wherever fighting was to be done, and when peace was at length concluded the losses of this brave regiment amounted to 48 officers, 83 sergeants, 86 corporals, 18 drummers, and 712 privates, making a total of 947.

After the Crimea, the 63rd passed many years in peaceful duties, their next active service being in the Afghan Campaign of 1879—80, in which their duties consisted principally of out-post service. Then followed the Egyptian Campaign of 1882, which earned for the gallant Manchester Regiment the last distinction on their colours.*

The Second Battalion of the Regiment, the old 96th Foot, dates from 1824. The first eleven years of its existence were passed in North America; then, after six years of home service, it was ordered to New South Wales. In 1845, the 96th saw some service in Auckland. With the exception of this and the Egyptian Campaign of 1882, the 96th have had no opportunity as yet of emulating the deeds of their predecessors in numerical title, whose distinctions they were authorized to adopt in 1874. The old 96th, the Queen's Own, which was disbanded in 1818, bore the familiar emblazonments of "The Sphinx," "Egypt," and the "Peninsula," and had acquired the sobriquet of "the British Musketeers." The present, or rather late, 96th, the subject of the present notice, has, since its formation, served—though not in actual warfare—at Gibraltar, the East Indies, Malta, and the Cape of Good Hope. In the Egyptian Campaign of 1882, the regiment performed arduous duties in Alexandria, where it was broken up into detachments occupying police forts, but took no active part in the Campaign.

* The nickname attributed to the 63rd is "The Bloodsuckers."

END OF VOL. I.

HER MAJESTY'S ARMY.

THE DUKE OF CAMBRIDGE'S OWN* (MIDDLESEX REGIMENT)—Regimental District No. 57—consists of two very famous regiments, of which the former, at any rate, is familiar by its sobriquet, "The Die-hards," to the most superficial student of the career of Her Majesty's Army. The 1st battalion—the 57th—was raised in 1755 by Colonel John Arabin, chiefly in the counties of Gloucester and Somerset, and the first service of the new regiment was as marines with the fleet in the Mediterranean. The following twenty years were passed chiefly in Gibraltar, Minorca, and Ireland. The 57th joined the force under Lord Cornwallis, and the following year took part in the battle of Brooklyn on August 26th, 1776. Afterwards they shared in the storming of Redbank, the capture of York Island, the attack on Powell's Hook, and the storming of Fort Montgomery, at which place they sustained heavy losses. In 1778 the flank companies were formed into separate battalions, and were busily engaged throughout the troublous times that followed, the light company being among the garrison at Fort York under Lord Cornwallis, who were taken prisoners in October, 1781. Even on the disaster at York Town we are able to look back without any feeling of humiliation. In September Lord Cornwallis was directed to make as good a defence as possible, receiving assurance of speedy and effective succour. "On the 28th of September," writes an author whose works of fiction contain historical sketches of which the accuracy is only equalled by the fascination of their style,† "the combined army of French and Americans, consisting

---

* The Duke of Cambridge's Own (Middlesex Regiment) bears as badges the coronet and cypher of the Duke of Cambridge, with the Prince of Wales's Plume and the word "Albuera" on cap and collar; the motto is that of the Prince of Wales. On the colours are: "Seringapatam," "Albuera," "Ciudad Rodrigo," "Badajoz," "Vittoria," "Pyrenees," "Nivelle," "Nive," "Peninsula," "Alma," "Inkerman," "Sevastopol," "New Zealand," "South Africa, 1879." The uniform is scarlet, with facings of white.

† G. A. Henty, "True to the Old Flag." Blackie and Son.

of 7,000 of the former and 12,000 of the latter, appeared before York Town and the post at Gloucester. Lord Cornwallis had 5,960 men, but so great had been the effects of the deadly climate in the autumn months, that only 4,017 men were reported fit for duty. The enemy at once invested the town and opened their trenches against it. From their fleet they had drawn an abundance of heavy artillery, and on the 9th of October their batteries opened a tremendous fire upon the works. Each day they pushed their trenches closer, and the British force was too weak in comparison with the number of its assailants to venture upon sorties. The fire from the works was completely overpowered by that of the enemy, and the ammunition was nearly exhausted. Day after day passed and still the promised reinforcements did not arrive. On the 16th, finding that he must either surrender or break through, Lord Cornwallis determined to cross the river and fall on the French rear with his whole force. In the night the light infantry (including the company of the 57th) and other regiments were embarked in boats, and crossed to the Gloucester side of the river before midnight. At this critical moment a violent storm arose which prevented the boats returning. The enemy's fire re-opened at daybreak, and the engineer and principal officers of the army gave it as their opinion that it was impossible to resist longer. Only one eight-inch shell and a hundred small ones remained. The defences had in many places tumbled to ruins, and no effectual resistance could be opposed to an assault." Accordingly, on the 19th, Lord Cornwallis surrendered, and five days later the long-promised reinforcements arrived —too late!

From 1783 to 1790 the 57th served in Nova Scotia, and in the latter year returned to England. In 1794 they joined the Duke of York's forces at Malines, and served in Flanders until the close of the year. In 1796 the regiment was ordered to Barbadoes, where they assisted in the capture of St. Lucia, returning, after a sojourn of a few years in Trinidad, to England in 1803.

Six years later, in 1809, commenced the era, glorious in the making of splendid names, amongst which none gleams with a clearer and more enduring brilliancy through the intervening years, than does that of the gallant 57th, the Die-hards of Peninsular fame.

The first scene of the war tragedy which was enacted after the 57th had joined Wellington's army was the battle of Busaco. "Nothing," writes Colonel Leith Hay, "could be conceived more enlivening, more interesting, or more varied than the scene from the heights. Commanding a very extensive prospect to the eastward, the movements of the French army were distinctly perceptible; it was impossible to conceal them. Rising grounds were covered with troops, cannon, or equipages; the widely extended country seemed to contain a host moving forward, or gradually condensing into numerous masses, checked in their progress by the grand natural barrier. In imposing appearance as to numerical strength, there has been rarely seen anything comparable to that of the enemy's army from Busaco; it was not an army alone encamped before us, but a multitude, cavalry, infantry, cars of the country, horses, tribes of mules with their attendants, sutlers, followers of every description crowded the moving scene." Yet ere many hours had passed this mighty host was in full retreat, beaten by the army whose honours the 57th had to share and increase.

The following year, the 57th joined in the pursuit of Massena, and at Albuera earned for themselves immortal fame by their conduct, the record of which is, so to speak, *crystallized* in their before-mentioned sobriquet of the "Die-hards." The fortunes of the day were wavering; everywhere the Spaniards were falling back, despite the dauntless courage and personal exertions of Beresford, who actually seized a Spanish officer and by main force carried him to the front, only for the dastard to run back again when the iron grasp was released. Then Stewart brought up Houghton's Brigade, with which were the 57th. Fierce, indeed, was the conflict! Cannon and musketry at *pistol range* belched forth death against the indomitable British regiments. Stewart was twice wounded, the gallant Houghton fell dead even as he called to the heroic 57th, "Die hard, my men, die hard!" And undismayed, with grim valour *dying hard* before the hurtling shower of grape and shot and shell, the 57th stood, giving back death for death and defiance for defiance, while officers and men were stricken down with awful quickness. Then came Cole's's splendid charge, before which the erst triumphing legions of France quailed and fled, and "like a loosened cliff went headlong down the steep; the rain flowed after in streams discoloured with blood, and one thousand eight hundred unwounded men, the remnant of six thousand unconquerable British soldiers, stood triumphant on the fatal hill." Of the five hundred and seventy of all ranks with which the 57th went into action that day, only a hundred and thirty remained to be marched off the field by the adjutant, while amongst the heaps of dead and wounded were Colonel Inglis, twenty-two officers, and over four hundred men of the regiment which had fought and died so hard. "It was observed that our dead, particularly the 57th Regiment, were lying as they had fought in the ranks, and that every wound was in front." The King's colour received seventeen shots, while the regimental colour was pierced by twenty-one. "Here was won the laurel wreath, of which any corps might well be proud."

It is impossible to dwell at length upon the prowess of the 57th throughout the Peninsular War; though not all of the battles are inscribed on their colours, there were but few places made famous by the gallantry of British troops where the 57th did not participate in that gallantry. Vittoria, the Pyrenees, Nivelle, the Nive—these are the triumphs recorded on the colours; but it must not be forgotten that "Peninsula" covers the countless smaller actions and operations performed by the Army, and in these the 57th ever gave evidence of the accuracy of the popular and professional judgment which then, as now, assigned them one of the foremost places amongst British regiments. At St. Pierre—the remarkable omission of which from the list of distinctions has been before noticed—the 57th were in the right wing under General Byng, which found itself opposed by the strong force led by d'Armagnac. During the action they were taken to strengthen Barnes's position in the centre, and materially aided in the repulse of Soult, which was practically the crisis of the battle which made "Hill's day of glory complete."

During 1814 the regiment was in Quebec, returning to England in August, 1815, immediately after which they joined the army of occupation in France, with which they served until November, 1818. From that date till the Crimea no particular fighting of note fell to their share, though they rendered good service at Mangalore in 1837. The entire regiment was garrisoned at Madras from 1840 to 1845, when they removed to Poonamalee; returned home in 1846, and during the disturbed period in Ireland in 1848. In September, 1854, the regiment joined General Cathcart's Division in the Crimea, and took up their position before Sevastopol. At Balaklava they acted as support to the Artillery. At Inkerman, when the Guards were maintaining their splendid resistance to the masses that threatened to overwhelm them, Sir George Cathcart led on his Division in the hope to relieve the Guards from the assault they were sustaining with such high valour; and despite the vast disparity of force—the Russians opposed to him numbered 9,000 men—he gave the order to charge, falling dead as he led on his men sword in hand. The 57th lost heavily; amongst the killed being their former colonel, Brigadier Goldie.

On the occasion of the assault on the Redan, the 57th led the assault on the right flank of the fort, and lost no fewer than six officers and a hundred and ten men. Amongst the numerous acts of individual heroism which redeemed the comparative failure of the attack must be mentioned that of which Colour-Sergeant Gardiner of the regiment was the hero.* When retreat became inevitable, Sergeant Gardiner persuaded some of the men of the regiment to delay returning to our lines and try the effect of a little more firing. The little band made such shelter as they could for themselves by taking advantage of the deep holes torn by the shells, by the side of which they improvised a somewhat ghastly breastwork with the bodies of their dead comrades; and here they remained, inflicting no little annoyance on the enemy till their ammunition was exhausted. This was done under a fire in which nearly half the officers and a third of the rank and file of the storming parties were put *hors de combat*. For this achievement, coupled with his gallant conduct on the 22nd of March, Sergeant Gardiner was rewarded with the Victoria Cross. During the siege, another soldier of the " Die-hards," Private M'Corrie, gained the same coveted honour for his coolness and courage in picking up a live shell which had fallen into the trenches and throwing it over the parapet—fortunately without injury to himself, though he subsequently died before receiving the coveted decoration.

The 57th took part, in the following September, in the expedition against Odessa, and were in the first brigade of the force which was despatched to effect the reduction of Kinburn, on which occasion, despite the small loss which our troops actually suffered, a rumour reached the camp that the 57th had been cut to pieces. From Kinburn, after a skirmish with some Cossacks near Shadoffka, they returned to Sevastopol, after the surrender of which they proceeded to Malta, and later on to India. Here they remained for three years, when they were ordered to New Zealand on the outbreak of the Maori war, where they performed some sterling service. But this service was not rendered without loss.

In 1863 Lieutenant Targett and a party of six men of the regiment, who were acting as escort in charge of a prisoner to be tried by court-martial, were all slain by Maories in ambush, one man only escaping to tell the tale and evoke a determination in the breasts of the gallant 57th to avenge the death of their comrades. General Warre, the historian of the regiment, thus describes the incident:—" On reaching the Wairau (the name of a small stream) the escort was suddenly fired upon by an ambuscade of thirty or forty rebel natives, and the whole party were killed or wounded.

---

* Sergeant Gardiner had before this greatly distinguished himself on the occasion of the sortie of the 22nd of March, when, seeing that the covering parties had been driven in and were in some confusion, he rallied them, and at their head attacked the Russians, who were speedily driven out of the trenches again.—*Knollys*.

Private Florence Kelly, although wounded, escaped into the fern, subsequently joining a party under Lieutenant Brutton, which had been sent on the report of the murders being conveyed by a mounted orderly." An opportunity for revenge occurred on June 4th, in the attack and capture of the rebels' pah, when the regiment fought with marked courage and dash. Later in the same year occurred a severe encounter with the natives at Pontoko, where the British gained a complete victory over much superior numbers, though the 57th suffered some loss. "Ensign Down and Drummer D. Stagpool were recommended for, and eventually received, the Victoria Cross, for their gallant conduct in rescuing a wounded comrade from the clutches of the rebel natives." On the occasion of the storming of the Otapawa Pah, the 57th, numbering one hundred and thirty rank and file under Colonel Butler, again distinguished themselves, though they had to mourn the death of Lieutenant-Colonel Hassard, who fell inside the pah, while leading on his men. It would seem on this occasion as though the natives had been studying the "*fas est ab hoste doceri*" doctrine, for they kept perfectly quiet till our men were within about thirty or forty yards, when they commenced a most severe and unusually well-directed fire. Lieutenant-Colonel Hassard, with a party of the regiment, drove out the enemy on the left, and then proceeded against those on the right. "At the same moment the remainder of the 55th, gallantly led by Lieutenant-Colonel Butler, reached the left angle of the work. The Maories fought desperately for a time, but in vain; a portion of the palisading being cut down by Private Doakes, 57th Regiment, the troops entered the works and carried all before them." In addition to Lieutenant-Colonel Hassard * the regiment lost two sergeants and five privates killed and many wounded. Amongst those killed was Private Doakes, whose gallantry had been such as to have decided the commander to recommend him for the Victoria Cross.

The regiment returned to England in 1866, remaining at home till the Zulu war. They arrived in South Africa from Ceylon shortly before the battle of Ghinglovo, and suffered somewhat more than the other troops from the wet and cold, in consequence of the greater change of climate. The 57th and 91st were stationed on that face of the lager on which the Zulus, after their repulse by the Rifles, hurled the whole force of their attack. How well that attack was repulsed is matter of common know-

---

* Colonel Hassard is thus referred to in the official despatch : "In Lieutenant-Colonel Hassard the service has lost one of its bravest officers : he led his men with the greatest gallantry, and fell inside the Pah, nobly performing his duty."

ledge now. From Ghinglovo they proceeded with Lord Chelmsford to the relief of Colonel Pearson at Etschowe. When Sir Garnet Wolseley took the direction of affairs, the command of one of the columns was given to Colonel Clarke of the 57th, and that of the regiment devolved upon Major Tredennick. Later on the regiment was actively employed in the pursuit of Cetewayo, and in September returned to England. The following year—to quote from Colonel Archer—"many deserved honours were bestowed on officers of the corps, including Lord Gifford, the pursuer of Ketchewayo, for services in the Zulu war; and the gallantry of Private Howard, who, with Lieutenant Torrens of the Scots Greys, assisted in rescuing the crew of the brig *Robert Brown*, wrecked off the Pigeon House Fort, was publicly commended by the commander-in-chief." Since the Zulu war the 57th have not been engaged in any active service.*

The 2nd battalion of the Middlesex Regiment is the 77th Foot, which was raised in 1787 for service in the East Indies. The regiment arrived in India in August, 1788, and joined the force under Abercromby. They were at the siege and surrender of Canonore, December 18th, 1790, and then advanced upon Periapatam; but, on Lord Cornwallis suspending operations returned to cantonments. In December, 1791, under Abercromby they entered Mysore and joined Lord Cornwallis before Seringapatam in February of the following year. Throughout the campaign against Tippoo, in which they lost over two hundred men, the 77th acquitted themselves with great credit, and on the conclusion of the campaign proceeded to Canonore, and thence to Bombay, a few

---

* On the occasion of fresh colours being presented to this splendid regiment, the old ones were deposited in St. Paul's Cathedral, under circumstances which provoked some remark. The following letter which appeared in the *Times* correctly represents the general feeling.—"Sir—Between one and two o'clock to-day was seen a small military detachment in uniform, marching from Cannon Street to the Mansion House. A field officer, three other officers, and about eight non-commissioned officers and men, were taking to their final resting place in St. Paul's Cathedral, the old colours of the 57th Regiment—the West Middlesex—the 'Die-hards.' They were cordially received by the Lord Mayor, and with equal cordiality at the Cathedral, where, after a short, impressive ceremony the colours were placed on its walls. They were the colours of the Crimea, and especially of Inkerman. They were accompanied on this their last march by the condition that 'no expense was thereby to be entailed on the public.' As this detachment of honour passed from the Mansion House and along Cheapside little did the rich and busy crowd think that the officers' private purses had saved to the country the railway fare from Woolwich, and thus added to our economical, if not quite to our military, credit." An influential paper of the time thus comments on the foregoing letter:—"It cannot fail to infuse into the breast of every Englishman who reads it a glow of pleasure. There is nothing like maintaining amongst our soldiery a sober enthusiasm for Queen and country; and by our own feelings as we read of this apparently trifling but truly significant little incident, we may judge of the sentiments which animated that small company of soldiers as they marched to the Cathedral—without parade, without ostentation; indeed, rather sneaking than marching—to place the colours that waved at Inkerman in their final resting place. Every heart beat high with the thought that although the dear flag was being carried through the streets as a pauper corpse is trotted to the grave, the noblest principles of government were vindicated in an almost pathetic manner, 'no expense was thereby entailed on the public.'"

months later taking part in the reduction of the Dutch settlements at Cochin. They took part in the operations under Colonel Stewart against the Dutch Settlements, and later on in the expedition against the Rajah of Cotiote. In January, 1799, the 77th joined the Bombay army and occupied the signalling station of Sudapore, between Stewart and Harris's forces. Here the enemy, headed by the Sultan in person, appeared suddenly in order of battle, and, being greatly superior in numbers, turned the position, and cut off its communications with the Bombay force. But the 77th, with whom were the 75th, by a brilliant effort recovered the advantage before General Stewart had reached them with his support. In 1799 they again found themselves before the walls of Seringapatam. The 77th furnished their flank companies for the storming party. The troops moved to the attack on the left under Lieutenant-Colonel Dunlop, of the 77th. Under a terrible fire from cannon, jingalls, and musketry the glacis and ditch were passed, and the storming party swarmed up the breach. "Lieutenant-Colonel Dunlop was here wounded by a Sidar of Mysore who met him scimitar in hand. Parrying a cut with his sabre the Colonel slashed open his antagonist's breast and mortally wounded him. The Sidar made another cut that nearly hewed off the head of the Colonel, and falling back into the breach was instantly bayonetted. Dunlop reached the summit and then fell from loss of blood."

In 1799 the regiment was quartered at Mangalore; "and in 1800, at Cochin and Calicut. In June, 1800, they captured Arrakerry; served under Wellesley at Dhoondra, and took part in the capture of Bednore, Coongull, Subtitee, and Humaul (at the assault of which latter Captain McPherson distinguished himself); and at the final defeat of Dhoondra." In 1801 they were engaged in operations against Coliote and Wynand, and in the attack of Panjalamcourchy, which was captured with a loss of two officers and fifty-one men. Subsequently the regiment operated against the Polygars, took part in the attack on Bollaum Rajah; and, in 1802, in the second capture of Arrakerry, and subsequently in the operations against the Mairs.

The 77th returned to England in 1807 after an absence of nineteen and a half years, during by far the greater part of which they had been actively engaged. Under the Earl of Chatham, they shared in the operations in Flanders in 1809, and were present at the capitulation of Ramakins and Flushing. After a few months in England the regiment went to Portugal in July, 1810, and very shortly after landing commenced war in earnest. At El Bodon in September, 1811, where "the action began disadvantageously for the allies," the 77th, under Lieutenant-Colonel Bromhead, evinced splendid valour. In conjunction with the 5th they several times *charged* the French Cavalry, on whose numbers neither artillery nor musketry volleys seemed to make any impression. At one time by a movement of the Portuguese, " the 5th and 77th, two weak battalions formed in one square, were quite exposed, and in an instant the whole of the French horsemen came thundering down upon them." Perhaps in all Napier's brilliant pages there is no passage which eclipses in beauty his description of the deeds of the 77th and their comrades on that day. " But how vain, how fruitless," he continues, " to match the sword with the musket, to send the charging horsemen against the steadfast veteran! The multitudinous squadrons, rending the skies with their shouts, closed upon the glowing squares like the falling edges of a burning crater and were as instantly rejected, scorched, and scattered abroad; then a rolling peal of musketry echoed through the hills, bayonets glittered at the edge of the smoke, and with firm and even step the British regiments came forth like the holy men from the Assyrian's furnace." At Ciudad Rodrigo, under Colonel Dunkin, the 77th with two other regiments pushed up the great breach amidst a whirlwind of death and horror and confusion, such as might have swept through a hell of warring demons. Curses and yells of anguish strove for the mastery over the crash of shell and shot; stones and pieces of masonry fell thick around, and gleaming amongst them through the heavy cloud of smoke came thick and fast the glint of gory bayonets, like the red lightning playing across the track of an avalanche. After Badajoz—the name of which they bear on their colours—the 77th returned to Lisbon, rejoining the army in the field in October, 1813, and being actively employed in the investment of Bayonne, where they assisted in carrying the entrenched works.

At the close of the war the 77th embarked for home, where they stayed until 1824, in which year they went to Jamaica, remaining there for ten years, losing during this period twelve officers, eleven sergeants, and two hundred and thirty of other ranks, and finding their only active employment in the operations which became necessary in 1831 against the insurgent slaves. On returning to England they were engaged on peace duties for twenty years, during which time they were stationed at Malta, Canada, Jamaica, the Ionian Islands and Nova Scotia. On the outbreak of the Crimean War they proceeded to the front, and were with the Light Division under Sir George Brown. At the Alma the advance of the Light Division was acknowledged to be one of the finest performances of the campaign, and right well did the 77th carry out their part in it. Again at Inkerman they distinguished themselves, some forty of the regiment following the heroic charge of Lieutenant Clifford of the Rifle Brigade against a strong force of Russians, who, unperceived, had approached dangerously near the camp of the Second Division. The right wing of the regiment received deserved commendation for the three brilliant charges it made against the enemy. On the occurrence of the sortie of the 22nd of March, 1855, the 77th again won deserved honour in the fierce fighting which ensued before the enemy were repulsed.

It was on the occasion of the above-mentioned sortie that Private Alexander Wright, 77th Regiment, performed one of the acts of valour which earned him the Victoria Cross. As mentioned in the account of the 97th Regiment—who with the 77th were guarding the trenches—our men were surprised by the Russians, who rushed in upon them before they had "barely time to snatch their arms and defend themselves." It was a time to try the mettle of the most seasoned soldier, and Alexander Wright proved himself to be, like William of Deloraine "good at need." At the affair of the rifle pits of the 19th April, the 77th were again to the fore. With a wing of the 33rd Regiment they carried the rifle pits at a rush, despite a fierce fire which the enemy directed on them. Colonel Egerton and Captain Lempriere were wounded,* as were other officers, including Sergeant Park of the regiment, who was awarded a Victoria Cross. Private Wright again distinguished himself on this occasion. At the assault of the Redan, a hundred and sixty of the regiment, under the gallant Major Welsford, formed part of the party in charge of the scaling ladders. Alas! scarcely had the order been given "Ladders to the front!" than their gallant bearers fell thick and fast. Major Welsford had his head blown off by a cannon ball fired by a Russian officer, who afterwards surrendered himself to a sergeant of the 97th. The stormers struggled on and gained the Redan, only, as is well known, to be driven out by overwhelming numbers after an hour and a half of such fighting as rarely falls to the lot of any soldiers. There was no need to carry out the intended re-assault on the morrow; the Russians had evacuated their city, and so closed a war which had gained for the 77th much glory, and had cost them the loss of fifteen officers and nearly nine hundred men.

Since the Crimea no war service has been demanded of the 77th, who have been stationed in various quarters of the globe, including India and New South Wales. "Peace hath its victories," however, and amongst these may be instanced that of the 77th in gaining for two successive years the honour due to the "best shooting regiment of the army." †

* These officers subsequently died.
† The nickname of the 77th is "The Pothooks," from a supposed resemblance of the figure 7 to a pothook.

THE ROYAL MUNSTER FUSILIERS*—Regimental District No. 101—consist of the 101st and 104th Regiments, both old regiments of the old East India Company.

The 1st battalion of the Royal Munster Fusiliers, the 101st Regiment, date their origin from December, 1756, when, amid the chaos of doubt and terror, of incapacity and impending ruin, the Man arrived with the Hour. As one of his first steps towards the salvation of British India, Clive organized the Bengal European Battalion, and placed in command Major Kilpatrick. Like another famous regiment whose career we have sketched,† though a date can be given with exact or approximate accuracy for its origination, yet that process in the case of the Bengal European Regiment partook rather of the nature of crystallisation. For many years prior to 1756 there had existed scattered, more or less independent, companies of Europeans in the military service of the Company; as in the days of the "blameless king"

> "here and there a deed
> Of prowess done redressed a random wrong,"

and Clive was the first who drew together this knighthood errant into the "glorious company" of the 101st Fusiliers. From its very commencement the 101st has been eminently a fighting regiment. From the interesting account which appeared of it a few years ago,‡ the Bengal European Regiment has fought in no fewer than eighty-three known engagements, omitting the less important items which swell the total list of a campaign. It is obvious therefore that in such a sketch as the present it will be impossible to do more than mention—and even that but shortly—the more important of the battles in which the famous regiment has been engaged. While yet only a few days old, the Bengal European Regiment fought at the battle of Baj-Baj, which was won by the British, not without some slight loss to the newly-formed corps. In this connection it may not be without interest to recall an incident referred to by Colonel Innes. After the battle had been fought and won, it became necessary to take the Fort of Baj-Baj, and the troops—amongst which was the Grenadier Company of the 101st§—were

---

* The Royal Munster Fusiliers bear as badges the Royal Tiger on a grenade on cap and collar and on helmet plate and glengarry three golden crowns on a blue shield (the ancient arms of Ireland). The motto is that of the Garter. On the colours, in addition to the Royal Tiger, is the Shamrock, with the names of the following battles: "Plassey," "Buxar," "Guzerat," "Deig," "Bhurtpore," "Afghanistan," "Ghuznee," "Ferozeshah," "Sobraon," "Punjaub," "Chillianwallah," "Goojerat," "Pegu," "Delhi," "Lucknow." The uniform is scarlet, with facings of blue.

† The 3rd Buffs.

‡ "History of the Bengal European Regiment." Lieutenant-Colonel P. R. Innes. Simpkin, Marshall & Co.

§ Here and elsewhere the modern denomination of the regiment has been for brevity's sake adopted. It will be of course borne in mind that the numerical title was not given till 1861, prior to which date the regiment was—first the

mustered early the following morning for the purpose. It appeared, however, that the fort had already been taken! A certain "sailor named Strahan, who with a few of his comrades had been drinking freely in anticipation of hard work, conceived the idea of seeing what was going on inside the Fort. Clambering through the breach, Strahan found the walls deserted, and shouting to his companions, proclaimed with cheers that he had captured the fort. His companions quickly followed, but soon found themselves hotly engaged with the enemy's rearguard, who were smoking over the fire before joining their comrades, who had evacuated the Fort during the night. More of our sailors soon followed, and after a short skirmish it was proved that the drunken sailor, Strahan, was right when he proclaimed that he had taken the Fort." Strahan is not the only warrior of ancient or modern times who has proved that '*in Vino Victoria*' can be as true as the kindred saying with regard to *Veritas*.

The 101st fought at the battle of Chitpore, which in its results must be considered as one of the most important of that eventful period; at the famous Council of War which preceded Plassey, the majority of the regiment present voted for immediate action; they assisted in the winning of that memorable battle itself. Not long afterwards, the regiment received a welcome addition to its strength by the acquisition of volunteers from H.M. 39th Regiment, and from the Bombay and Madras European Regiments, the detachments of which Clive "annexed"—"finding it inadvisable to send them back." At Condore, the 101st were, with the exception of one company of Artillery, the only British soldiers present at the battle, "justly ranked amongst the decisive Battles of India," for it was one between the English and French for supremacy. Undoubtedly, the skilful change of front which the regiment made, and the daring courage with which they pressed on the bewildered French, were the chief factors in obtaining the victory. The loss of the regiment in the action was forty-five men killed and wounded. At the storming of Mussulipatam, the regiment acquitted themselves with signal heroism, the gallantry of Yorke, Fischer, and Moran being specially conspicuous. The siege of Mussulipatam was under the direction of Colonel Forde, the French Commander being Conflans. The following description of this important stronghold will serve to emphasize the gallantry of the besiegers. "The fort of Mussulipatam stood in an extremely defensible position. It was surrounded by a swamp on three sides, the other face rested on the river. From the land side it was only approachable by a causeway

Bengal European Regiment, then the 1st Bengal European Light Infantry, and lastly the 1st European Bengal Fusiliers.

across the swamp, and this was guarded by a strong cavalier, which is the military name for an outwork erected beyond the ditch of a fortress. It was in all respects capable of a prolonged defence. In form it was an irregular parallelogram about eight hundred yards in length and six hundred yards wide, and on the walls were eleven strong bastions. The morass which surrounded it was of from three to eighteen feet in depth."

There were only about three hundred and eighty Europeans and seven hundred natives composing the attacking party, which was under the command of Captain Callender, an officer of the Madras Army. One of the most remarkable occurrences connected with the siege was the disappearance of this officer just when the attack was ordered to begin. Where he was, what was the reason of his failing to appear at such a critical moment, was never known. From the following account of the capture of the fort, which we have condensed from histories of the time, it will be seen that when the fighting was at its height he reappeared, but gave no explanation, and before many minutes was shot dead. "The hour of midnight was fixed for the attack, as at that time the tide was at its lowest, and the water in the ditches round the ramparts not more than three feet deep. The French, in their belief in the absolute security of the place, had taken but few precautions against an attack, and it was not until the leading party had waded nearly breast-high through the ditch, and begun to break down the palisade beyond it, that they were discovered. Then a heavy artillery and musketry fire from the bastions on the right and left was opened upon the assailants." Fischer's party soon gained the breach, and were speedily joined by that under Yorke; the two parties then charged together, and captured an important bastion. Then Yorke and Fischer separated. As the former was moving forward, he saw a strong body of French Sepoys advancing towards the foot of the ramparts and the buildings of the town. These had been sent to reinforce the bastion just carried. Without a moment's hesitation Yorke ran down the ramparts, seized the French officer who commanded, and ordered him to surrender at once, as the place was already taken. Confused and bewildered, the officer gave up his sword, and ordered the Sepoys to lay down their arms. They were then sent as prisoners into the bastion. Then followed an incident almost identical with that related in the account of the 4th Regiment and their heroism at Badajoz. Some one called out " A mine ! A mine ! " and the soldiers of Yorke at Mussulipatam behaved just as, more than sixty years after, Walker's splendid troops behaved at Badajoz. Literally " frighted with false fire " they fell back in hopeless confusion, these men who unmoved had faced sweeping volleys, to whom morass and rampart had proved no obstacles, fled in unreasoning terror, scared—as Napier puts it—"by a chimera of their own raising." Yorke was left alone save for two plucky native drummer boys who stood by him. Threats and remonstrances soon brought the stormers back to a sense of their duty, and "they charged the bastion, Yorke leading with a drummer on each side playing the Grenadiers' March." The brave Yorke fell desperately wounded, shot through both thighs; with him fell dead the two brave drummer boys and many others, but it was in the moment of victory, for with loud hurrahs of triumph, and with a rush that none could withstand, the 101st and their comrades carried the formidable bastion. Meanwhile Captain Fischer had not been idle. He pressed on towards the works where was the great gate of the town. The French made strenuous efforts to resist his progress, but in vain. Reserving their fire till within a few yards of the enemy, his men threw in a staggering volley, and with a sudden charge cleared the bastion. Then Fischer at once closed the great gates and thus isolated and completely imprisoned the troops within. "Just as the division was again advancing, Captain Callender, to the astonishment of every one, appeared and took his place at its head." He offered no explanation of his absence, doubtless postponing it to a more convenient season. But such season never came; only a few shots more were fired by the already defeated garrison, and by one of these Captain Callender was killed. So ended the siege of Mussulipatam, one of the most memorable sieges and brilliant achievements in the long catalogue of British triumphs in India. The town taken by our troops had ten times as many guns and nearly twice as many men; save at certain times it was unassailable otherwise than by boats; not far distant was another large hostile force, our provisions were scanty, the fidelity of our allies more than doubtful, and some of our own force were beginning to murmur at the withholding of the long arrears of pay. Yet we took the town, and with it more than three thousand prisoners (five hundred being French), with a loss to our own men—exclusive of Sepoys and allies—of only twenty-two killed and sixty wounded. Well may it be said that "the capture of Mussulipatam may claim to rank among the very highest deeds ever performed by British arms." And in this capture none played a more prominent part than the splendid regiment now known as the 101st.* In dealing with a regiment such as that now under consideration, one feels a sort of Aladdin-like bewilderment at the amount and variety of the dazzling treasures gathered for our choice. At Biderra, near Chandernagore, they completely worsted the Dutch; at the

---

* More strictly as the "1st Battalion of the Royal Munster Fusiliers." Chroniclers of regimental histories may, however, be pardoned for sometimes ignoring the rather cumbrous and not very comprehensible modern titles.

siege of Patna they gloriously distinguished themselves. Captain Cochrane was in command of a portion of the regiment forming part of the garrison, the remainder of which consisted of the troops of our ally, the Rajah Ram Narian. Strict orders had been given that for the present no engagement with the besieging force was to be attempted. The over-confident Rajah, however, thought he saw an opportunity, and sallied out, soon to find himself utterly overmatched by the Emperor's troops. He himself was soon surrounded and in grievous straits, and thereupon sent back to Captain Cochrane, who, conceiving that the prohibition did not extend to a case in which the Rajah's life was imperilled, went out with his companies. The Rajah's disregard of orders was to be productive of sad results for the 101st. Fighting his way gallantly to the rescue of his ally, the brave Cochrane fell dead, and with him fell his three subalterns. A sergeant of the regiment at the head of twenty-five Sepoys charged through the surrounding foes, and, rescuing the Rajah, brought him back in safety to the English lines, now commanded by a non-combatant officer, Dr. Fullerton, of the Company's medical service.

"Dr. Fullerton's name," writes the historian of the regiment, "is known to history as a brave, gallant soldier, and his military prowess never shone with greater lustre than when he brought the remnant of the Ram Narian's defeated force into the city of Patna, not, however, without leaving one of his disabled guns in the hands of the enemy; but before abandoning it, he had spiked it with his own hands. There is something most touching in the record of this great sacrifice of life of the Bengal European Regiment. Four officers gave their lives in attempting to perform a simple act of duty; the officer commanding the Sepoy regiment was also killed, as well as the only artillery officer with the force; none were left but that brave man Fullerton, who, when he saw all his comrades dead, manfully fulfilled the duty to perform which these six officers had given their lives." The command of the garrison at Patna then devolved upon Dr. Fullerton, and most ably did he acquit himself in the well-nigh desperate position. The besiegers, elated with their victory outside the walls, attacked with redoubled ardour. So fierce was the assault that the Emperor's colours were once planted on the ramparts, when Fullerton rushed to the spot, and after a fierce hand-to-hand conflict captured them and drove back the assailants. Affairs began to look hopeless; it seemed impossible for the weak garrison much longer to resist, but, as often happens, "just when help was so much needed a joyful cry was raised that relief was at hand. A cloud of dust and the glitter of the sun on bayonets was seen on the other side of the river; the shouts of the Europeans and the inspiring sound of the fife and drum were distinctly heard, reviving the spirits and hopes of the besieged, who, rushing to their deserted posts, defended them with renewed vigour." Relief was not long delayed now. The sound of the familiar British cheer grew clearer and stronger, and Knox with the rest of the 101st, their colours flying, broke through the beleaguering lines, and clasped hands with their gallant comrades of long-enduring Patna. Next day French and Imperial troops gave way before the strengthened British force, and abandoned their position. At Beerpur, after six hours of tremendous and doubtful fighting, a charge of the grenadiers of the 101st obtained the victory for the British. At Bhirboom, Yorke, happily recovered from his severe wound at Mussulipatam, and White, though their forces only consisted of the 101st and a few Sepoys, routed the Rajah's army of twenty thousand foot and five thousand horse. At Suan, in January, 1761, they formed an all-important part of the force which utterly defeated the forces of the Emperor, thanks, however, in great measure to the cannon shot which killed the mahout of his Majesty's elephant, and impressed upon the sensible beast itself the advisability of executing a well-defined, even ostentatious, strategic movement to the rear. Under Law, the band of French, fighting in the Imperial army, gathered on an eminence, and from thence kept up a brisk fire at the advancing columns of English.

The 101st charged up the hill and captured the French guns. And now occurred an incident worthy of the palmiest days of knightly chivalry. The French, be it remembered, were the most formidable of our opponents; they had done their best to check the flight of the Emperor's troops, and for the last half-hour had been pouring grape and musketry into our ranks. Yet—" the Bengal Europeans now advanced with *shouldered* arms towards the French officers, thirteen or fourteen of whom stood by their commander and colours on the rising ground, with some fifty French soldiers in their rear. The Frenchmen, wearied with the vagrant, profitless life they had been leading since we had captured their possessions at Chundernagore, seemed determined to sell their lives as dearly as possible; but when they saw the English soldiers advancing with shouldered arms they were amazed at the generosity of their conquerors. Major Carnac, now ordering his soldiers to halt, advanced towards the French officers, and saluting, told them he did not wish to take their lives if they would surrender. M. Law replied that he and his comrades would submit only on the condition that they might retain their swords; but this stipulation not agreed to, they would resist to the last. The terms were accepted; and M. Law and his officers giving themselves up as prisoners of war were placed on their parole. All our officers now advanced, cordially shaking hands with their prisoners, and the British troops were marched back to their camp, where the French officers were hospitably entertained by those of the English army."

At Patna, when Major Adams had rightly and contemptuously refused the terms begged by Mir Kassim, the latter carried out the terrible massacre he had threatened on the prisoners, most of whom were men of the 101st Regiment. The Alsatian Sumru, the only man whom Mir Kassim had found willing to carry out his fiendish mandate, proceeded, in October, to the prison where the captives were confined. He told them he had "planned an entertainment to enliven their captivity, and that knives and forks were essential to the feast in order to entertain them in the English manner." The ruse was only to disarm suspicion, and render the victims an easier prey. Then the massacre began, the bodies being hacked to pieces and thrown into a well, women and children finding sex nor youth protection. "When one of the prisoners, named Gulston, was found still alive, the men employed in clearing away the bodies would have saved him, but he declined their proffer of assistance and was thrown into the well alive." Amidst the horror inspired by this sickening tale comes, like a gleam of pure, unearthly light in some devil's Sabbath, the pride and thankfulness inspired by the description given by a native of the way the men of the 101st and their comrades met their death. "Without losing courage," says the account, "they marched up to the murderers, and with empty bottles, stones, and brickbats fought them to the last man, until they were all killed."

It was obviously necessary to take Patna and to signally punish Mir Kassim and the "infamous Sumru,"* and though Adams's health was terribly shattered he felt that till this had been done his task was yet uncompleted. In the following November, by splendid fighting and magnificent heroism, the 101st (with whom were H.M.'s 84th and some Sepoys) took Patna, though with heavy loss.

Passing over, as we are compelled to do, the many and interesting incidents of the war then raging, we come to the battle of Buxar, the second distinction on the heavily blazoned colours of the regiment. At the first glance at the picture of this battle, handed down by past and present writers, we notice the features common to all the "battle-pieces" of the time—of overwhelming odds against the British. On this occasion the numbers were between 40,000 and 50,000 as against 7,080! The splendid cavalry of the enemy charged again and again, striving fruitlessly to break by sheer

---

* It is interesting to note that a descendant of Sumru became a colonel in the army, and married the daughter of an English Peer.

VOL. II.

weight of men and horses—exceeding in number our whole army—the stubborn British phalanx. "A desperate struggle ensued,"—after a temporary success over our native allies emboldened the foe with the fancy of victory—"several of the men of the Bengal European Regiment being sabred in the ranks; but the British line remained firm and unbroken. The charge was again renewed with increased vigour, but the leader, in making a vigorous dash at the English line was received on the bayonet of one of our Europeans, who at the same moment discharging his musket, the chief fell a lifeless corpse amongst his gallant followers." A brilliant charge by Major Champion, with whom were two companies of the 101st, gave a favourable turn, at a critical moment, to the wavering battle. The enemy were soon in retreat, which rapidly degenerated into flight, and then followed a scene which can hardly be matched for its sickening horror. "The Nawab, accompanied by a strong party of chosen horsemen, crossed the Torah River with some of his most portable treasures, and as soon as he had ascertained that his trained brigades had followed him, *ordered the bridge of boats to be destroyed, thus completely cutting off the retreat of his infantry and camp-followers.* A fearful scene of carnage ensued: elephants, camels, bullocks, horses, men, women, and children, all pressing forward to gain the opposite bank of the river, were precipitated into the stream; indeed, so great was the indiscriminate rush that the weaker fell under the strong, so that, at last, a *mole three hundred yards long was formed by the dead and dying, across which the remnants of the fugitives made their escape.*"

The British captured on this occasion a hundred and seventy-two guns; the loss to the 101st was thirty-seven men killed, and one officer and fifty-eight men wounded.

At the battle of Deeg Colonel Macrae and Captain Kelley won high fame by desperate fighting. During the prolonged siege of Bhurtpore with its renewed assaults, many were the acts of bravery chronicled of the 101st, and the names of Colonel Ryan and Lieutenants Morris, Brown, and Moore were mentioned again and again in despatches. There was yet another name—that of Sergeant Allen, of whom the historian of the regiment writes: "The gallantry of Sergeant Allen of the grenadier company should ever be remembered by the regiment with pride." It was during this siege that the 101st won their cherished sobriquet of "Dirty Shirts." The similarity of the circumstances under which they fought and worked at Delhi during the Mutiny has caused the latter occasion to be given as the date of its origin. Colonel Innes' account, however, seems definitely to fix the earlier date. The work in the trenches was intense and prolonged, and the labours of the soldiers knew scarcely an hour's intermission. On one occasion the Commander-in-Chief, visiting the trenches as was his wont, was addressed by some of the men of the 101st, who "apologised for their dirty appearance, urging as an excuse that they had not found time to change their shirts for several weeks. General Lake remarked approvingly that they were an honour to the wearers, showing that they had willingly sacrificed comfort to their duty in dirty shirts.

It was indeed a terrible undertaking, that storming of the maiden fortress of Bhurtpore. Lord Lisle writes in his despatches: "The troops, most confident of success, commenced the attack, and persevered in it for a considerable length of time with the most determined bravery; but their utmost exertions were not sufficient to enable them to gain the top of the breach. The bastion, which was the point of attack, was extremely strong; the resistance opposed to them was vigorous; and as our men could only mount by small parties at a time, the advantages were very great on the side of the enemy. Discharges of grape, logs of wood, and pots filled with combustible materials, immediately knocked down those who were ascending, and the whole party, after being engaged in an obstinate contest for two hours and suffering very severe loss, were obliged to relinquish the attempt, and retire to our trenches."

The siege was turned into a blockade, and terms subsequently agreed upon. The next of this famous regiment's many distinctions is "Afghanistan," and closely to follow their career throughout the campaign would be to write afresh, and in laudatory terms, the history of the war. At Ghuznee they fought; at Ferozeshah they again—the phrase becomes gloriously monotonous—greatly distinguished themselves. They supported the memorable charge of the 80th, which elicited such high praise from the Governor-General, and, throughout, manfully played their part in the fierce game at which our troops "within thirty hours stormed an entrenched camp, fought a general action, and sustained two considerable combats with the enemy; within four days dislodged from their position 60,000 Sikh soldiers, supported by 150 pieces of cannon, 108 of which the enemy acknowledge to have lost, and 91 of which are in our possession" (Sir Hugh Gough: Despatches). They fought at Sobraon, where the heaviest brunt of the battle seems to have fallen on them and on the 29th Regiment. Under General Gilbert they were ordered to advance, and came in front of the centre and strongest portion of the Sikh encampment, unsupported either by artillery or cavalry. Rushing forward with incredible bravery they crossed a dry nullah, and found themselves opposed to one of the hottest fires of musketry that can possibly be imagined. Retreat became inevitable; the enemy were safely ensconced behind high walls; "to remain under such a fire without the power of returning it would have been madness." In retreating, the 101st had "their ranks thinned by musketry, and their wounded men and officers cut off by the savage Sikhs." It is not remarkable after reading this to hear that the losses of the regiment were nearly the heaviest on the field.

At Chillianwallah they were surrounded on all sides, and "were compelled to have recourse to so many formations to repel the enemy that they were obliged to charge with the rear rank in front." At Goojerat, perhaps one of the most important battles ever fought in India, they were with Penny's Brigade, and had some terrible fighting in the village of Barra Kabra, which they carried at the point of the bayonet, taking three colours, and losing 149 of all ranks killed.

In the Burmese War, which is commemorated by "Pegu" on the colours, the 101st were at first in garrison at Rangoon under Colonel Tudor. In November of the same year the expedition against Pegu was decided on, and three hundred of the regiment joined the force to which this duty was confided. The Bengal and Madras detachments pushed forward, beneath the most intense heat, and exposed to the fire of a concealed enemy, till they reached the gateway of the town; here, however, they were so exhausted that a rest was absolutely necessary. Then General Godwin rode up, and after some words of deserved praise for the "superhuman exertions" they had gone through, addressed the fusiliers. "*You,*" said he, "are Bengalies, and *you* are Madrassies, let's see who are the best men." The regiments addressed responded by that most eloquent and characteristic of all replies—a hearty cheer, "and the Bengal and Madras Fusiliers led the assault towards the city gate, which was after a short struggle captured; the Burmese soldiers being forced back, and seeking shelter under the walls of the Pagoda on the platform above. About noon the whole of the town and Fort of Pegu was in our possession." Sergeant-Major Hopkins of the 101st gained his commission this day, and died, thirty years later, a lieutenant-colonel in Her Majesty's army. Subsequently a detachment of the regiment under Major Gerrard relieved the garrison which had been left in Pegu, and in its turn besieged by the enemy. Early in the following year Major Seaton of the regiment led the storming party which captured Gongoh, penetrated into the very heart of the country, reducing scattered towns and villages to a peaceful recognition of our supremacy, though not without many severe skirmishes and much arduous labour. Majors Seaton and Gerrard, Captain Lambert, and Lieutenant Dairson earned the special recognition of the authorities.

We now come to the crowning epoch of the regiment's splendid service—that of the

Mutiny. When the outbreak at Meerut gave unmistakable evidence at once of the fact and extent of the Mutiny, the 101st were at Dugshai and received orders to march to Umballah. Within a few hours of receiving the order they started, eight hundred strong, under Major Jacob, and reached their destination early on the next day but one after their start. From thence they were moved on to Kurnaul, and "it was from this place that Lieutenant W. S. Hodson, of the 1st Bengal Fusiliers, performed the daring feat of riding by himself with despatches through a hostile country to Meerut and back, 150 miles."

Later on Lieutenant Butler arrived at the head-quarters from leave of absence, having in his anxiety to be at his post ridden across country on one horse, 110 miles in forty hours. The 1st Bengal Fusiliers were with the 1st brigade under Brigadier Showers, Colonel Welchman being in command of the regiment, and both they and their comrades of the 2nd Bengal Fusiliers experienced some severe fighting at Budlee-Ka-Serai, from which they completely routed the enemy. While before Delhi the regiment was engaged in daily skirmishes with the enemy, in which countless acts of valour were performed, and more than one Victoria Cross was awarded to the gallant Fusiliers. One notable feat was the capture of the works called Ludlow Castle. The official report speaks of the "steadiness, silence, and order with which the 1st Bengal Fusiliers advanced to the attack on the enemy's guns, which was well conceived and gallantly executed by Major Jacob and the officers and men of the regiment under his command, and Captain S. Greville of the regiment, commanding the skirmishers who made the first attack upon the guns." Of these latter Private Reagan was, perhaps, the most distinguished. "Rushing," writes Colonel Innes, "upon a 24-pounder howitzer, which was charged with grape, he attacked the gunners single-handed, and bayoneted one of them just as he was applying the portfire." At the battle of Nujjufghur, on the 24th of August, the 101st were again conspicuous by their valour. Previous to the engagement General Nicholson addressed the troops, and turning to the regiment he said, "I have nothing to say to the 1st Fusiliers, they will do as they always do." The result of the "doing" on this occasion was that the enemy fled "leaving the whole of their camp equipage, baggage, and 13 guns in our possession." An officer of the regiment who was present adds that we "reached our camp after an absence of 41 hours, during which time our men had only partaken of one meal." At the assault of Delhi the 1st Bengal Fusiliers were divided between the first and fourth columns, of which the former, under General Nicholson, was to "storm the breach by the Cashmere Bastion," and the latter under Major Reid "to enter the city by the Lahore Gate." The 2nd Bengal Fusiliers were with the second column under Brigadier Jones, to whom was committed the charge of storming the "Water Bastion."

The story of the capture of Delhi is too familiar to allow us to dwell upon it, identified though it so greatly is with the gallant Munster Fusiliers. At the assault the brave Speke, Nicholson, and Jacob fell, mortally wounded; Greville was shot through the shoulder; Captain Caulfield, Lieutenants Wemyss, Butler, and Woodcock all fell at this time, as well as a large proportion of rank and file. The second column, in which were the 2nd Fusiliers under Boyd, pressed forward as far as the Kabul Gate, and had somewhat less desperate fighting; the fourth column, in which were the remainder of the 1st Fusiliers under Captain Wriford, had a terrible struggle. So fierce was the fire of the enemy that the road became well-nigh impassable from the number of the dead bodies. "Reid now gave the order, 'Fusiliers to the front!' and with a wild rush they charged across the bridge, unavoidably treading under foot the wounded men who lay on the road. . . . Captain Wriford and many of the officers in advance were engaged in single combat with the mutineers, who pelted our troops from behind their breastworks with brickbats and other missiles, whilst our ranks were being rapidly thinned by the musketry fire poured upon us by the thousands of the enemy behind their barricades. Here Lieutenant Owen was severely wounded in the head, but was saved from falling under the tulwars of the enemy by Lieutenant Lambert's protection. . . . Here also fell Sergeant Dunleary of the 1st Bengal Fusiliers, whose distinguished bravery was formally mentioned in the despatches of the commander of the column." There is, however, one incident of the capture of Delhi that, associated as it is with the 101st Fusiliers—the prime mover and instigator in this incident, which materially affected the future, being an officer in the regiment—it is not out of place to relate somewhat at length; the more so as, strange though it might seem, considerable controversy has arisen concerning it. We refer to the execution of the Delhi princes by Lieutenant Hodson of the 101st, the famous organizer and commander of "Hodson's Horse."

Hodson seems to have entertained from the first a sort of prescience that some crisis would arise which would call for the exercise of *one* controlling will. Accordingly he was immeasurably relieved and delighted when he obtained full discretion to deal as he thought best with the fugitive king and princes of Delhi, the only condition being that the former's life was spared. The king came forth from his hiding-place towards the glorious gateway of his captured city, still in all seeming a king in verity, surrounded by attendants and populace far outnumbering the small band of resolute British. But Hodson was a born king of men; numbers were of comparatively small account to him; his was the dominant will in that vast assembly, and he knew it. Sitting calm and unconcerned upon his horse, he had just before turned to one of the scowling crowd—a sentry of the Royal Guard—and ordered him to fetch a light for his cigar. At the right moment he demanded the king's arms, promising that his life should be spared. Then, having intimated that this promise was conditional on absolute and effective surrender, and that if any attempt at rescue was made, the royal captive would be shot like a dog, he rode back to the gates of Delhi and handed the king to the representative of the civil power. But, though the king was secured, the three princes, the prime instigators of the rebellion, had escaped. Tidings were brought to Hodson of their whereabouts. He took with him one subaltern and a hundred men, and rode straight for the tombs where the miscreants had taken shelter. At least six thousand adherents remained with the princes—odds of sixty to one! Yet Hodson sent in word demanding unconditional surrender. This was agreed to, and Hodson started back with his prisoners to Delhi. But on the way the crowd of rebels increased, and the escort was stopped. It was the moment for action, and Hodson was the man of all others fitted for the emergency. Another minute's delay and the princes would have been rescued and their captors not improbably annihilated. Riding up, with only Lieutenant Macdowel and four troopers, he turned to the crowd with the words: "These are the men who have not only rebelled against the Government, but ordered and witnessed the massacre and shameful exposure of innocent women and children, and thus therefore the Government punishes such traitors taken in open resistance." He ordered them to strip, so as still further to degrade them, and then, with his own hand, regardless of appeals, regardless, too, of the sanctimonious horror of fireside sentimentalists or jealous compeers, he shot them dead. The effect is said to have been instantaneous. The Mohammedans of the troop and some influential moulvies among the bystanders exclaimed, "Well and rightly done! their crime has met with its just penalty. These were they who gave the signal for the death of helpless women and children, and now a righteous judgment has fallen upon them." Such was the execution of the princes of Delhi, monsters to whose hideous cruelty and more hideous lust numbers of gentle English women had been sacrificed with tortures to them worse than death. Such was their execution, executed by the dauntless courage of an officer of the 101st, and applauded by all whom a spurious sentiment has not induced to consider other nationalities first and their own—nowhere.

In all the subsequent operations up to the siege of Lucknow, Hodson was pre-eminent for valour and capability. With the fall of Lucknow came the end of a glorious career. "He entered the breach with General Napier and several others, just as a party was starting to attack the Begum's palace; he fell in with them. The place was quickly taken, and as he was searching for concealed rebels, he looked into a dark passage full of them. A shot was fired from the inside; he staggered back some paces and fell. He was carried by his faithful orderly out of danger. At first hopes were entertained that he might recover, but he rapidly sank from internal bleeding. His last words were: 'My love to my wife. Tell her my last thoughts were of her. Lord, receive my soul!' Thus, on the 12th of March, 1858, in his thirty-seventh year, closed the earthly career of one of the best and bravest of England's sons—one of her truest heroes," * one of the ablest and bravest officers that even the 101st Fusiliers have ever possessed.

After Delhi the 101st had some severe fighting at Namoul, where the brigade was under the command of Colonel Gerrard of the regiment. This brave officer was killed, and the command of the regiment devolved upon "Lieutenant McFarlane, an officer of only six years' standing." Many were the brave deeds done at Namoul by officers and men of the 101st. Lieutenant F. D. M. Brown won the Victoria Cross for rescuing a wounded soldier under a heavy fire; Private McGovern—who had already won the same distinction—volunteered to dislodge three of the enemy who had retired to a small turret. Avoiding by sheer quickness and presence of mind the fire of their three rifles, he dashed forward before they could reload, "shot the man in front, and, rushing on the other two, bayoneted them without giving them time to recover." Some of the regiment were with Havelock when he effected the first relief of Lucknow; subsequently the 101st formed part of Colonel Seaton's column, and at Allyghur and Puttialee earned great credit. On the occasion of the final assault on Lucknow, they were attached to the 5th brigade. On the 9th of March they were hotly engaged, and it was on this occasion that Lieutenant Adair Butler won the Victoria Cross. It was necessary to ascertain the state of defence in which a strong battery of the enemy's was. Captain Salisbury of the 101st expressed the opinion that it was deserted, and Butler volunteered to test the accuracy of this surmise. He swam a rapid stream sixty yards wide, clambered up the

* Sketches from the "Life of the late Major W. S. R. Hodson."

works regardless of the extreme probability that every corner might conceal an ambushed enemy, and finding Captain Salisbury's views correct waved his *cummerbund* as a signal. To insure its being seen he remained in a most conspicuous position under a heavy fire of musketry. The city was finally captured with but small loss, three officers and twenty rank and file of the 101st being wounded, and eight rank and file killed. Lieutenant MacGregor "greatly distinguished himself by engaging in single combat with one of the bravest of the rebels, whom he reduced to eternal submission by sending his sword through his body up to its hilt, returning to his comrades looking 'very warm and exceedingly wild and happy.'" During the following months the regiment was engaged in various skirmishes with vagrant bands of mutineers, in which Captains Cunliffe and Trevor, and Lieutenants Brown and Warner earned great distinction. When it was found that the terrible Sepoy Mutiny had been completely crushed, and men had leisure to take stock of their credit account in the lists of worthful and memorable deeds, it was found that no fewer than five individuals of the 101st had gained the envied Victoria Cross. These men—their names, even if space forbids the enumeration of their triumphs, must be recorded—were Lieutenant Adair Butler, Lieutenant F. Brown, Sergeant J. M. Guire, Private J. McGovern, Drummer M. Ryan. After the rebellion had been crushed came the Royal Proclamation by which the Majesty of England announced that, "We have resolved to take upon ourselves the government of India," and simultaneously, so to speak, therewith came the transformation of the Bengal Fusiliers into H.M.'s 101st and 104th Regiments. For a few years no serious warfare engaged the services of the regiment, for we will still look on it as a whole, but in 1863 the 101st were engaged in the Umbeyla Campaign. "An account of the campaign," quoted by Colonel Innes, has the following remarks, which throw a descriptive light on the then composition and *morale* of the regiment. "It was well known that, whatever service was to be performed, the 101st would share in it, and the young soldiers—for with very few exceptions the whole of the regiment was composed of very young soldiers who had never seen service—burned with ardour for their maiden fight, and, remembering the gallant deeds of the old regiment, were eager to have their first brush with the enemy under the new colours of the 101st." The same account gives a graphic account of the difficulties that beset our troops. The jungle was so thick that the men could only go in single file—the duties "were far harder than usually fall to the lot of soldiers"—for nearly a month accoutrements were uncharged. In November of that year, the 101st carried the "Craig Piquet" with conspicuous dash, losing in the enterprise five killed and twenty-six wounded. In a subsequent engagement, Lieutenant Chapman lost his life. He was mortally wounded, and he knew it. Beside him fell another officer, Captain Smith of the 101st, whose hurt was not necessarily fatal. Even while the cold, unrelaxing hand of death was clutching closer and closer about his own throat, Chapman knelt by his wounded comrade and began to dress his wounds, declining to be moved as ' it was useless," but begging for the removal of Captain Smith. A sudden rush of the enemy frustrated this intention; "both officers fell into their hands and were hacked to pieces, their heads being cut off and their bodies shockingly mangled." Well may the writer conclude his account of this incident with the words: "In Lieutenant Chapman the 101st lost an officer of rare ability, of untiring energy, the perfect type of an English gentleman and a British officer." Before this troublesome "little war" was ended, two more officers, Ensign Sanderson and Surgeon Pitt, were killed, with many of the rank and file; the total loss in killed and wounded being eighty-seven officers and men.

So ends the military record of the 101st Regiment, which in 1871, for the first time, visited England. Since that date only the ordinary services of a regiment in peace time have fallen to their lot.

The 104th Regiment, the 2nd battalion of the Royal Munster Fusiliers, boast a record which may almost claim to vie in brilliancy, though not quite in age, with their brethren of the 1st battalion. The present 2nd battalion is the successor of previous 2nd battalions of the Bengal Fusiliers, which from time to time have become absorbed in the first. The 104th dates from 1859, and at the time of their consolidation into the Imperial Army bore on their colours "Punjaub," "Chillianwallah," "Goojerat," "Pegu," "Delhi." For their gallant services during the campaign commemorated by "Punjaub," the 2nd Bengal European Regiment were created Fusiliers, at their own request, and to mark the approbation of the Government "of their gallant, exemplary, and praiseworthy conduct." So much of the career of the gallant 104th has been noticed in dealing with the 101st that further notice is unnecessary. Together the two regiments preserve and uphold the splendid traditions of the Bengal Fusiliers of glorious memory.

We have dealt with the Royal Munster Fusiliers somewhat at length, but it must be remembered that in a sense, and that sense a military one, their history is the history, executed in relief, of the acquisition of British India; they are the representatives of the regiments which upheld, however irregularly and spasmodically, British power against French and natives, and thus, before ever a Royal regiment appeared upon the scene, laid firm hold on the glorious heritage which we of to-day enjoy, thanks to the stubborn valour of the East Indian Regiments.

THE NORFOLK REGIMENT*—Regimental District No. 9—consists of the 9th Foot, which dates from 1685, when it was raised—chiefly in Gloucestershire. On the occasion of the abdication of James II., Colonel Nicholas, of the 9th, was one of the officers who could not reconcile it with their oath to the absent King to renew it to his successor, and the colonelcy of the regiment consequently devolved upon Colonel Cunningham. It would almost seem, however, that Colonel Cunningham's view of duty was somewhat too unaccommodating for William III. The 9th were sent to subdue Londonderry, whose governor, being attached to King James, had incurred the resentment of the inhabitants. The latter accordingly determined to take the law into their own hands and to depose him, and they then offered the government to Colonel Cunningham of the 9th. He replied that, "being himself commanded by the King to obey the governor, he could not receive any application from persons who opposed that authority." The 9th thereupon returned to England. King William was so displeased that Colonel Cunningham, together with the Colonel of another regiment, the 17th, was deprived of his commission.

After some further service in Ireland, whither the regiment was again sent under a less punctilious commander, during which they fought at the Boyne, Morhill, Balleymore, Athlone, Galway, and Limerick, the 9th went in 1701 to Holland, where they shared in the siege of Kaiserswerth, and afterwards formed part of the covering army during the sieges of Venloo, Ruremonde, Stevenswart, and Liege, at the last named of which places the grenadier company of the regiment highly distinguished itself.

In 1703 they served at the siege and subsequently in the campaign under the Archduke Charles of Austria in Portugal, during which they experienced one of the more unpleasant "fortunes of war," by being made prisoners—through an act of treachery—at Castel de Vide. After being exchanged they took part in all the actions and sieges of that campaign, fighting over a district which the wars of a hundred years

---

* The Norfolk Regiment bears as a badge the figure of Britannia on cap and collar, and on the waistplate the Castle of Norwich. The motto is that of the Garter. On the colours are " Roleia," " Vimiera," " Corunna," " Busaco," " Salamanca," " Vittoria," " St. Sebastian," " Nive," " Peninsula," " Kabul, 1842," " Moodkee," " Ferozeshah," " Sobraon," " Sevastopol," " Kabul, 1879," " Afghanistan, 1879—80." The tunic is scarlet with facings of white, and the officers wear a black line on the gold lace of the tunics.

later were to make familiar to all, and where we find records of the gallantry of the regiment at Valencia, Badajoz,* Albuquerque, and Ciudad Rodrigo. In 1707 was fought, on Easter Day, the battle of Almanza, the peculiarity of which was that the English commander, Lord Galway, was by extraction a Frenchman named Rouvigny, whom the anti-Protestant policy of Louis Quatorze had driven to England, while the leader of the French army was the Duke of Berwick, an Englishman, and a Royal Stuart to boot, though with the bar sinister across his escutcheon. To the 9th Regiment, however, the defeat of Almanza only brought honour and fame. They went into action 467 strong; only one hundred were left to retreat with their commander, Colonel Stewart, to Tarragona. It was necessary for the regiment to recruit, and they accordingly returned home, and for many years no fighting fell to their lot. In 1761 the 9th, then known as Whitmore's Regiment, joined the expedition under General Studholm Hodgson, against Belle Isle, and fought gallantly in the fierce engagement which preceded the capitulation. The following year they joined the army under the Earl of Albemarle against the Havannah, where, in common with the rest of our forces, they endured great hardships, and where Lieutenant Nugent particularly distinguished himself in the capture of the Morro. The regiment was stationed in Florida from 1763 to 1769, when they returned to Ireland, and in 1776 embarked for Canada. Here they took part in the engagements at Fort Ticonderago, Skenesborough, Castletown, and Fort Anne, Wood Creek; at the last-named place greatly distinguishing themselves by "standing and repulsing an attack six times their number. In the height of action Lieutenant-Colonel Hill found it necessary to change his position. So critical an order was executed by the regiment with the utmost steadiness and bravery. They also captured the colours of the 2nd Hampshire (American) Regiment," and despite the arduous nature of the struggle lost only one officer and twelve rank and file. The 9th returned to England in 1781, where they remained till 1788, in which year they embarked for the West Indies. The grenadier and light companies took part in the expedition against Tobago, under Admiral Sir John Cafney and Major-General Cuyler and received high praise in the Commander-in-Chief's despatches. In 1794 the 9th were with Sir Charles Grey's army in the attack on Martinique. In the sharp fighting which followed an unexpected onslaught of the enemy Lieutenant-Colonel Campbell of the regiment was killed. After the conquest of Guadeloupe, General Sir Charles Grey said in his despatch that he " could not find words adequate to convey an idea, or to

* Where their colonel, the Earl of Galway, lost his right hand from a cannon ball.

express the high sense he entertained of the extraordinary merit evinced by the officers and soldiers in this service."

The 9th were subsequently stationed at Grenada, not returning to England till 1796, having suffered severely from the climate. In July, 1799, the regiment was formed into three battalions. The 1st and 2nd battalions embarked for Holland in the autumn and advanced with the force under the Duke of York to attack the French and Dutch forces at Bergen, taking part the following month in the capture of Egmont-op-Zee. After this no important fighting fell to their share till 1808, when the 1st battalion embarked for Portugal. At Roleia, the first battle whose name is on their colours, the 9th formed part of the centre column under Brigadier Nightingale, and with the 29th greatly distinguished themselves. It soon became evident that the battle would be fought in the rocky passes of the hills overlooking the town. Here the two regiments were, by what Napier characterizes as a "false movement,"* suddenly exposed to the full brunt of Laborde's attack. Many fell, including the colonel of the 29th; then "the oppressed troops rallied on their left wing and on the 9th Regiment, and all rushing up the hill together regained the tableland, presenting a confused front, which Laborde vainly endeavoured to destroy; yet many brave men he struck down, and mortally wounded Colonel Stewart of the 9th, fighting with great vehemence." The loss of the regiment in this engagement was five men, including Colonel Stewart, killed, and fifty-two, of whom three were officers, wounded.

The 2nd battalion arrived in Portugal in August, 1808, and on joining the army took up a position at Vimiera, the 1st battalion being posted on the mountain on the right of the village. On the morning of August 21st, the soldiers were under arms before daybreak, and at seven o'clock the French army was seen advancing " in two great columns, supported and flanked by a cloud of skirmishers, and dressed in long white linen coats and trousers." The hill, on which the 2nd battalion of the 9th was posted, was attacked by the enemy, who were repulsed with severe loss.

"The 1st battalion proceeded to Spain, and, though stationed at Corunna, were not engaged in the battle on January 16th, but their conduct during the expedition procured for them the honour of bearing the word 'Corunna' on their colours" (*Official Record*). It was a party of the 9th that dug the grave of Sir John Moore—literally "the sod with their bayonets turning"—and attended to his obsequies. After this they returned to

---

* The nature of this false movement is finely described in the historian's inimitable style as a "fierce neglect of orders in taking a path leading immediately to the enemy."

England, embarking six months later, with the expedition against Holland, where, however, they only remained three weeks.

In April, 1810, the light company of the 2nd battalion, which had been stationed at Gibraltar, was withdrawn from there to take part in the defence of Tarifa. The 1st battalion meanwhile landed at Lisbon in March of the same year to join Wellington's army.

On the 26th of September, the eve of the battle of Busaco, "the armies lay down for the night on the ground under the open sky. In the balmy autumn night none complained of nature's couch, and before dawn 100,000 men stood quietly to arms. While the grey mist of early morning still shrouded the ridge the French lines were formed for the attack, and their forward movement began. Ney was to make an assault on the allies' left, and, at a distance of three miles from him, Reynier on the allies' right, while Junot was kept in reserve."

The distinguished conduct of the regiment on this occasion is thus described in the official record of its career: "Major-General Leith led the 9th Regiment to attack the enemy on the rocky ridge, which they did without firing a shot. That part which looks behind the sierra was inaccessible, and afforded the enemy the advantage of out-flanking the 9th on the left as they advanced, but the order, celerity, and coolness with which they attacked panic-struck the enemy, who immediately gave way on being charged with the bayonet, and the whole were driven down the face of the sierra, in confusion and with immense loss from the destructive fire which the 9th opened upon them as they fled with precipitation after the charge. The steadiness and accuracy with which the 9th attended to the direction of the march which, before they were engaged, was continually changing, in order to form in the most advantageous manner for the attack of the enemy; the quickness and precision with which they formed line under a heavy fire; their instantaneous and orderly charge, by which they drove the enemy, so much superior in number, from a formidable position, and the promptitude with which they obeyed orders to cease firing, was, altogether, conduct as distinguished as any regiment could have shown." Afterwards the 9th were posted at Alcantara, and in December went into quarters at Torres Vedras, where they remained three months.

The 2nd battalion meanwhile embarked from Gibraltar early in 1811 to take part in an attack on the rear of the enemy's lines before Cadiz. At Barossa the flank companies of the 9th were with the force under General Browne, which "Graham's Spartan order had sent headlong" against the French, and of which nearly one-half went down under the first fire. Then when the 87th under General Dilkes forced their way to the rescue, the whole British force rushed up to the summit of the slope, where 'a dreadful, and for some time doubtful, combat raged, but the English bore strongly onward, and their incessant slaughtering fire forced the French from the hill with the loss of three guns and many brave soldiers.' Subsequently they embarked for Tarifa, and, after a short stay, returned to Gibraltar. The 1st battalion remained at Torres Vedras until the French army began to retreat towards Spain, when it followed with the army in pursuit, and on April 3rd, 1811, came up with a body of French at Sabugal. In the fierce combat that ensued, described by Wellington himself as "one of the most glorious actions British troops were ever engaged in," the 9th did their service gallantly, driving their opponents over the bridge at the point of the bayonet. After taking part in the battle of Fuentes d'Onor they went into cantonments, their next piece of important fighting being at the storming of Ciudad Rodrigo and Badajoz. In neither of these exploits, however, do they seem to have taken any prominent part. Very different, however, was the case at Salamanca. Here the 9th were a quarter of a mile in front of the other regiments, when a forward movement became of vital importance. One of Wellington's aides-de-camp rode up and said, "The 9th is the only regiment formed, advance!" And advance they did, though for a time comparatively unsupported, and throughout the engagement fought most gallantly, moving forward in pursuit of the enemy on the day following. They were with the force which compelled Clausel to abandon Valladolid, and then joined in the advance on Madrid. In October, the 9th, "not mustering 300 men, with scarcely an officer to a company," were ordered to take an active part in defending the bridge of Muriel and the fords. The contest was so obstinate that the men were twice supplied with ammunition. The regiment lost 1 sergeant and 16 rank and file killed; 8 officers, 4 sergeants, and 50 rank and filed wounded. During the retreat from Burgos the 9th were distinguished for the order and discipline they observed, and in consequence did not consider themselves implicated in the severe censure published in general orders.

In the spring of 1813, 10 sergeants and 400 rank and file from the 2nd battalion joined the regiment in Portugal in time to share in the memorable battle of Vittoria, where they behaved with their customary courage. At the siege of San Sebastian one of the first objects was the reduction of San Bartolomeo, and here the 9th gained conspicuous honour. Colonel Cameron led the grenadier company down the face of the hill, exposed to a heavy cannonade from the horn work. His spirited advance occasioned the French to abandon the redoubt, and the grenadiers of the 9th jumped over the wall and assaulted both the convent and the houses of the suburb with the most heroic gallantry. A fierce struggle took place in the suburb. Capt. John Woodham of the 9th fought his way into the upper room of a house and was there killed; Lieutenant and Adjutant Thornhill was also killed: in the meantime the grenadiers carried the convent with such rapidity that the French had not time to explode some mines they had prepared. The companies of the regiment with the right attack were no whit behind their brethren in gallantry and dash, and the severity of the fight may be judged from the fact that in this encounter the regiment had upwards of seventy officers and men killed and wounded.

On the renewal of the siege the following month a determined sortie of the French was repulsed by the bayonets of the 9th. The terrible and dramatic features of this siege are familiar to all from the pages of Napier. The singular distinction gained during its progress by the 9th Regiment will be most effectively shown by an unvarnished extract from the official record, the stern simplicity of which has an eloquence all its own. At the storming there was in command of a forlorn hope a Lieutenant Colin Campbell,* known to after days as Field-Marshal Lord Clyde. His position was in the centre of the Royals, for the purpose of carrying the high curtain work after the breach should be won. Lieutenant-Colonel Cameron and Lieutenant Campbell distinguished themselves on this occasion, the latter receiving a cut from a sabre and a stab from a bayonet. On the morning of August 27th, 1813, a hundred soldiers of the 9th, commanded by Captain Hector Cameron, proceeded to attack the island of Santa Clara in the bay of San Sebastian. As the boats approached the shore a heavy fire was opened upon them. The island was, however, captured and the French garrison made prisoners, and the conduct of Captain Cameron on this occasion was commended by Wellington in his despatches. San Sebastian was again attacked by storm on August 31st, when the 9th lost 4 officers, 5 sergeants, and 42 rank and file. Lieutenant-Colonel Campbell and five other officers were wounded, and over a hundred men.

At the passage of the Bidassoa on October 7th, the 9th took post in the left wing of the allied army. The German light troops had driven the French back to the important post of the Croix des Bouquets; this, however, was the very key of the position and the

* It has been asserted of the East Norfolk Regiment that it "may be said to have commenced its military career with his arrival, as its colours, then virgin, were only about to be decorated with the names of the battles in which he first saw fire." This is somewhat hard on a regiment which has a previous history of over a hundred years, but the *distinctions* certainly synchronise with the joining of the future hero of the Crimea and Lucknow.

enemy made a stubborn and effective resistance. Led by the gallant Colonel Cameron the 9th rushed up the height "with a furious charge" and cleared it, when the French infantry fled to a second ridge, where they could only be approached by a narrow front. Colonel Cameron then formed the regiment into one column and advanced under a concentrated fire. The 9th moved steadily forward until they arrived within a dozen yards of their antagonists, when, "raising a loud shout, they rushed on the opposing foe. The enemy fled and the ridges were won. The conduct of the 9th elicited the commendations of the general officers who witnessed their intrepid bearing, and the regiment was thanked in the field by Wellington." They subsequently took part in the battle of the Nive, and at Biaritz captured no fewer than one hundred and sixty prisoners.

Immediately after the termination of the war in the Peninsula, in which they had won so fair a renown, the 9th were ordered to Canada, returning the following year, though too late to take part in the battle of Waterloo. They served, however, with the army of occupation, and were stationed at Paris, Compiegne, and St. Armand successively, returning to England in October, 1818.* Three months later they proceeded to the West Indies, where they remained for eight years, being stationed at St. Vincent, Dominica, and St. Lucia, Grenada, and Trinidad. After a short stay in the United Kingdom, in 1833 the regiment went to the Mauritius, leaving there two years later for Bengal. Some six years passed before an opportunity occurred for them to share in any fighting. In December, 1841, however, they proceeded from Meerut *en route* to Ferozepore, for the purpose of being employed on active service beyond the Indus, and were engaged at the Khyber Pass, and in the actions in the Valley and Pass of Tezeen. The regiment then proceeded to Kabul, where they arrived on September 15th, and the following month assisted at the assault and capture of Istalif. In 1845, after being stationed in and about Kabul since its capture, the 9th joined the army of the Sutlej, and took part in the battles of Moodkee, Ferozeshah, and Sobraon.

The particulars of these battles are elsewhere given, and it need only be here observed that the 9th acquitted themselves as they have ever done. They returned to England in 1847, and found their next warlike service in the Crimea, where they arrived in November, 1854, and from the time of their arrival to the evacuation of Sevastopol, took part in all the arduous and dangerous duties which devolved upon our gallant army. In 1858 a second battalion was raised chiefly in Yarmouth, and has

* The 2nd battalion was disbanded at Chatham at the end of 1815.

added to the distinctions the two last names on the colours of the regiment ; previously to which it had served in China and Japan, and in the Jowaki expedition of 1877—78. In the Afghan war of 1879—80, the 9th were with General Gough's column, which arrived at Kabul on Christmas Day, "sorely disappointed at being too late to share in the recent action," when the British reoccupied the city. Later on they formed part of the force under General Ross, which two days before the battle of Ghazni marched to join the force under Sir Donald Stewart. The junction, however, was prevented by the unexpectedly hostile attitude of the chiefs of the intervening territory. After the order to evacuate Kabul had arrived the 9th had a fierce skirmish with the Ghilzies at a place called Syazabad. It was after this encounter that Lieutenant Lorne Govan attacked a couple of Ghazis who had just murdered a man of one of our Ghoorka regiments. One he killed and the other was shot by the infuriated comrades of the murdered man. The Afghan war terminates the active service record of the gallant Norfolk Regiment, as it is beyond the scope of this work to treat of hostilities which— at the time of publishing—are still in operation.

THE NORTHAMPTONSHIRE REGIMENT *—Regimental District No. 48— consists of the 48th and 58th Regiments of Foot. The former dates from 1740, and a year after its formation, received its numerical distinction. There seems, according to Archer, whose sketch is the most readily available, to be some doubt whether they actually participated in the battles of Fontenoy or Culloden. It is, however, certain that they took part in the campaign in Flanders of 1747—48, and at Laffeldt distinguished themselves under Colonel Seymour Conway, who was taken prisoner. In 1755 they went to America and shared in the disaster which overtook our forces at Fort Duquesne, afterwards— such as were left—being ordered to Albany. Two years after they were at Louisburg, and in 1759 were with Wolfe in the immortal struggle of Quebec. After seeing some service at Martinique and the Havannah, the regiment returned home in 1763 and were next employed under Abercromby in the West Indies. As a two-battalion regiment, they were represented (by the 1st battalion) in the war in Portugal in 1809, and were present at the passage of the Douro, the name of which only three regiments besides the

* The Northamptonshire Regiment bears as badges the Castle and Key, with the name "Gibraltar" above, and " Talavera " below, on the cap, and the Cross of St. George with a horseshoe on the collar. The motto is *Montis insignia Calpe*. On the colours are the Sphinx and the names of the following battles: " Louisburg," " Quebec, 1759," "Gibraltar," " Egypt," " Maida," " Douro," " Talavera," " Albuera," " Badajoz," " Salamanca," " Vittoria," " Pyrenees," " Nivelle," " Orthes," " Toulouse," " Peninsula," " Sevastopol," " New Zealand," " South Africa, 1879." The uniform is scarlet with facings of white.

Northamptonshire bear on their colours. In July of the same year was fought the bloody battle of Talavera, which yielded to the 48th perhaps the fairest flower in their chaplet of honour. It was at the critical moment of the fight, "when the British centre was absolutely beaten, that Colonel Donellan, who fell mortally wounded a few minutes later, led up the gallant 48th Regiment. Wheeling back into open columns of companies to let the disordered masses of the Guards pass through, the 48th assailed the enemy's flank with heavy volleys." The effect was to give the gallant Guards time to reform, and before long the enemy were in headlong retreat. As Wellesley declared, the day was saved by the "advance, position, and steadiness of the 1st battalion of the 48th under Major Middlemore," who had taken command of the regiment on the death of Colonel Donellan. With regard to the last-named officer, the account of the incident given by Grant has a certain pathos. He was the last officer in our service who adhered to the old Nivernais, or three-cornered cocked hat, and on the order to succour the Guards being given, executed the requisite manoeuvres with consummate skill. At the moment of advance "he fell mortally wounded, and lifting his old Nivernais to Major Middlemore, requested him to take the command." Both battalions were at Albuera, where the second was with Stewart's first brigade, which, under Colonel Colborne, was "almost annihilated," while the 1st battalion charged under General Houghton and its own officers, Colonel Duckworth and Major Way, to "turn the doubtful day again." At Badajoz, to the 1st battalion under Major Wilson was assigned the storming of the San Roque, and such was the fury of their assault, that "resistance was almost instantaneously overpowered;" at Salamanca they gained yet another distinction for their honour-heavy colours. At Vittoria, St. Sebastian, Nivelle, at Orthes, Toulouse, and the battles of the Pyrenees they fought, ever foremost in the fray. At the close of the Peninsular War they repaired to India, where, in 1834, they served "in the brief but arduous campaign of Coorg," which was the last warlike service demanded of them till the Crimea, the intervening years being spent in Malta, the West Indies, and Jamaica. They landed in the Crimea in April, 1855, and from that date to the close of the war were actively engaged. Since then their time has been spent chiefly in India, but no active service of importance has fallen to the lot of the gallant 48th.

The 2nd battalion of the Northamptonshire Regiment, the 58th Foot, dates from 1755, and is the third regiment which has borne that number. In 1758 they joined the expedition against Louisburg under General Amherst, and the year following were in the famous British line which, on the heights of Abraham, gained Quebec and "the princely dominion of Canada" for the crown of Great Britain. In 1762 they fought in the Havanna, and during the following years were variously engaged. In 1781 they shared in the memorable defence of Gibraltar, being one of the five regiments which bear the "Castle and Key" in commemoration thereof. While engaged here they received the territorial designation of the Rutlandshire Regiment. When peace was concluded the 58th spent ten years at home, during which time amongst the captains appointed to the regiment was "Arthur Wellesley, from the 12th Light Dragoons." In 1794 the 58th were with the forces under Sir Charles Grey in the West Indies, and shared in the conquest of Martinique. After seeing some service in Minorca and the Mediterranean, the Rutlandshire Regiment were ordered to Egypt, and were placed in the reserve under Major-General, afterwards Sir John, Moore. On the occasion of the landing at Aboukir the fire of the 58th effectually checked the French cavalry which were seriously harassing the Guards. At the battle of Alexandria they, with the 28th, were posted amongst some ruins on the right of our line and here it was that the heaviest of the fighting took place. Under Colonel Crowdjye the 58th "manned the breaches in the ruined wall, and after three rounds of ball cartridge rushed on the enemy with the bayonet." But the struggle was by no means over. So impressed was the French General Menou with the importance of the position, that he promised a louis d'or to every soldier who should penetrate within the enclosure. At last, attacking on three sides at once, they got in—but few got out again. Our men closed up behind them; "when powder and shot lasted no longer, our people had recourse to stones and the butt-ends of their muskets. It was a hand-to-hand fight, a *mêlée* in which the French found they had not a chance either of victory or escape. They were knocked down in heaps, they were transfixed with the bayonet against the walls of the old building; the entire area was covered with their blood and their bodies. Seven hundred Frenchmen were slain amongst these dismal ruins, scarcely a man of them that entered got off, for the few who were not killed or prostrated by their wounds surrendered and cried for mercy." (*Low*.)

On the renewal of the war with France, a second battalion was enrolled and fought in many of the famous battles of the Peninsular War. The 1st battalion, meanwhile, was in Sicily, and under Sir John Stewart took part in the memorable battle of Maida. Here they were commanded by Sir John Oswald, and, with the 78th, formed Acland's brigade, which so splendidly seconded the brilliant efforts of the Light Infantry under Kemp. The 2nd battalion fought at Salamanca and at Burgos, during the disastrous retreat from which they suffered very heavily. After this they were attached to General

Barnes' Brigade. At Echellar they gained the praise of Lord Wellesley for the share they took in that splendid charge, which ended in "the astonishing spectacle being presented of fifteen hundred men driving, by sheer valour and force of arms, six thousand good troops from ground so rugged, the numbers might have been reversed and the defence made good without much merit." The Nivelle and Nive, Orthes and Bordeaux, witnessed their prowess and discipline, and at the close of the war the 2nd battalion was disbanded, having done well for its country and the honour of the regiment. The 1st battalion was engaged in Canada, and so were unable to share in the victory of Waterloo; they formed part, however, of the army of occupation. For the next twenty-two years or so their sphere of service lay in Jamaica and Ceylon, and during their sojourn at the latter station, they were engaged in quelling one of the periodic outbreaks of the Candians. In 1843 they were ordered to New South Wales, and took part in the first New Zealand War, returning home in 1859. After a peaceful interval of about twenty years they joined the British forces engaged in the Zulu War, during which—and the subsequent operations against the Boers—few regiments gained greater renown or suffered more severely. They were with the reinforcements which arrived in April, 1879, and were placed in the Second Division under General Newdigate. After the melancholy death of the Prince Imperial of France, it was by a party of the 58th that his body was escorted to Pietermaritzburg. On the 6th of June, occurred a somewhat regrettable incident—yet one to which, as history tells us, the best troops are liable—from a false alarm given by a sentry. Under the impression that the camp was surrounded, the officer in command ordered a random fire, from which the only victims—for no Zulus were near—were some nine men of the regiment. At the battle of Ulundi they were at the right rear angle of the square, on which the Zulu force desperately hurled itself, but the steady fire of the 58th and their comrades repulsed them just when a fierce hand-to-hand fight seemed imminent. When the war with the Boers broke out the 58th were amongst the three British regiments then in the Transvaal, and in January, 1881, some of the regiment were with Sir Pomeroy Colley at the disastrous affair of Laing's Nek. Terrible was the upshot of the day to the gallant Rutlandshire! They led the way up the steep slope, the grass of which was wet and slippery, the surface swept with bullets. For five minutes, the men endured a scathing fire from front and flank; then Colonel Deane gave the word to charge. Scarcely had he uttered it than he fell, mortally wounded; the command devolved upon Major Higginson, but ere long he, too, fell. Major Poole and Lieutenant Dolphin were shot dead; "Captain Lovegrove was wounded and nearly every non-commissioned officer was killed or wounded;" the colours were taken. "Lieutenant Bailie, a mere boy subaltern, but a gallant one, who carried one of the colours, on falling mortally wounded, was succoured by Lieutenant Peel who carried the other. 'Never mind me,' he exclaimed, while choking with blood, 'save the colours.'" Peel then took both colours, but he, too, soon fell; then Sergeant Brindstock seized them, and they were at last rescued by a desperate sally. The command of the regiment devolved upon Captain Hornby, who had been acting with a mounted body, and besides the casualties before referred to Lieutenant O'Donnell was wounded. Lieutenant Peel, it appeared, had not been shot when he fell, but had stumbled into a hole, and he was one of the ten officers who survived that terrible day. The accounts of fiendish cruelty on the part of the Boers were so frequent, that it is with a certain amount of grim satisfaction one reads that "Private Brennan bayoneted a Boer when in the act of shooting at a wounded soldier who lay helpless on the ground, and calling out for mercy." At Majuba Hill there were one hundred and fifty of the terribly attenuated regiment. The tale of that mad but heroic struggle has been before told: of the 58th, Captain the Hon. C. Maude (attached) was killed, Captain Morris and Lieutenants Hill and Lucy wounded, and Captain Hornby prisoner. Of these Lieutenant Lucy was specially complimented in the dispatches of Sir Evelyn Wood for his conspicuous valour. Meanwhile, Captain Saunders of the regiment had been gallantly holding Wakkerstroom, aided by Captain Power and Lieutenant Read, while a detachment under Lieutenant Compton had been with the force, which for twelve weeks had been besieged in Standerton.

Since the war in the Transvaal, in which they suffered so terribly, and fought so bravely, the 58th have not been engaged in any warlike operations which call for notice.*

THE NORTHUMBERLAND FUSILIERS †—Regimental District No. 5—consist of the famous old 5th Foot, and date their corporate existence as a regiment from 1674, though it was not till eleven years later that they were permanently placed on the British

---

* The sobriquets of the 58th are "The Black Cuffs" and "Steelbacks." The former recalls the original facings; the latter is said to have originated in the old flogging days, when the men of the 58th used to pride themselves on bearing the lash without wincing.

† The Northumberland Fusiliers bear as badges on cap and collar St. George and the Dragon on a grenade. The motto is *Quo fata vocant*. On the colours are the Rose and Crown and the King's Crest, with the following distinctions: "Wilhelmstahl," "Roleia," "Vimiera," "Corunna," "Busaco," "Ciudad Rodrigo," "Badajoz," "Salamanca," "Vittoria," "Nivelle," "Orthes," "Toulouse," "Peninsula," "Lucknow," "Afghanistan, 1878—80." The uniform is scarlet with facings of white, and Fusilier's cap with red and white feather.

Establishment. The British legion, which at the first-named date was in Holland, was formed into four regiments—"two English, one Scots, and one Irish. The latter is now designated the 5th Regiment of Foot, or Northumberland Fusiliers" (*Cannon*). They soon, however, dropped the Irish appellation and nationality, and as Fenwick's Regiment gained a high reputation in the wars fought by the Prince of Orange. On this period of their career, however, it is not our purpose to linger, as they were not at that time, strictly speaking, a regiment of the British Army. They accompanied the Prince of Orange when he landed in England, previously to accepting the Crown abandoned by his father-in-law, and from that date the career of the Northumberland Fusiliers is wholly identified with this country. They fought in the Irish Wars against the adherents of James II., and in the abortive foreign expeditions undertaken about that time. In 1693 they went abroad, where they served till the peace of Ryswick. After passing some nine years at home, principally in Ireland, the 5th were ordered, in 1706, to Portugal, where the mere fact of their presence imbued the enemy with a wholesome awe. At Caya, in 1709, the regiment is reported to have "acquired great honour by its signal gallantry;" later on, the attempt made by the Spaniards in 1727 to capture Gibraltar provided another opportunity for the gallant 5th to distinguish themselves. They took part in the expeditions against St. Malo and Cherbourg in 1758, and in 1760 joined the army in Germany and fought at Corbach, Warbourg, Zierenberg, Campen, Kirch-Denkern, Copenhagen, and other places. At Wilhelmstahl they gained their first "distinction," an honour rendered the more valuable since the 5th are the only regiment which bear that name on their colours. An artillery officer, writing at the time, says: "The 5th Foot behaved nobly, and took above twice its own number prisoners." They were allowed to change their caps for those of the French grenadiers they had conquered, and from that time dates the unique privilege they enjoy of wearing a red and white hackle feather on their fusilier caps. This was originally white, but when all infantry regiments were ordered to wear a white feather, the distinctive character of the badge in the case of the Northumberland Fusiliers was perpetuated by theirs being changed to red and white. It is illustrative of the tardiness which characterizes official recognition of military merit that though Wilhelmstahl was fought in 1762, it was not till 1836 that the 5th were allowed to bear the name on their colours. Visitors to Brighton will remember seeing in old Hove Churchyard the tombstone to the memory of Phœbe Hassell. This veritable Amazon had a share in the glories of Wilhelmstahl, having fought in the ranks of the 5th on that occasion. The regiment returned to England in

1763, remaining at home for some ten years, during which time they acquired the nickname of the "shiners," from their remarkable smartness of appearance. In 1767, the regimental order of merit, which has been found to work so well, was instituted. They were dispatched to America in 1774, and came in for the full of the fighting to be had there, taking part in the battles at Concord, Lexington, Bunker's Hill (where it was said that "the 5th behaved the best, and suffered the most"), Long Island, Brooklyn, Whiteplains, and Germantown. They distinguished themselves greatly at St. Lucia, where Brigadier-General Meadows, taking the colours and planting them in the ground, addressed the 5th in the following words: "Soldiers, as long as you have a bayonet to point against an enemy's breast, defend those colours."

The next eighteen years were passed at home and in Canada, and in 1799 the Northumberland Fusiliers were ordered to Holland, where, at Egmont-op-Zee and Winkle, under Colonel Bligh, they earned special praise. In 1806 they served at Buenos Ayres, and two years later joined Wellington's army in Portugal. At Roleia, they were to have formed one column with the 9th and 29th. The two latter regiments, however, by their "fierce neglect of orders" (referred to in treating of the Norfolk Regiment), took another path; the 5th, adhering to the plan marked out, appeared at the critical moment on Laborde's left, and he was eventually forced to retire. They fought at Vimiera; at Corunna the names of Mackenzie and Emes of the regiment were not dimmed even by the brilliant glory which surrounded that of Moore. They were at Flushing. Under Colonel Copson a detachment fought at Talavera; at Busaco they did sterling service; at Redinha and Sabugal they fought. At El Bodon Major Ridge led them forward to charge the French cavalry, retaking the Portuguese artillery that had been captured; later on in the day they successfully resisted, in conjunction with the 77th Regiment, the furious charge of the French horsemen. At Ciudad Rodrigo Ridge again led them to the desperate conflict. At Badajoz, again, though for the last time, he fought at their head, in the thick of the unholy turmoil that raged. The ladders put against the walls were, with their living freights, hurled backwards by the triumphant defenders. Shrieks, groans, oaths, the sickening thud of live, writhing bodies dashed against stone or earth, the clash of steel, the clang of stormers' axes, the crash of musketry, the clamour of cries and curses—amidst all this, "the British, baffled yet untamed, fell back to take shelter under the rugged edge of the hill. There the broken ranks were reformed, and the heroic Colonel Ridge, again springing forward, called with stentorian voice on his men to follow, and, seizing a ladder, raised it against the castle to the right of the former attack, where the wall was lower, and an embrasure offered some facility. A second ladder was placed alongside by the grenadier officer Canch, and the next instant he and Ridge were on the rampart, the shouting troops pressed after them, and the garrison, amazed and in a manner surprised, were driven fighting through the double gate into the town. The castle was won. Soon a reinforcement from the French reserve came to the gate, through which both sides fired, and the enemy retired; but Ridge fell, and no man died that night with more glory--yet many died, and there was much glory." (*Napier*). The 5th fought at Salamanca, and it would seem that it was at this battle that the glorious deception practised by one James Grant, a bandsman, was discovered. According to custom, the bandsmen were invariably left to guard the baggage during an engagement. This did not suit Grant, who was a fine man physically as morally, and, accordingly, he was wont to steal after the combatants, appropriate the first uniform whose wearer was *hors de combat*, and fall in with the grenadier company of the regiment. He fought with the most reckless courage throughout all the battles in which the 5th were engaged, but, strange to say, was never wounded. The 5th fought at Vittoria, at Nivelle, at Orthes and Toulouse. They were then ordered to Canada, the operations in which caused them to miss Waterloo. After serving in the army of occupation for some time, they were quartered in the West Indies, and their next active service (for they were in the Mauritius during the Crimean War) was in India at the Mutiny. They were with Havelock in his march to relieve Lucknow, and vied with the gallant Madras Fusiliers in their splendid courage. They remained in garrison at Lucknow till its final relief by Colin Campbell, and many are the acts of individual heroism recorded of men of the 5th. One of the regiment, Private McManus, was with the gallant little band which, under Surgeon Home, fought so nobly against such overwhelming odds in guarding and rescuing the wounded; at the fight at the Alumbagh, Sergeant Ewart, with some more men of the 5th, rescued their comrade, Private Deveney, who was lying, with a leg shot away, at the mercy of the rebels, who knew not what the term mercy meant. Private McHale on several occasions distinguished himself by his dauntless courage. His speciality seems to have been capturing guns, for at the Alumbagh, and again on the occasion of a sortie from the Lucknow Residency, he took some pieces from the rebels. "On every occasion of attack," says the official report, "Private McHale has been the first to meet the foe, amongst whom he caused such consternation by the boldness of his rush as to leave little work for those who followed to his support. By his habitual coolness and daring and sustained bravery in action, his name has become a household word for gallantry amongst his comrades."

After the relief of Lucknow, the 5th served in Oude, and throughout proved themselves worthy of their lofty traditions. Passing over the intermediate years, during which no active service of note fell to their lot, we find them with the Peshawur field force in the Afghan War of 1878—9, and with the Khyber line in 1880.*

The Oxfordshire Light Infantry† consist of the 43rd and 52nd Regiments. The former—the 43rd—date from 1741, the year following which they embarked for Minorca, where they stayed till 1749, though without seeing any active service. In 1757 they were ordered to Louisburg, having passed the intervening eight years in Ireland, and on the temporary abandonment of that expedition repaired to Nova Scotia. Various skirmishes of no great importance occupied their time here, and the regiment were getting weary of the comparative inaction when the welcome news arrived in 1759 that they were to join the army under General Wolfe. At first it seemed as though their initiation into the severe mysteries of warfare was to be identified with a failure, but the happy inspiration of scaling the heights of Abraham did more than nullify failure, it transformed it into success. At the battle of Quebec the position of the 43rd was in the centre of the first line. The incident and result of that battle are matter of general history. What may not be so generally known is the compliment—recorded by Sir R. Levinge, the historian of the 43rd—made to that regiment by the defeated French. "Never had they known," they admitted, "so fierce a fire or such perfect discipline; as to the centre corps, they levelled and fired *absolument comme un coup de canon.*" Another testimony from our foes is recorded by Sir R. Levinge. Almost the last words of the brave Montcalm were, "If I could survive this wound I would engage to beat three times the amount of such forces as I commanded with a third of their number of British troops." After the fall of Quebec the 43rd fought at Sillery, and on peace being signed remained at the former station, from whence in 1762 they proceeded to Mar-

---

* In addition to the nickname above mentioned, the 5th were, during the Peninsular War, known as "The Old Bold Fifth," "The Fighting Fifth," and "Lord Wellesley's Body-Guard"—the last referring to some supposed preference of Lord Wellesley for the gallant regiment.

† The Oxfordshire Light Infantry bear as badge the bugle characteristic of Light Infantry. The motto is that of the Garter. On the colours are the Tudor Rose with the following names :—"Quebec, 1759," "Hindoostan," "Vimiera," "Corunna," "Busaco," "Fuentes d'Onor," "Ciudad Rodrigo," "Badajoz," "Salamanca," "Vittoria," "Nivelle," "Nive," "Orthes," "Toulouse," "Peninsula," "Waterloo," "South Africa, 1851-2-3," "Delhi," "New Zealand." The uniform is scarlet with facings of white. The officers wear shirt collars in "undress" uniform.

tinique.* They fought there and in the Havannah, and in 1764 returned to England, where they remained for ten years, when the troubles of the War of Independence summoned them to America, which they reached the first of all the regiments from England. Under Captain Lawrie they fought at Lexington and Concord; at Bunker's Hill they fought side by side with their future comrades and present 2nd battalion, the 52nd,† and suffered severely. They fought at Long Island with but little loss, at White Plains, Fort Washington, and New York Island, they shared in the victories won by the Royal troops. At Quaker's Hill, in 1778, they particularly distinguished themselves, as, indeed, they did throughout the unfortunate war which resulted in the independence of America. After the termination of the war they remained in England ten years, and in 1794 were ordered to Martinique, where they suffered terribly from the climate, an experience which was renewed three years later when they again served in the West Indies. Despite, however, the hostility of the climate, not a few—when the regiment was, in 1800, ordered home—elected to stay and volunteer into the West India regiments. In 1803 they received the formal denomination of Light Infantry, which in the case of the 43rd, more perhaps than in that of any other regiment, has remained as an especially distinctive appellation. In the following year there joined the ranks of the 43rd, as captain, their future commander and eulogist, Sir W. Napier, from whose brilliant pages we have so often quoted. The regiment was amongst those stationed at Shorncliffe during the scare of the threatened French invasion, and, like their companions of the Rifles, acquired considerable proficiency as marksmen. Under Colonel Stewart they took part in the expedition against Copenhagen in 1807, and with the 52nd and 92nd were brigaded under Sir Arthur Wellesley. On their return to England the ship, in which a considerable number of the regiment were, struck and for some time it seemed as though all on board would be lost. With Ensign Neale, however, the approach of death in no wise abated either his pluck or sense of the proprieties. Amongst his baggage was a flute on which he was no bad performer; routing it out he proceeded to play the "Dead March in *Saul*." *Abfuit omen!* The crew and soldiers were saved, and Ensign Neale, some years after, exchanged the sword for the stole and took holy orders.

* A curious incident is related by the writer above quoted. In 1761 the 43rd, under Major Elliott, were wrecked on Sable Island. In 1842 a violent storm swept over the island and completely swept away a big pyramid of sand, which had always excited curiosity. Huts were disclosed, and on investigation countless relics of the dead-and-gone warriors of the old 43rd were discovered—furniture, boxes, bullets, clothes, shoes, and innumerable smaller articles, including "a tiny brass dog collar with 'Major Elliott, 43rd Regiment,' engraven."

† Sir R. Levinge states that each regiment had at one time been numbered 54th.

With the Peninsular war proper the most brilliant glories of the 43rd may be said to commence. There was scarcely a combat or a skirmish in which they were not engaged, scarcely—if, indeed, even that limitation is not too exclusive—a report in which they were not praised. With the 52nd and 95th they formed the famous Light Division, to whose splendid prowess so much of the success of the British Army was due. It scarcely needs an apology under any circumstances to quote from a writer like Napier, but in dealing with the 43rd—his own regiment—quotation ceases to be merely allowable and becomes obligatory. It is not our province to attempt nicely to discriminate between the relative merits of strategic movements, or to question how far the loyalty of the warrior to his own corps may instinctively guide the pen of the military historian; in Napier's pages the deeds of the Light Division, and notably of the 43rd, are portrayed in colours brilliant and undying, and the Peninsular record of the 43rd will be best given, by presenting that portraiture as it came from his pen. At Vimiera the attack of the regiment was well timed. The steadfast hail of our artillery had thrown the French into some confusion; "the moment was happily seized by the 43rd; they poured down in a solid mass and with ringing shouts dashed against the column, driving it back with irrecoverable disorder, yet not without the fiercest fighting. The loss of the regiment was a hundred and twenty, and when the charge was over, a French soldier and the Sergeant-Armourer, Patrick, were found grimly confronting each other in death as they had done in life, their hands still clutching their muskets, and their bayonets plunged to the socket in each manly breast! It is by such men that thousands are animated and battles won." It was about this time that Sergeant Newman of the regiment gained his commission. He had been left behind in charge of a company of invalids, and by his energy and endurance beat off continued charges of French cavalry. As an example of the martial ardour that animated the regiment may be instanced the fact that, in their eagerness to be in time for the fight at Corunna, many men came to take their places in the ranks *crawling on hands and knees*, so fearfully lacerated were their feet!

The 2nd battalion—for the 1st had not hitherto been engaged in the Peninsula—was ordered home to recruit, and subsequently took part in the Walcheren expedition. The disastrous nature of that exploit has been before referred to: the historian of the 43rd throws an additional light on the ghastly picture when he tells us that, so fatal was the climate, in a fortnight no fewer than twelve thousand men were stricken down.

Fearfully sudden, too, were the attacks of the dread pestilence. Men would be marching gaily in the ranks or sitting idly in camp when they would reel and stumble, and a few hours afterwards only a livid corpse or a human wreck, whose days were surely numbered, remained to bear witness to the soldier that had been. Years after, when the terrible Crimean cholera was filling hospitals and cemeteries by that "dolorous midland sea," a writer*—whose works make us sigh regretfully "for the touch of a vanished hand"—wrote of two young soldiers who sat chatting together in the sweltering, death-fraught, heat. "And Charles told his comrade about Ravenshoe, about the deer and the pheasants and the blackcock, and about the big trout that lay nosing up into the swift places in the cool, clear water. And suddenly the lad turned on him, with his handsome face livid with agony and horror, and clutched him convulsively by both arms, and prayed him, for God Almighty's sake—There, that will do. The poor lad was dead in four hours." The passage is from a work of fiction—*oh, si sic omnia!*—it is true, but it was a faithful description of what took place in the Crimea, and might, with equally exact veracity, have been penned about Walcheren.

After this, both battalions of the regiment joined the allied forces in the Peninsula. The Douro was forced and Talavera won; and though the regiment was not at the latter battle, the march they made in their endeavours to be in time is reckoned one of the most remarkable in military annals. As a matter of fact, about a hundred of the regiment *were* present, having been earlier separated from the main body.

The combat on the Coa, where the 43rd were under command of Major M'Leod, "a young man endowed with a natural genius for war," may almost be said to have been won by them and the gallant 52nd. Two incidents related by Napier may be given, each illustrative of what manner of men the 43rd were composed. A soldier named Stewart, nicknamed "the Boy," because of his youth and gigantic stature and strength, was one of the last men who came down to the bridge, but he would not pass. "Turning round, he regarded the French with a grim look and spoke aloud as follows: 'So! this is the end of our boasting. This is our first battle, and we retreat. "The Boy" Stewart will not live to hear that said.' Then striding forward in his giant might he fell furiously on the nearest enemies with the bayonet, refused the quarter they seemed desirous of granting, and died fighting in the midst of them. Still more touching, more noble, more heroic, was the death of Sergeant Robert M'Quade. During M'Leod's

* Henry Kingsley, "Ravenshoe."

rush, this man* saw two Frenchmen level their muskets on rests against a high gap in the bank awaiting the uprise of an enemy. Sir George Brown, then a lad of sixteen, attempted to ascend to the fatal point, but M'Quade, himself only twenty-four years of age, pulled him back, saying, with a calm, decided tone, 'You are too young, sir, to be killed.' And then offering his own person to the fire, fell dead, pierced with both balls.''

The 43rd fought at Busaco and Redinha; at Cazal Novo Napier was wounded; at Sabugal Captain Hopkins of the regiment did much to win the fight described by Wellington, "as one of the most glorious actions British troops were ever engaged in." Under Colonel Patrickson they captured a howitzer round which, when the battle ended, most of the slain were found heaped. Great was their glory at Ciudad Rodrigo, greater still at Badajoz, where the heroic Macleod, "whose feeble body would have been quite unfit for war if it had not been sustained by an unconquerable spirit," fell dead; where the "intrepid Lieutenant Shaw" stood for awhile alone on the ramparts he only had gained; and where Ferguson, "who having at Rodrigo received two deep wounds, was present, with his hurts still open, leading the stormers of his regiment, the third time a volunteer and the third time wounded." The loss of the 43rd exceeded that of any other regiment, twenty officers and three hundred and thirty-five sergeants and privates were killed and wounded. At Salamanca it is recorded of the regiment that the "43rd made a very extraordinary advance in line for a distance of three miles under a cannonade with as clear and firm a front as at a review." When, during the retreat from Madrid, the disgraceful ingratitude of the Spaniards culminated in wanton insults and outrages upon our troops—to whom they well-nigh owed their existence—the 43rd were conspicuous in teaching the insolent Don that the British and their allies were not to be thus treated with impunity. On one occasion, "the Prince of Orange remonstrating about his quarters with the sitting Junta, they ordered one of their guards to kill him; and he would have been killed had not Lieutenant Steele of the 43rd, a bold, athletic person, felled the man before he could stab." At the Huebra they and the Riflemen supported the guns defending the higher fords; at Vittoria the gallant regiment was for awhile "in a most extraordinary situation, at the elbow of the French position, isolated from the rest of the army, within a few hundred paces of Joseph with his 5,000 Guards." At Echellar—one of the battles of the "Pyrenees"—Sergeant Blood undoubtedly saved the British cause from the incalculable disaster that would have ensued from the capture of Wellington. The great general had taken half a company of the 43rd as an escort

* Both Stewart and M'Quade hailed from the North of Ireland.

while he examined his plans of the country. The French stealing on in force would inevitably have made him prisoner, had not Sergeant Blood, leaping headlong down the precipitous rocks adjoining the pass, given timely and effective warning.

Amongst the killed at St. Sebastian was Lieutenant J. O'Connell of the 43rd, a near connection of the Agitator. He had been in several storming parties before this, and seeking here again "in such dangerous service the promotion he had earned before without receiving—he found death." They fought on the Bidassoa; at Vera a strong force of Spanish was kept in check by a formidable abbatis, from behind which two French regiments poured a heavy fire. Despite all exhortations from their own officers they would not advance; "but there happened to be present," says Napier, "an officer of the 43rd regiment named Havelock. His fiery temper could not brook the check. He took off his hat, called upon the Spaniards, and, putting spurs to his horse, at one bound cleared the abbatis, and went headlong among the enemy. Then the soldiers, shouting for 'the fair boy,' so they called him, for he was very young and had light hair, with one shock broke through the French." The mere mention of "Nivelle" brings to mind the splendid heroism the regiment there displayed. The defences were well built and strongly manned, "but strong and valiant in arms must the soldiers have been who stood in that hour before the veterans of the 43rd." Throughout that day the famous Light Division fought, as even the heroes who composed it had scarcely fought before; pitted against overwhelming odds they forced the French back till the victory was won. Heavy was the loss, and amongst the slain were Freer and Lloyd of the 43rd, of whom their comrade in arms writes with a power and pathos all his own: "The first, low in rank, being but a lieutenant, was rich in honour, for he bore many scars, and was young of days. He was only nineteen, and had seen more combats and sieges than he could count years. Slight in person, and of such surpassing and delicate beauty that the Spaniards often thought him a girl disguised in man's clothing, he was yet so vigorous, so active, so brave, that the most daring and experienced veterans watched his looks on the field of battle, and would obey his slightest sign in the most difficult situations. His education was incomplete, yet his natural powers were so happy that the keenest and best-furnished intellects shrank from an encounter of wit, and all his thoughts and aspirations were proud and noble, indicating future greatness if destiny had so willed it. Such was Edward Freer of the 43rd, one of three brothers, who all died in the Spanish war. Assailed the night before the battle with that strange anticipation of coming death so often felt by military men, he was pierced with three balls at the first storming of the Rhune rocks, and the sternest soldiers in the regiment wept even in the middle of the fight when they heard of his fate."

The regiment fought at the Nive; at Arcangues, some of the regiment and a few Riflemen—about a hundred in all—were cut off by the French. The officer commanding the little British force was Ensign Campbell of the 43rd, a boy of eighteen, and the French seemed to entertain no doubt that so youthful a commander would surrender to their vastly superior number. But British pluck and dash, contempt of death and scorn of odds, do not "tarry till the beard be grown," or man's estate attained. Ensign Campbell was a brave gentleman and an officer of the 43rd to boot, so with shout and waving sword he led his seemingly doomed band against the astounded French, broke through them and reached a position of safety, though half of his followers were taken prisoners. There remained but a few more laurels to be won in the Peninsula; they were to gain "Toulouse" on their colours before the hardly won peace allowed of the return to England of her conquering army. But the stay there of the 43rd was little more than a flying visit. They were ordered to America, where dissensions were still rife, and thus missed being present at Waterloo. For a long time after that their victorious weapons were idle; in 1837 they took part in the suppression of the revolt in Canada, and fifteen years later were engaged in the Kaffir War. Here they were under Lieutenant-Colonel Skipwith, and in the attack on the Water Kloof formed part of the right column, losing in the assault a very promising officer, the Hon. H. Wrottesley, who fell mortally wounded. A sergeant and forty men under Lieutenant Giradot were on the ill-fated *Birkenhead*, and the Lieutenant was one of the fortunate few that escaped. From the Cape the regiment was ordered to India, and it is needless here to dwell on the sterling service they performed during and after the mutiny.* The next warfare in which "the fighting 43rd" were engaged was in New Zealand, 1861—3, and the campaign was in many respects a disastrous one for the regiment. The unfortunate repulse our troops experienced at the Gate Pah in April, 1861, caused at the time a bitter disgust amongst the troops, and none deplored it more keenly than the men of the 43rd. Lieutenant-Colonel Booth commanding the regiment was mortally wounded; amongst the killed were two brothers, R. C. Glover and F. S. G. Glover, both subalterns of the 43rd. The elder fell "in the foremost of the fray, and the younger, who loved him with more than a

---

* Amongst the Victoria crosses gained by our soldiers during that eventful time was one presented to Private H. E. Addison of the 43rd for gallantly defending a political officer in an engagement near Kuncreah in January, 1859. Addison, besides losing a leg, received two serious wounds.

brother's love, rushed forward with a loud and bitter cry. It was in vain that he raised him in his arms and strove to bear him from the field; a hostile bullet brought both the brothers to the ground, and left them side by side with the tide of life ebbing fast away." Captain Hamilton, "one of a race of soldiers, and who had marched with Havelock to Lucknow," was shot through the head; seven men were taken prisoners by the fierce foe. When New Zealand was quiet again the regiment returned to England, leaving again a few years later for India, where, in 1873, they shared in the fighting consequent on the troubles in Malabar. Since that time no campaign of note has claimed the services of the 43rd.

The 52nd Regiment, the 2nd battalion of the Oxfordshire Light Infantry to which it gives the title, dates from 1775, when it was formed and numbered the 54th. Immediately after its completion the regiment was ordered to America, and throughout the war the gallant Oxford Light Infantry of the near future gave ample promise of the fame they were to win. At Bunker's Hill they won particular distinction, the whole of the grenadier company, with the exception of eight men, being either killed or wounded. It is not our purpose to follow the fortunes of the 52nd throughout the war. In all the battles they fought well and bravely, and when, in 1778, they returned home, it was acknowledged that few regiments with only a history of three years could show its page more fairly writ. Five years later—by which time they had received the title of the Oxfordshire Regiment—they were ordered to India, and participated in the siege of Cannanore, at which the forlorn hope supplied by the regiment had nearly every man killed or wounded. They fought in the subsequent campaign against Tippoo Sahib, being frequently brigaded with the 36th Regiment under Major Shelley. Lieutenant J. Evans of the 52nd was second in command of the storming party which forced its way into Bangalore; at Savendroog they were hotly engaged; at Seringapatam they not improbably saved the day by rescuing the Governor, Lord Cornwallis, from the imminent danger in which he was placed. After seventeen years of service in India the regiment returned home in 1800, many of the effective rank and file being transferred to the 77th and 80th Regiments. In 1803 a 2nd battalion which had been formed was constituted, as has been before mentioned, the 96th Regiment, and the remaining battalion received the distinctive appellation of "Light Infantry."

They were brigaded under Moore at Shorncliffe, and on the occasion of a review by the commander-in-chief, His Royal Highness was so impressed with their soldierly appearance that he recommended to the King that "promotion should be more extensive in that corps than had been usually granted." They served in Sicily and at Copenhagen; they were amongst the troops ordered to form General Moore's force for the defence of Sweden; and then the 2nd battalion, at that time recently formed, commenced the tale of Peninsular triumphs by its participations in the battle of Vimiera, where the 52nd and their present 1st battalion fought together under Anstruther. Both battalions were at Corunna, where they made some prisoners, and lost in the brilliant general, to whom the famous victory was due, the Colonel-in-chief of their regiment. After returning home the 1st battalion repaired to Portugal, and formed with the 43rd and 95th the famous Light Division.

It will be seen, from what has been said in dealing with the 43rd, that to write anything like a full account of the doings of this division would be to transcribe the history of the Peninsular War. We must be content with noticing here and there some—and those but a few—of the incidents in which the 52nd were more particularly concerned. At the combat on the Coa, they and the 43rd particularly distinguished themselves at the bridge, and after the battle was over, Lieutenant Dawson of the regiment gained great credit by the masterly manner in which, after being isolated from the main body of the army, he effected a junction with it, though to do so necessitated passing through the enemy's posts. At Busaco their splendid charge resulted in the defeat of the French, whose General Simon surrendered to Privates Hopkins and Harris. At Redinha, by some oversight they were placed in a position of extreme danger, being ordered to move forward blindly into a mass of fog, which, when it rose, " disclosed the 52nd on the slopes of the opposite mountain closely engaged in the midst of an army." They fought with great credit at Caza Nova and Sabugal, and a somewhat amusing anecdote is related of a private of the regiment in the latter battle. Private Patrick Lowe, though he had, as beseemed a 52nd man, the soul of a hero, was, in his physical formation, round and small and fat. During a skirmish his company, being threatened by a cavalry charge, fell back, but Pat, unfortunately, could not beat a sufficiently speedy retreat, and an impetuous dragoon was rapidly gaining on him. Undismayed, however, he faced about and covered his pursuer with his musket. Vainly did the dragoon try to disconcert his aim; wheel and curvet as he would that grim piece of gun metal and Pat's grimmer face behind it threatened him with certain death if he came on. So he fell back, and Pat rejoined his comrades without—to every one's surprise—shooting his antagonist. An officer took him roundly to task for this omission: " You were a fool to let the man go without shooting him." "Och, then, an' is it shooting ye mane?" responded Pat; "shure an' how could I shoot him *when I wasn't loaded at all, at all!*" At Marialva Captain Dobbs, with a single bayonet company and some riflemen, held the bridge against two thousand French; at Fuentes d'Onor the enemies' cavalry strove in vain to break the resolute squares of the Light Division. At Ciudad Rodrigo the ardour of the stormers of the Division would not allow them to wait for the hay-bags; they "jumped down the scarp, a depth of eleven feet, and rushed up the *fausse braie* under a smashing discharge of grape and musketry." Lord Wellington, in his dispatches, was betrayed into praises of a degree unusually high for him. "I cannot," he wrote, "sufficiently applaud the conduct of Colonel Colborne and of the detachment under his command." Napier and Dobbs and Gurwood were the other officers of the 52nd that forced themselves to the front at Ciudad Rodrigo; to the last named surrendered the French commander, Barrie, whose sword Wellington publicly presented to his gallant captor "on the breach by which Gurwood had entered, a fitting and proud compliment to a young soldier of fortune." At Badajoz—the assault of Picuria—Stewart and Nixon greatly excelled, while at the final storming the splendid gallantry of the Oxfordshire may be gauged by the fact that the 43rd and 52nd Regiments of the Light Division alone lost more men than the seven regiments engaged at the Castle. They fought at Salamanca and the Huebra; at Vittoria the 52nd Regiment, with an impetuous charge, carried the village of Margarita; the courage of the stormers at St. Sebastian has passed into a proverb; at Schelar and Vera and throughout the battles of the Pyrenees, the Oxfordshire Light Infantry were ever foremost; at the Nivelle, under their gallant leader Colborne, they were severely and gloriously engaged. An untoward occurrence cost the lives of many of their brave band to be needlessly sacrificed. A staff officer, acting on some misunderstanding, ordered Colborne to advance against the signal redoubt which was being obstinately defended by the enemy. "It was not a moment for remonstrance; on the top of the hill the troops made their rush, but then a ditch, thirty feet deep, well fraised and palisaded, stopped them short, and the fire of the enemy stretched the foremost in death." Colborne—who escaped by a miracle, as he was ever at the head of his men on horseback—made three different attempts to carry the work; then, calling the fox to the aid of the lion, he advanced alone with a white flag of truce, and showing the French commandant that he was completely surrounded, persuaded him to surrender. This he did, "only having one man killed, but on the British side there fell two hundred soldiers, victims to the presumptuous folly of a young staff officer." At Orthes, "Colonel

Colborne, so often distinguished, led the regiment across the marsh under a skirmishing fire, the men sinking at every step above the knees, in some places to the middle; yet still pressing forward with that stern resolution and order to be expected from the veterans of the Light Division, soldiers who had never yet met their match in the field." They fought at Toulouse; at Waterloo " the fate of the battle seemed to hang in the balance when the gallant 52nd, under Colborne of Peninsular glory, moved down upon the left flank of the Imperial Guard." The fire of such a regiment gave pause to the splendid column of the foe; the Rifles and other regiments coming up joined their volleys with those of the 52nd; the enemy wavered and swayed, and ere long their colonel's well-known voice called upon the regiment to charge, and the last great battle between the English and French had been fought and won.

The 52nd went into battle probably the strongest numerically of any regiment present, numbering, as they did, upwards of a thousand men; the casualties were one officer, one sergeant, and thirty-six rank and file killed; eight officers, ten sergeants, and a hundred and fifty rank and file wounded.

The 2nd battalion meanwhile had been engaged in Holland under Lieutenant-Colonel Gibbs. They distinguished themselves at Merxem, and Captain Diggle, who commanded on that occasion, mentions in his account that King William IV., then Duke of Clarence, was often to be seen "riding about the village, the skirts of his great-coat perforated by a bullet and wholly regardless of danger, as is the wont of the Royal family."

After Waterloo the 52nd were stationed in various places, including America, Canada, the West Indies, and India. At the time of the mutiny, they showed that the forty years which had passed since Waterloo had wrought no deterioration in their matchless efficiency. It is impossible to dwell upon all the varied proofs they gave of this; one will speak for all, and their deeds at the capture of Delhi rank with any in the long struggle in the Peninsula. The blowing open of the Cashmere Gate was entrusted to a party amongst which was Bugler Hawthorne of the 52nd. Under a heavy fire they proceeded to lay the powder against the gates; officer after officer fell before the massive gate was blown up; then Hawthorne was ordered to sound the advance to his regiment. Three times had he to sound before the notes could be heard amidst the din; then, under Colonel Campbell, the regiment dashed forward like greyhounds from the leash, and secured the barrier. For this feat Hawthorne received the Victoria Cross, and on the same occasion Corporal Henry Smith gained the same distinction for gallantly bearing off a wounded comrade. The histories of the mutiny teem with the deeds of the regiment, telling how Seymour and Blanc, Vigors, Synge, Monsoon, Crosse, and Bayley were brave amongst the brave, but our sketch must here cease. No important service has since then fallen to the lot of the old Oxfordshire Light Infantry—"a regiment never surpassed in arms since arms were first borne by men."

THE RIFLE BRIGADE,* the Prince Consort's Own, takes precedence after the Argyll and Sutherland Highlanders, its number when first formed being the 95th. In the case of such a "regiment" as the Rifle Brigade, the compiler of any *short* account suffers from a veritable *embarras de richesses*. The Rifle Brigade, under its present or former designation, has fought everywhere; its doings have been chronicled by an enthusiastic historian,† it is a *corps d'élite*, and the various battalions of which from time to time it has been composed —the present number is four—have been, each of them, practically distinct regiments in all but name. In 1800 the commanders of fourteen regiments (2nd battalion Royals, 21st, 23rd, 25th, 27th, 29th, 49th, 55th, 69th, 71st, 72nd, 79th, 85th, and 92nd) received a communication from the Horse Guards, to the effect that it was intended to form a corps "to be instructed in the use of the rifle," and requesting them to select four non-commissioned officers and thirty men, and to recommend three officers for the purpose of forming the corps. This was in January, and so favourably was the project viewed, and so apt in their new duties did the new regiment prove, that in the following August three companies embarked with the expedition under General Pulteney against Spain. Shortly after this service—in which the chosen companies most creditably acquitted themselves—the regiment was formed, and the commissions of the officers dated the 25th August, the day on which they had a skirmish with the Spanish. The first duty of the corps as a perfected body seems to have been a sort of marine service at the bombardment of Copenhagen. In December, 1802, they were numbered the 95th, and

---

* The Rifle Brigade bear as badges a bugle on the glengarry. On the helmet plate is a bugle with strings on a Maltese Cross "surmounted by a wreath of laurel, with which is intertwined a scroll bearing the battles of Sebastopol, Alma, and Inkerman. The other battles are recorded on the arms of the cross, the whole is surmounted by the Prince Consort's coronet with 'Waterloo' below it. A lion is placed between each division of the cross." The motto is "Treu und fest." The following are the battles inscribed: "Copenhagen," "Monte Video," "Rolcia," "Vimiera," "Corunna," "Busaco," "Barossa," "Fuentes d'Onor," "Ciudad Rodrigo," "Badajoz," "Salamanca," "Vittoria," "Nivelle," "Nive," "Orthes," "Toulouse," "Peninsula," "Waterloo," "South Africa, 1846–7," "South Africa 1851–2–3," "Alma," "Inkerman," "Sebastopol," "Lucknow," "Ashantee," "Ali Masjid," "Afghanistan 1878–9." The uniform is dark green with facings of black. The black racoon skin caps were exchanged for the helmet three or four years ago, but it is hoped that before long the more distinctive head-dress will be resumed.

† Sir Wm. Cope.

the following year, in Sir John Moore's camp of instruction at Shorncliffe, " first met and were brigaded with, as their compeers, the 43rd and 52nd, in united action with whom, as the Light Division in the Peninsula, so many of their laurels were won." In 1805 a second battalion was formed, and the first battalion was ordered to Germany, where, however, nothing more arduous than a military promenade occupied its attention. In 1807 the 2nd battalion joined the force under Sir Samuel Auchmuty destined for South America, and greatly distinguished itself at the taking of Monte Video. In 1807 the regiment* fought at Monte Video with the most marked valour, losing ninety-one of all ranks killed, and having double that number wounded and missing. Meanwhile, other companies of the regiment joined Lord Cathcart's expedition against Copenhagen, " where they first served under the immediate command of the great chief who commanded the advance; under whose eye they were so often to fight, whose praise they were so often to receive, their future Colonel, then Major-General Sir Arthur Wellesley," and during the campaign their " gallant style," their "conduct and steadiness," were more than once referred to in dispatches. The following year they joined the British Army in Portugal, and first engaged the enemy at Obeidos, in conjunction with their comrades of the King's Royal Rifle Corps. They fought with great dash and spirit at Roleia; at Vimiera the historian of the regiment relates that " three brothers of the name of Hart, privates in the 2nd battalion, pressed on the French with such daring intrepidity that Lieutenant Molloy, who himself was never far from his opponent in action, was obliged repeatedly to rebuke them. ' D—n you!' he cried, 'keep back and get under cover. Do you think you are fighting with your fists that you run into the teeth of the French?'" The 2nd battalion suffered very severely that day, one fourth of their number being put *hors de combat*. During the retreat to Corunna, under Moore, the 95th proved themselves invaluable, covering the movements of the other troops, and holding positions against the utmost efforts of the foe. During the battle at Corunna itself, the 1st battalion had a sort of duel with two battalions of Voltigeurs. The 95th had just made a brilliant charge against the enemy's artillery, when the Voltigeurs came to the rescue, causing them to fall back for a moment. They soon rallied, and for two hours kept up a sharp skirmish with their opponents, and in the end gained a complete victory, taking prisoners seven officers and one hundred and fifty-six men. The 95th was the last corps to enter Corunna, having acted as the rear-guard, and almost before they were embarked the enemy were firing on the ships. Their losses during the past

* Space will not allow of the battalions being in all cases particularized.

twenty days were one hundred and thirty-six killed or prisoners and thirty-five wounded.*

About this time—such was the popularity and evident value of the regiment—a third battalion was raised, the command of which devolved upon Andrew Barnard of the Royals, whose name in connection with the deeds of the Brigade is so familiar to all readers of the history of the Peninsular War. In May, 1809, the 1st battalion were brigaded with the 43rd and 52nd into the Light Brigade, to relate whose prowess would be to write anew the campaign which ended at Waterloo. Very severe were the hardships which the battalion experienced from the very first. In addition to the enemy, they had daily to reckon with that terrible foe—threatening Starvation. The discipline enforced by Cranford, their brigadier, was "Draconic" in its severity. Almost their first feat was, in their haste to reach Talavera, "in heavy marching order, under a burning sun, and with a most insufficient supply of food, to march upwards of fifty miles with only two short halts in twenty-five hours." Soon afterwards, at Barta del Puerco, they elicited praise even from the stern Cranford; in the battle on the Coa, they again fought splendidly and suffered severely. At Busaco, the charge of the Light Division was one of the most brilliant episodes of the war. Meanwhile, the 2nd battalion had been fighting in the Walcheren expedition, on its return from which, detachments were sent to join their comrades in Portugal, whither the 3rd battalion, under Barnard, proceeded in July, 1810. At Barossa, this battalion and some of the 2nd particularly distinguished themselves, the brave Barnard being twice wounded. After Redinha, an incident occurred which shows in a marked way the courteous feeling reciprocated by the English and French. The 1st battalion were driving the French before them, when the officer commanding the latter waved his handkerchief at the end of his sword. On the officer of the 95th coming up, the Frenchman suggested that both sides would be the better for a night's rest, and proposed a truce. The Rifles consented, and invited the French officers to share their mess, an overture which was gladly accepted, though the menu only disclosed ration beef, and little enough of that, with rum to wash it down. After dinner they separated, and the next morning the French resumed their retreat, and the Rifles their pursuit. The 95th distinguished them-

* In the account of the battles one is apt sometimes to lose sight of the less romantic aspect of the horrors of war. The following description shows it in all its naked hideousness. "The appearance of the battalion on their arrival in England was squalid and miserable. Most of the men had lost some of their appointments; many were without shoes, and their clothing was not only tattered and in rags, but in such a state of filth and so infested with vermin that on new clothing being served out it was burnt at the back of Hythe barracks."

selves at Sabugal; at Fuentes d'Onor, the repulse they inflicted on a strong body of French infantry was mentioned in Lord Wellesley's dispatches. In the various engagements which preceded the storming of Ciudad Rodrigo they rendered sterling service. At that storming, there is no need here to dwell upon the brilliant achievements of the Rifles—how Uniacke was killed, and Cox and Hamilton, Mitchell, M'Gregor, and Bedell were wounded; how Crauford, the gallant though stern commander of the Light Division, fell, cheering on his men; or how many brave men of the 95th slept that night the "sleep that never wakes." At the storming of Badajoz, again, the part they played is well known. Some led the Light Division; seven officers and a hundred men of the 95th formed part of the storming party. With the forlorn hope were nine non-commissioned officers of the regiment. The incidents of that direful day are history; twenty-three officers and two hundred and ninety-two non-commissioned officers and men of the Rifles were killed or wounded. Napier's splendid description is aptly quoted by Cope in its relation to the regiment. "Who shall measure out the glory of . . . . O'Hara of the 95th, who perished in the breach at the head of the stormers, and with him, nearly all the volunteers for that desperate service? Who shall describe . . . . the martial fury of that desperate soldier of the 95th who, in his resolution to win, thrust himself beneath the chained sword-blades, and there suffered the enemy to dash his head to pieces with the ends of their muskets?" To these might be added—only to mention the names of the killed—Stokes and Diggle, Hovenden, Cary, Alix, Crondace, Macdonald and Macpherson, of the last of whom it was said that "he had been true to man, and true to his God, and he looked his last hour in the face like a soldier and a Christian." It might be mentioned here that Sir Harry Smith, the hero of Aliwal in after years, gained his wife in a way that recalls the pages of some romance. After the terrible sack which followed the capture of Badajoz, two Spanish ladies of rank, the younger about fourteen, approached Smith, then a captain in the Rifles, who was talking with another officer, and threw themselves on the protection of the English. Their appearance showed the cruelty to which they had been subjected; their ears were bleeding from the brutal gash which had torn away their earrings, and to avoid worse and nameless shame, they had resolved to confide to the honour of the first British officer they met. The younger of the two ladies became, ere two years had passed, the wife of the officer who had saved her. In the battle of Salamanca, the brigade was not very actively engaged, and from that date till the battle of Vittoria, though privation and arduous labour, enough and to spare, fell to their lot, their participation in actual warfare was limited to a few skirmishes. Their historian claims for them that theirs was the regiment which commenced the battle of Vittoria, during which their dark uniform more than once exposed them to the fire of our own men, who mistook them for the enemy. They also captured the first guns which were taken from the French in the engagement, and throughout the day fully merited the enthusiastic praise which has been awarded to them. Their loss was twelve of all ranks killed; seven officers and sixty men wounded.

During the pursuit of the flying foe, some of the Riflemen were mounted behind the troopers of the Royal Dragoons, and it is interesting to note that in the sharp skirmish which they had on the Camino Real, they were fortunate enough to take "the last and only gun which the French carried off from Vittoria." At Schelar, one of the battles included in the "Pyrenees," they greatly distinguished themselves; but perhaps the combat at the Bridge of Jansi, where they had marched under a hot sun, and with frequent want of water, about eight leagues, "considering that it was made in the heat of an August sun, and that at the end of the march the men had four or five hours' hard fighting, may hold its place with the famous march from Calzada to Talavera . . . . It was said that two hundred men of one regiment of the Light Division fell out. But the Riflemen had a resolution to excel, and many held on till they died." At the storming of St. Sebastian, the regiment was represented by a subaltern and fifty men from each battalion. The names of the officers were Percival, Hamilton and Eaton, and the two former were desperately wounded. At the Bridge of Vera, the regiment suffered terrible loss, which their historian attributes in great measure to the ill-advised order of General Skerrett, by which Captain Cadoux, whose company held the bridge, was compelled to withdraw. The order was so peremptory that he had no choice left, but even while obeying, he remarked that "but few of his party would reach the camp." And so it proved. Up till then he had not lost a man; before many minutes had elapsed, Cadoux himself and sixteen others were killed, three officers, nine sergeants and thirty-four rank and file wounded out of a total of a hundred, all told. Again, at the battle of the Nivelle, where their gallant leader Sir Andrew Barnard was severely wounded, the regiment incurred very heavy loss. Sundry sharp skirmishes preceded the battle of the Nive in which the regiment played a leading part. They were not very actively employed at Orthes, the 1st battalion, indeed, being absent altogether. At the hard-fought battle of Tarbes, however, on the 20th of March, 1814, they had most of the fighting to themselves, and after a fierce struggle, during which "they fought muzzle to muzzle, and it was difficult to judge at first who would win," drove the French before them in disordered flight. At a skirmish which took place a few days afterwards a most extraordinary incident occurred, which—were it not for the character of the narrators and the evidence adduced—one would be tempted to ascribe to some latter-day Munchausen. "A Rifleman of the name of Powell was shot in the mouth, the ball knocking several of his teeth out. One of these struck a Portuguese and wounded him in the arm. The surgeon of the 43rd, who happened to be at hand, dressing the wound of the Portuguese, found in it not a bullet but a tooth. On this the cry went among the Riflemen that 'the French were firing bones and not bullets.'" At the battle of Toulouse the regiment was again actively engaged, and on the termination of the war returned to England. Meanwhile the 95th had been represented by detachments which gloriously upheld the honour of the regiment at Bergen-op-Zoom, Merxem, and other places in Holland. Scarcely had peace been secured with France than some of the regiment—the 3rd battalion—were ordered to New Orleans, and in the very arduous and not altogether satisfactory campaign which was sandwiched in between the war in the Peninsula and Waterloo proved themselves of the utmost value. At Quatre-Bras the 1st battalion enjoyed the distinction of being the first to engage with the enemy. At Waterloo the 1st battalion was with Picton, and the 2nd and part of the 3rd with Sir Frederick Adams. Very early in the day did the former come into action, while the latter were engaged in the fierce fighting that raged round Hougoumont, and in the splendid charge which completed the discomfiture of the Imperial Guard.* The losses of the regiment during the day were very severe, and their conduct was most highly praised. They stayed with the army of occupation, and in the February following Waterloo were removed from the regiments of the line, ceasing to be known as the 95th and receiving their present appellation of the Rifle Brigade.

The years following Waterloo must be passed over rapidly. There were disturbances in Ireland, *émeutes* in Birmingham, sundry and divers other occasions on which the Rifle Brigade was engaged, but it was not till 1846 that they were again employed in foreign service. At that date troubles arose in South Africa, and we wish that space would allow us to recount in detail all the brave deeds and services performed by the Rifle Brigade. It

---

* Another remarkable occurrence is narrated by Sir W. Cope, quoting Kincaid, which, he adds, has been confirmed to him by independent testimony. Lieutenant Worsley, of the 3rd battalion, "had at Badajoz received a shot in his ear which came out at the back of the neck, which on his recovery had the effect of turning his head to the right ; at Waterloo he received exactly a similar wound in the left ear, the ball coming out near the exit of the former, which restored his head to its original position."

must suffice to repeat the dictum of an historian quoted by the chronicler of their deeds. "It was the useful green jacket, the untiring Rifle Brigade, who worried Sandilli out of his hiding place among the mountains." After fighting the natives it became necessary to teach the Boers a lesson, and this was most effectually done at Boemplatz, though the result to the representatives of the Rifle Brigade was that the command of both companies devolved upon second lieutenants. The general orders issued on the departure of the Rifles for England contained the following paragraph: "In 1805 the commander-in-chief, Sir H. Smith, joined this (1st) battalion. . . . He has served with it during the most eventful period of its career, and has never worn the regimental uniform of any other corps." The Rifles are to be congratulated on being thus complimented by a chief who had not learnt the lessons enforced by politicians of after years, that these same rebel Boers whom he hanged with such good will were, because they had beaten us, to have all they asked for. Then again the Kaffirs had to be dealt with, and the share the Rifle Brigade (with the sister corps, the 60th) had in the lesson taught is written large in the annals of the war. Gladly would we quote from the graphic accounts which exist of this arduous campaign,* but we must leave them to tell their own tale of the achievements of the Brigade and pass on to the war in the Crimea, in which the 1st and 2nd battalions gained so glorious a renown. At the Alma it was the 2nd battalion that was principally engaged, and amongst the many names which might be singled out are those of Colonel Lawrence, Major Norcott, Captain Syers, Captain the Earl of Errol, and Lieutenant Ross. Major Norcott was recommended for the Victoria Cross, and Sir George Brown testifies that "Major Norcott's conduct was not only conspicuous to the whole division but attracted the notice of the enemy, for the officer in command of the Russian battery, who was subsequently made prisoner, informed Lord Raglan that he had laid a gun especially for "the daring officer in the dark uniform on the black horse." In the approach to Balaclava, at which no serious fighting occurred, a rather amusing incident happened. As Captain Vigers was taking his men into the town "a baker, evidently in great terror, came out of his house and, notwithstanding the early hour of the morning, produced a roast turkey which he offered him, and a great number of loaves. These Vigers desired him to break into two and to give half to each man, so that all the men of his company had a good meal." Many were the incidents of daring which are to be credited to the Brigade during the battle of Inkerman and the first stages of the siege of Sebastopol: Wheatley's presence of mind,

* Notably from those of Mrs. Wood and Captain King.

in flinging a live shell over the parapet, Herbert's wonderful shooting, Harman's and Ferguson's close struggle with the Russians, the brave deeds of Powell, Godfrey, Alrington, Hewitt, and Markham. Some were officers, some privates, but no distinction is necessary where each and all added to the proud record of their regiment. At Inkerman the 1st battalion—recommended by their leader as one "which could do anything" —fought splendidly, and their fierce struggle may be estimated by the fact that the 2nd company was brought out of action by a colour sergeant.* The "affair at the Ovens" was one in which the 1st battalion was almost exclusively engaged, and Lieutenants Tryon, Bourchier, and Cuninghame, with four sergeants and a couple of hundred men, performed the arduous task which was not only eulogised by the commander-in-chief of the British army but formed the theme of an *Ordre Général* published by General Canrobert.† At the storming of the Redan a detachment of the 1st battalion under Stuart and Boileau and Sanders, and one of the 2nd under Blackett, Macdonell, Forman, and Freemantle, were engaged, and with the Rifles to be "engaged" is to be distinguished. Amongst so much that is worthy of record the account given of the deaths of Captain Hammond and Lieutenant Ryder claims mention. "Hammond had only been in the Crimea forty-eight hours when he was killed. When the Rifles were forming for the assault on the Redan a young subaltern addressed him, 'Captain Hammond, how fortunate we are! We are just in time for Sebastopol.' Hammond's eyes were gazing where the rays of the sun made a path of golden light over the sea, and his answer was short and remarkable, and accompanied by the quiet smile which those who knew him so well remember. 'I am quite ready,' he said." He was seen afterwards fighting like a hero at the embrasures, his gleaming sword flashing, his form conspicuous even in the awful hurly-burly from amongst which brave men's souls flew thick and fast to the gates of "the hereafter." "The next morning he was found in a ditch beneath a dozen of the slain with a bayonet wound through his heart." Ryder was scarcely eighteen when he fell. He had been severely wounded, but could not brook the necessary delay in attending to him. Binding his wound himself as best he might he again mounted the scaling ladder, "and when he was found next day in the ditch a bayonet thrust had transfixed his forehead."

After the fall of Sebastopol came peace, and with it the thanks of the Sovereign and the gratitude of the nation for the heroism which, at the cost of so many

---

* Colour-Sergeant Higgins, afterwards Captain W. Higgins.

† Bourchier and Cuninghame received the V.C., and Colour-Sergeant Hicks the French war medal.

brave lives, had added yet more names to the long roll of the Brigade's distinctions.*

On the outbreak of the Indian Mutiny, the 2nd and 3rd battalions of the Brigade were ordered to embark, and on arriving in India were pushed on to Cawnpore. It was soon found that not only their fighting but their marching powers were destined to be tried to the uttermost. One wonders as one reads of the long marches under blazing sun, with the heavy European clothing unchanged for days together, while want of sleep caused men now and again to stumble through sheer drowsiness even while marching in the ranks—one wonders how it came to pass that when they met the enemy, these weary, footsore, sleep-bereaved men brightened as with a flash into that activity the rebels found so deathful. When they fought at Cawnpore the 3rd battalion were almost starving, and frequently a biscuit and ration of rum formed the only meal during the day. The regiment captured Etawah, fought on the Ramgunga, and under Colonel Horsford engaged in the resultless pursuit of Nana Sahib. Under Outram they fought at the capture of Lucknow, and earned that commander's highest commendation for their spirit and dash. Two hundred men from the regiment with the same number of Sikhs were formed into a camel corps under Major Ross, and proved a most useful addition to the effective force of the British army. After the capture of Lucknow, the Rifles were engaged in constant skirmishes and sudden and fatiguing marches, during which many deaths occurred from disease and sunstroke. At the battle of Nawabgunga they gained special praise for the splendid manner in which, unaided, they kept at bay a vastly superior force of the enemy. At last, when their sorely-taxed strength was well-nigh failing, the 7th Hussars, with Sir C. Russell at their head, came thundering to the rescue. Their losses were heavy that day; far worse than the injuries done by the enemy's fire were the sufferings of the men from exposure to the sun. Numbers of the gallant Rifles lay seemingly dead—with many, alas! it was no mere seeming—others were raving mad. Had they not deserved it by their valour, it might almost be said that their sufferings alone merited the laudatory reference they received in the dispatches of Sir Hope Grant. At Jamo, Lieutenant Andrew Green engaged in a conflict which recalls something of the warrior tales told in 'chronicles of old.' Rushing to the rescue of some men of his party who were surrounded by the enemy, he found himself attacked by six rebels. Two he shot; he was then cut down by the others, who hacked viciously at him while prostrate. Springing up he knocked down

* At the first distribution of V.C.'s no fewer than eight fell to officers and men of the Brigade.

two more with the butt of his revolver, and was keeping the others at bay with his sword when he was attacked by three fresh arrivals. Again he was cut down, and again he struggled to his feet and shot another of his assailants. When found by Colour-Sergeant Mansel, who gallantly fought his way to the rescue, Green was lying bathed in blood, having received fifteen wounds, of which all except one were sword cuts.

The Brigade captured Birwah, again suffering heavy loss; they fought at Hyderguh; Mejidia fell before their conquering arms. But it is impossible even to mention the names of all the places where they fought, or to tell of the sterling service rendered by the camel corps under Ross. When the mutiny was over no regiment had better earned the "Well done!" that echoed through the length and breadth of the Empire. Four of the Victoria Crosses fell to the share of the Brigade; while, in addition to those who were killed in action, two officers and a hundred and thirty-two men fell victims to disease. Afterwards—in 1861-2—the 1st battalion was ordered to Canada during the alarm caused by the "*Trent* affair," while the 2nd and 3rd battalions were engaged in various encounters with the Mohmunds and other hostile Indian tribes. Later on the 1st and 4th battalions assisted in teaching the Fenians a salutary lesson in Canada. The next operations of any magnitude in which the Brigade were represented was the Ashanti war in 1874, throughout which the 2nd battalion served. To quote the words of Sir Archibald Allison, "it is needless to speak of the steadiness and high discipline," of the courage and cheerfulness they displayed. The campaign was emphatically a trying one, and King Koffee's terrible ally, Disease, vanquished many a brave rifleman, whom shot and spear passed by. The final exploits of the Brigade are commemorated by "Ali Musjid" and "Afghanistan." In concluding this notice of the Rifle Brigade we cannot summarize its character and achievements better than in the words of King William IV., who, when Duke of Clarence, reviewed them at Plymouth: "What more can I say to you, riflemen, than that whenever there has been fighting you have been employed, and wherever you have been employed you have distinguished yourselves."

THE ROYAL FUSILIERS* (City of London Regiment)—Regimental district No. 7—are comprised of the old 7th Foot. In 1685 a large regiment was formed, chiefly from

---

* The Royal Fusiliers bear as badges " The White Rose of York (in the Garter) on a grenade, the flame of which is crowned," on cap and collar, with the White Horse on the helmet plate. The mottoes are those of the Garter and *Nec aspera terrent*. On their colours is the White Horse and "Martinique," "Talavera," "Albuera," "Badajoz," "Salamanca," "Vittoria," "Pyrenees," "Orthes," "Toulouse," "Peninsula," "Alma," "Inkerman," "Sevastopol," "Kandahar, 1880," "Afghanistan, 1879—80." The uniform is scarlet with facings of blue, and Fusilier's cap.

the old London bands, and designated the Ordnance Regiment, receiving at the same time the appellation of Royal Fusiliers. Their first service was at Walcourt, then in the Irish wars consequent on William's accession to the throne. After this they joined the troops in Holland, where they experienced some severe fighting. They were represented at Steenkirke; at Landen they fought with unexampled courage, nearly all their officers being either killed or wounded; for their gallantry in storming Namur they received the special thanks of William. They took part in the Duke of Ormond's expedition against Vigo, and in 1703 served as marines. Hurrying over the following years—during which we note that the regiment served as marines on board the fleet of the unfortunate Byng, which did *not* relieve Minorca—we come to the era of the war in America and Canada, during which they experienced some severe reverses, though throughout their consistent courage gained them unqualified praise. In the defence of St. John's a great number were made prisoners; they fought at Staten Island; at the capture of Fort Clinton—where our troops, unsupported by artillery, "crossed ground swept by ten guns, and without firing a shot pressed forward to the foot of the works, climbed over each other's shoulders on to the walls and drove the enemy back"—the 7th gained great distinction. At Cow Pens, in December, 1781, the regiment suffered severely from the unfortunate repulse experienced by our troops under Colonel Tarleton; their colours were taken, and many of their number killed and wounded. Shortly after that they returned to England and were on duty in various places, being for some time under the command of the Duke of Kent, father of Her present Majesty. In 1807, they were with the forces dispatched against Copenhagen, and a couple of years later under Colonel Packenham to Martinique. Here, at the stubborn fight on the heights of Surirey, the Royal Fusiliers gave striking evidence of their splendid fighting capacity. Meanwhile, the 2nd battalion of the regiment was with Wellesley in Portugal, and first met the foe at Talavera. Here, we learn from the Official Record, the Royal Fusiliers "met the storm of war with unshaken firmness," and succeeded in capturing seven guns. Both battalions were at Busaco; where, however, they did not come in for very much actual fighting. After a sharp skirmish at Burlada, the 7th and 23rd were formed into the famous Fusilier Brigade, under Pakenham, the command of the battalions being given to Vigers and Blakeney. At Albuera, the account of the magnificent charge of that Fusilier Brigade still kindles into enthusiasm the most listless and unemotional. The tide of war seemed turning steadily against us : " we had lost a whole brigade of artillery ; a large number of our men were prisoners ; a deep gully prevented the British from using their bayonets, and affairs wore a most unpromising appearance." As the history of the Royal Fusiliers expresses it, a crisis had arrived, and a mighty, a determined, a desperate effort alone could save the allied army from defeat. Sweeping onward in seemingly resistless force were three columns of exultant French, supported by cavalry and artillery, each column mustering about twice the number of the force that was about to check their insolent progress. That force was the Fusilier Brigade. In front of the advancing French were their lancers surrounding our guns that they had captured.

Their pride was short-lived; the stern, avenging British line swept them aside and recovered the guns, then moved forward against the dense columns of the enemy. "Such a gallant line startled the enemy's masses, which were increasing and pressing forward as to an assured victory; they wavered, hesitated, and then vomiting forth a storm of fire, hastily endeavoured to enlarge their front, while the fearful discharge of grape from all their artillery whistled through the British ranks. Myers was killed, other officers fell wounded, and the Fusilier battalions struck by the iron tempest reeled and staggered like sinking ships. Suddenly and sternly recovering they closed on their terrible enemies, and then was seen with what a majesty the British soldiers fight! . . . . Nothing could stop our astonishing infantry. No sudden burst of undisciplined valour, no nervous enthusiasm weakened the stability of their order, their flashing eyes were bent on the dark columns in front, their measured tread shook the ground, their dreadful volleys swept away the head of every formation, their deafening shouts overpowered the dissonant cries that broke from all parts of the tumultuous crowd, as foot by foot, and with a horrid carnage, it was driven by the incessant vigour of the attack to the farthest edge of the hill. In vain did the French reserves . . . . endeavour to sustain the fight. Their efforts only increased the irremediable confusion, and the mighty mass, like a loosened cliff, went headlong down the ascent. The rain flowed after in streams discoloured with blood, and fifteen hundred unwounded men, the remnant of six thousand unconquerable British soldiers, stood triumphant on the fatal hill" (*Napier*). Well may the record of the Royal Fusiliers assert that they "exceeded anything that the usual word 'gallantry' can convey." Thirty-two officers, thirty-four sergeants, six hundred and thirty-eight soldiers, express the loss in killed and wounded the 7th sustained that day.*

* Amongst the killed was Myers, Lieutenant-Colonel of the 1st battalion. The depreciators of "boy officers" may be interested to note that he was only twenty-eight years of age.

They fought again with great credit at Aldea de Ponte and at Ciudad Rodrigo, though in the latter operations they were not largely engaged. At Badajoz it was Captain Mair of the 7th who led the storming party against the Trinidad bastion, while others of the regiment under Captain Cholwick attacked the breach in the curtain. Two hundred and thirty-two were killed and wounded during the assault. At Salamanca Captain Crowder gained his majority for dislodging, with only two companies of the regiment, a force of five hundred Frenchmen from a village they occupied. At Vittoria their position was against the enemy's centre, and materially assisted in the crushing defeat of Joseph's army; while, as evidence of the splendid state of discipline which they had attained, it may be mentioned that amidst the dazzling temptations which surrounded them, no case of that plundering on which the British commander commented so severely was reported in the ranks of the 7th. They fought in the battles of the Pyrenees, notably at Roncesvalles and Villalba, on the Bidassoa and at Orthes. At Toulouse they were not seriously engaged, and with this battle ended their glorious Peninsular record, for their services in the West Indies prevented their participating in Waterloo. In the expedition against New Orleans, which, barren of profitable result as it was, reflected nothing but credit on the troops engaged, the Royal Fusiliers again distinguished themselves, at the same time incurring considerable loss. From that time till the war with Russia in 1854 the 7th were not engaged in any warlike service. In the Crimea they were in the Light Division under Sir George Brown. Their splendid charge at the Alma, under Lacy Yeo, will long be remembered—how in the teeth of a storm of bullets they pressed on, though those who bore the colours were shot down in terrible succession, and how Private Lyle of the regiment helped Captain Bell to capture the Russian guns. At the famous sortie from Sebastopol of the 26th October and at Inkerman they fought, and throughout the prolonged siege acquitted themselves as might have been expected from their history and tradition. In the "affair at the Quarries" Captain Mitchell Jones gained the V.C. for the dauntless way in which, despite his receiving a wound in the early stage of the fighting, he led his men to the numerous attacks, and at the assault of the Redan Lieutenant Hope and Private Hughes gained the same priceless decoration. In the following September a non-combatant officer of the regiment, Assistant-Surgeon Hale, gained another Cross for his unremitting care of the wounded whom the heavy fire, which drove all but himself and Lieutenant Hope away from the spot, could not induce him to leave for a moment. During the Indian Mutiny the 7th were employed in Scinde, and a few years later in the disturbances on the

North-west Frontier. Passing over fifteen years, during which the history of the 7th was that of any distinguished regiment in times of peace, we find them next employed in the Afghan campaign of 1878—80. In the sortie from Candahar of 16th August, 1880, under General Brooke, the Royal Fusiliers were commanded by Major Vandaleur. The admirable courage and dash they displayed were unable to prevent the effort from being a failure, a failure, moreover, which cost the lives of Major Vandaleur and Lieutenants Wood and Marsh—"two gallant officers, mere lads,"—and numbered Lieutenant de Trafford amongst the wounded. But Lieutenant Case and Private James Asford each earned the Victoria Cross for rescuing a wounded comrade under a searching fire. With Afghanistan ends the long roll of warlike achievements which are to be credited to the Royal Fusiliers.

THE BLACK WATCH (ROYAL HIGHLANDERS)*—Regimental District No. 42—are composed of the 42nd and 73rd Regiments and date from 1729, when six companies were raised for "local service." Originally, doubtless, care was taken to enlist none except those unfriendly to the Jacobite cause; after a time, however, this restriction was dropped as regarded the rank and file, though the officers were still chosen from Whig families.† The proposal made in 1743 to send the regiment abroad gave rise to some disturbance, the Highlanders being not unnaturally keenly jealous at anything that looked like sharp practice. But it is not our purpose to dwell upon these earlier years of a regiment, whose historians are both numerous and enthusiastic, interesting as such early records undoubtedly are. The disturbance was terminated, and shortly after the battle of Dettingen had been fought the Black Watch,‡ then consisting of ten companies,

---

* The Black Watch have as badges St. Andrew and Cross on Star of the Order of the Thistle over the Sphinx on glengarry, St. Andrew and Cross on collar. The mottoes are those of the Order of the Thistle and—*Am freiceadan dubh*—The Black Watch. On their colours are the royal cypher within the Garter and the names, "Mangalore," "Seringapatam," "Egypt," "Corunna," "Fuentes d'Onor," "Pyrenees," "Nivelle," "Nive," "Orthes," "Toulouse," "Peninsula," "Waterloo," "South Africa, 1846—7," "South Africa, 1851—3," "Alma," "Sevastopol," "Lucknow," "Ashantee," "Egypt, 1882, 1884," "Tel-el-Kebir," "Nile, 1884—5," "Kirbekan." The uniform is scarlet, with facings of blue, feather bonnet, and kilt.

† The privates were in most cases men of good social position. On one occasion George II. expressed a desire to see some of these famous soldiers, and two privates were sent to St. James's Palace, where they showed some of the national sword exercises. On leaving they were given a guinea apiece, but these *private soldiers* as they strode out threw the guerdon to the porter at the door.

‡ The Black Watch is the English equivalent of the Gaelic *Friceadan Dugh*, which they were called in distinction to the *Saighdearan Dearg*, Red Soldiers. Their uniform at this time was a scarlet jacket and waistcoat with buff facings, with a tartan plaid of twelve yards long wound round the middle of the body, the upper part being fixed on the left shoulder, with flat beaver bonnets, bordered by the fess check of the Royal Stuarts, with a tuft of black feathers.

joined the allied forces in Flanders. At Fontenoy they fought with such marked heroism as to be saluted by the Duke of Cumberland himself with a loud cheer in acknowledgment of their chivalrous devotion. Their colonel, Sir Robert Munro, seemed to bear a charmed life. Suiting their tactics to the exigencies of their position the Highlanders, after delivering a volley, threw themselves flat on the ground while the return fire passed over them, but Sir Robert's enormous bulk, which had necessitated his being hauled out of the trenches by his own men, rendered this manœuvre impossible for himself to practise. He had perforce to stand there "like an invincible Ajax, and guarding the colours of his regiment faced unmoved the enemy's fire." In 1756 the Black Watch were ordered to America, and at Ticonderoga elicited unstinted praise for their valour. In that disastrous combat they lost six hundred and fifty killed or wounded. Others of the regiment* served in 1759 at Martinique, and greatly distinguished themselves by the "characteristic impetuosity" with which they fought. Their next service was in Canada, where they fought under General Amherst, and two years later they took part in the expedition against the Havannah. Many of the laurels of the Black Watch have been gained in America. In 1763 and subsequently they fought against the Indians, particularly distinguishing themselves at Bushey Run, and again in 1776 when the War of Independence gave them severe and constant work. "In every field," writes a chronicler of the regiment, "the Black Watch maintained their hardly-earned reputation," and numerous are the instances recorded of deeds of individual courage and readiness. As an example may be quoted the following:—

"In a skirmish with the Americans in 1776 Major Murray of the 42nd, being separated from his men, was attacked by three of the enemy. His dirk had slipped behind his back, and, like Colonel Munro before referred to, being very corpulent he could not reach it. He defended himself as well as he could with his fusil, and, watching his opportunity, seized the sword of one of his assailants and put the three to flight."

This same Major Murray found his Falstaffian dimensions again embarrassing at Fort Washington.

"The hill on which the fort stood was almost perpendicular, but the Highlanders rushed up the steep ascent like mountain cats. When halfway up the heights they heard a melancholy voice exclaim, 'Oh, soldiers, will you leave me?' On looking down they saw Major Murray, their commanding officer, at the foot of the precipice; his extreme obesity prevented him from following them. They were not deaf to this appeal;

* A second battalion had been raised consequent on the severe loss experienced at Ticonderoga.

it would never do to leave their corpulent commander behind. A party leaped down at once, seized him in their arms and bore him from ledge to ledge of the rock till they reached the summit, where they drove the enemy before them and made two hundred prisoners."

"In a skirmish with the American rebels in 1777 Sergeant Macgregor of the 42nd was severely wounded and remained insensible on the ground. Unlike Captain Crawley, who put on his old uniform before Waterloo, the sergeant, who seems to have been something of a dandy, had attired himself in his best as if he had been going to a ball instead of a battle. He wore a new jacket with silver lace, large silver buckles in his shoes, and a watch of some value. This display of wealth attracted the notice of an American soldier, who, actuated by no feeling of humanity, but by the sordid desire of stripping the sergeant at leisure, took him on his back and began to carry him off the field. It is probable that the American did not handle him very tenderly, and the motion soon restored him to consciousness. He saw at once the state of matters and proved himself master of the occasion. With one hand he drew his dirk, and grasping the American's throat with the other he swore that he would stab him to the heart if he did not retrace his steps and bear him back in safety to the British camp. The *argumentum ad hominem* in the shape of a glittering dagger before his eyes was too much for the American. On the way to the camp they were met by Lord Cornwallis, who thanked him for his humanity; but he had the candour to admit the truth. His lordship, who was much amused at the incident, gave the American his liberty, and, on Macgregor retiring from the service, procured for him a situation in the Customs at Leith."

In 1794 they fought in Holland, and in that terrible march through Westphalia rendered great service, especially at Gildermalsen, where they scattered a regiment of French Hussars. A Scotch officer records the fact that though the Highlanders all wore the kilt, and the men of the 42nd were principally very young soldiers, the loss they experienced from the terrible cold and privations " was out of all comparison less than that sustained by other corps." The following year they again served in the West Indies, and fought with their usual courage at St. Lucia and St. Vincent, and in 1800 joined Sir Ralph Abercrombie, with whom the following year they landed in Egypt. Here they were brigaded under Sir John Moore, and at the landing at Aboukir vied with the Welsh Fusiliers in their gallant onslaught on the French. The story of the battle of Alexandria has too often been told, and in the telling the deeds of the Black Watch enumerated, to need dwelling on here; it will suffice to say, that they undoubtedly are second to none of all the regiments that bear on their accoutrements the eloquent emblem of the Sphinx. It was to Major Sterling of the 42nd that the standard of the "Invincible Legion" was delivered; it was a corporal of the 42nd who shot one of the dragoons that attacked Abercrombie, and it was on the blanket of Donald Roy of the 42nd, that the loved general was borne away to die.

In 1808 the Black Watch joined the army in Portugal, and were with Sir John Moore at Corunna, and a tradition, tinged with the weird superstition of the Highlands, tells that there were not wanting those in the ranks of the Black Watch who, even as their gallant commander turned to them with the confident exhortation—"Highlanders, remember Egypt!" saw rising before his manly form the prophetic, shadowy shroud which foretold his coming death. The 2nd battalion of the regiment took part in the Walcheren expedition, while the 1st joined the allied army in Portugal. At Fuentes d'Onor, under Lord Blantyre, they vigorously repulsed and swept backward in disorder a formidable charge of French cavalry; at Burgos Major Dick, with the men of the Royal Highlanders under his command, were praised in dispatches for their gallantry at the assault. They fought in the picturesque battles of the Pyrenees and Nivelle, at the Nive and Orthes. At Toulouse General Pack, who commanded the Brigade, addressed the regiment as follows: "I have just now been with General Clinton, and he has been pleased to grant my request that in the charge which we are about to make upon the enemy's redoubts, the 42nd regiment shall have the honour of leading on the attack. The 42nd will advance!" Such a regiment needed no repetition of such an order; they advanced with a magnificent charge, and the redoubt was taken, but so terrible was the fire, that "out of about five hundred men which the 42nd brought into action, scarcely ninety reached the fatal redoubt from which the enemy had fled." At Quatre Bras they were subjected to a furious charge from the French Lancers, which came upon them before they could form square. The two flank companies were ridden down, but then the Highlanders formed square, and hemming the cavalry within, killed or made them prisoners. So fierce was this brief conflict that in the space of a few minutes the command of the regiment devolved upon four officers, of whom two were killed and one severely wounded. At Waterloo it suffices to say that they were in Picton's division. The two days' fighting cost the Black Watch in killed and wounded three hundred men.

Interesting though it would be to dwell on many of the occurrences of the intervening years, we must pass on to 1854, when the 42nd formed part of the famous

Highland Brigade in the Crimean War. Throughout the fascinating pages of the author of "Eothen" are numerous mentions of this splendid regiment, of which one of the earliest is the passage which tells how on that first trying march which preluded the Alma, when the troops arrived gasping and fainting with heat and thirst and weariness at their resting-place by the Bulganak River, the stern discipline of Sir Colin Campbell "would not allow even the rage of thirst to loosen the high discipline of his splendid Highland regiments. He halted them a little before they reached the stream, and so ordered it that . . . . they gained in comfort, and knew that they were the gainers." The next day was to be known throughout the centuries as the Battle of the Alma, and in the sweet, quiet fragrance of the morning air, while, though the enemy was in sight, nature seemed unready for war, and stillness pervaded the warrior-covered slopes, the quiet tones of Sir Colin were heard, remarking, "This will be a good time for the men to get loose half their cartridges." Before the day ended many pouches were empty, and their owners refilled them, recalling with pride "the deeds they did that day;" others were well-nigh full, but the hands that had so gleefully opened them in the morning, lay stiff for ever on the Russian hills. When the time came for the Highlanders to charge, matters were looking serious. Thistlethwaite and Lindsay of the Scots Guards had saved their colours, though torn and pierced with shot. The Guards, like wounded demi-gods, were resting, scornfully defiant, despite the terrible gaps in their ranks. Twelve battalions were before the Highland Brigade, which numbered three, yet there was no thought of the possibility of failure in Campbell's mind, as he wound up his short address to his men with the words: "Now, men, the army is watching us. Make me proud of my Highland Brigade!" Then the historian of the war tells us:—"Smoothly, easily, and swiftly, the Black Watch seemed to glide up the hill. A few instants before, and their tartans ranged dark in the valley; now their plumes were on the crest." A few deadly volleys, and the Russians fled in sheer confusion, followed by the exulting shout of the triumphant Scots. Neither Balaclava nor Inkerman are amongst the distinctions borne by the Black Watch, but the comprehensive "Sevastopol" covers many a deed of heroism done during the long months that elapsed before it fell. At the storming of the Redan, they were in reserve at the right attack, and, had it been necessary, would have shared with the Guards the renewed attack that was planned for the following morning.

Again passing over some years, we take up the thread of the record of the 42nd in 1873, when, under Colonel MacLeod, they served in the Ashantee War. At the battle of

Amoaful in January, 1874, the Black Watch were in the leading column under Alison, their own officers present being Majors Macpherson and Scott.* They soon experienced to the full the severe nature of the combat in which they were engaged. A correspondent wrote at the time that so hot was the fire, had the enemy used bullets instead of slugs, "scarcely a man of the Black Watch would have been left to tell the tale." Major Band was severely wounded, Major Macpherson was hit in several places, nine officers and nearly a hundred men were shot. For some time the firing was heavy and seemingly confused; at last the time came for a charge. Sir Archibald, at the head of the Black Watch, bade the pipes strike up "The Campbells are coming," and with a dash and a cheer the regiment charged straight for the foe. Throughout the fighting that preceded the taking of Coomassie, they were to the fore whenever fighting was to be done. In the advance on the capital, a well-known "Man of the Time"†—whose opinion on daring and self-possession is to be valued as coming from one who combines both qualities in so rare a manner—said, "their audacious spirit and true military bearing challenged admiration." "One man—Thomas Adams—exhibited himself eminently brave among brave men." After the town had fallen, the 42nd remained for a time as rear guard.

Their next—and concluding—campaign took place in Egypt, and it may well be imagined that we do not propose to dwell upon what is practically history of to-day. They were again under the command of Sir Archibald Alison, and at Tel-el-Kebir gave evidence that they were still the same formidable "Black Watch" as of yore. We learn from the official dispatches that the Highland Brigade was the first to reach the works, and that the fighting there was no mere child's play is evidenced by the fact that nine of all ranks were killed and forty-one wounded or missing. Amongst the former may be reckoned Lieutenant Graham, Sergeant-Major MacNeill, and Lieutenant Allen Park, though the last-named did not succumb to his wounds on the spot. They were engaged at El Teb and Tamai; at the latter place experiencing some very severe fighting, in which they lost, amongst others, Major Walker Aitken and Lieutenant Ronald Fraser, and nearly ninety others of all ranks. Private Edwards earned the Victoria Cross for "conspicuous bravery" in defence of a gun. Still later on they again won the distinction of Kirbekan on their colours.

The 2nd battalion of the Black Watch, the 73rd Regiment, dates its separate existence from 1786, when the 2nd battalion of the Black Watch was formed into a distinct

* Colonel M'Leod led the left column, and Captain Furse of the regiment was in command of a native regiment in the right column.
† Mr. H. M. Stanley.

regiment with the number 73. It is to the 2nd battalion that the Black Watch owe "Mangalore" and "Seringapatam." The defence of the former—described as one "that has been seldom equalled and never surpassed," and "as noble an example as any in history"—might of itself be sufficient to entitle the 73rd to the epithet "distinguished." At this time, however, they were the 2nd battalion of the 42nd. The Europeans fit for duty were about two hundred and fifty, and there were fifteen hundred natives. Against this handful Tippoo brought ninety thousand men, exclusive of two corps of European infantry, and one—under Lally—of Europeans and natives. He had besides eighty pieces of cannon. Mangalore was invested by this army about the 16th of May; for nine months Colonel Campbell and the 73rd, with the Sepoys, kept this huge host at bay; then they capitulated, but not before "the natives became so exhausted that many of them dropped down in the act of shouldering their firelocks, while others became totally blind." Food was exhausted; for some time the bill of fare had been dependent on frogs, dogs, crows, and similar delicacies; small wonder that even from the savage Tippoo they were granted "highly honourable terms." Of the 250 which the regiment numbered in May, nine officers and seventy rank and file were killed or wounded. As the 73rd the regiment fought at Pondicherry, were in Ceylon in 1793 under General Stuart, and at Seringapatam aided in the brilliant victory won over Tippoo. In the accounts of this most important battle the name of Colonels Sherbrooke and Major M'Donald, with other officers of the 73rd, are referred to in most laudatory terms. After this they were employed under the future Duke of Wellington in completing the subjection of the hostile tribes. Returning to England in 1806, the following eight years were passed in this country and New South Wales. A second battalion meanwhile had been formed, and under General Gibbs served in the Stralsund expedition of 1813, and was "the only British regiment present in the victory gained by Count Walmoden over the French in the plain of Gohrde, in Hanover, 16th September, 1813, to which the 73rd materially contributed." After serving under Sir Thomas Graham, the 73rd (2nd battalion) fought at Quatre Bras and Waterloo.

How well they fought at Waterloo may be gathered from the fact—referred to in our notice of the 30th Regiment—that the Duke at one time during the day sent to Halkett, in whose brigade they were, to inquire which of his regiments it was that was formed in square so far in advance. The answer revealed the actual state of the case, the square was formed of the dead warriors of the 30th and 73rd. "The last named regiment sustained no less than thirteen charges from Cuirassiers, and seven hours of a cannonade, and so greatly were both corps cut up, that at half-past seven their colours were sent out of the field and taken to the rear." After Waterloo peaceful duties occupied the 73rd till the Cape War, which commenced in 1846. They served throughout the campaign, which did not practically terminate till 1853, and to Lieutenant-Colonel Eyre of the regiment was given the command of the right wing in the operations in the Amatolas. Space will not permit of a detailed account of the doings of the 73rd during the war, their valuable services in which consummated in the dashing attack on the fastness of the rebel chief Macomo, which, despite its seeming impregnability, was taken by storm by the regiment and their gallant companions. Their next service was in the operations in Nepaul immediately following the suppression of the Mutiny, in which they earned great credit. Since then their career has been unimportant, but it is interesting to note that on the resumption of their original position as the 2nd battalion of the Black Watch, they again adopted the kilt, which since 1809 had been discarded.

THE ROYAL SCOTS FUSILIERS*—Regimental District No. 21—date from 1678, though they were not put on the English establishment till ten years later. Their first experience—as a regiment, for the stalwart recruits were no novices in the art of fighting—of actual warfare, seems to have been Bothwell Bridge, where the Earl of Mar's Fusiliers, as they were then styled, with the battalions of the Scots Guards under Lord Livingstone, shared in all the varied fortunes of the day. At the time of the Revolution the then colonel of the 21st adhered to King James, and was accordingly superseded by the new Government. The regiment fought with distinction at Walcourt; at Steinkirke they were in the advanced guard and were one of the "five fine regiments" that were entirely cut to pieces owing to the infamous behaviour of Count Solmes, the Dutch Commander; they were represented in the bloody conflict of Landen; at Blenheim they were with the gallant Lord Cutts in the splendid infantry charge which hurtled against the well-defended village; it was the gallant colonel of the Scots Fusiliers—General Rowe—who, ere he fell mortally wounded, "struck his sword into the enemy's palisades before he gave the word 'Fire!'" After the battle, the 21st were amongst the regiments which escorted the enormous band of prisoners to Holland. At Ramillies again they fought,

---

* The Royal Scots Fusiliers bear as badges the thistle on a grenade on cap and collar. On the waist-plate is St. Andrew with the cross, and on the cap-plate the Royal Arms. The motto is that of the Order of the Thistle. On the colours are the Royal cypher, and "Blenheim," "Ramillies," "Oudenarde," "Malplaquet," "Dettingen," "Bladensburg," "Alma," "Inkerman," "Sevastopol," "South Africa, 1879." The uniform is scarlet with facings of blue and Fusilier's cap.

distinguishing themselves by their extraordinary gallantry; at Oudenarde they were with those stern, immovable bodies of foot before whom the French cavalry fled, broken and demoralised; at Lisle and Wynendale they shared in the glories of the victories won. At Malplaquet six of their officers fell, and the records of the time are eloquent over the heroic bravery they there displayed. At Sheriffmuir the Fusiliers, then known as Orrery's Regiment, found themselves opposed to the son of their first colonel, the Earl of Mar, under whose command the Jacobite army was drawn up.

The 21st, then General Macartney's Regiment, were with the Force under General Wade in 1724, though their share was limited to enforcing the due payment of taxes in Aberdeenshire. In 1742 they were ordered to Flanders, and the following year fought at Dettingen, the first occasion, it is said, when the Fusilier Regiments wore those peculiar conical caps which came into vogue with the Prussian tactics. They suffered severely at Fontenoy; at the fratricidal conflict of Culloden they were one of the four Scottish regiments present in the army of King George. In 1761 the Scots Fusiliers, then the Earl of Panmure's Regiment, greatly distinguished themselves under Major Purcell at Belleisle, where they were amongst "the first on shore, and attacked the enemy with great intrepidity."

The campaign in America and Canada next claimed their services, and throughout the war their conduct elicited unstinted praise, especially at Stillwater, where they remained with the 10th and 62nd Regiments under a heavy fire for over four hours. At Saratoga they shared the fate of the remainder of the garrison, and were made prisoners of war.

In 1793 they repaired to the West Indies, and were represented in the fighting which centered about Martinique, gaining particular praise in the capture of Guadeloupe, in which Captain M'Donald of the regiment was killed. Then after a period of comparative inaction, they served in Sicily, and at Ischia, Scylla and Genoa gave evidence of the sterling qualities which have ever distinguished them. In 1814 they were with the army under Sir Thos. Graham which effected the reduction of Bergen-op-Zoom, and the same year fought again in America. At Bladensberg and Baltimore they gained great credit, at the latter place being opposed by the flower of the American army, and as a result suffering severe loss. The 21st were not at Waterloo, and the next distinction on their colours belongs to the wars of our own day. Between Baltimore and the Crimea their time was passed principally in the West Indies and Australia, in the last named of which stations they had a good deal of exciting employment in connection with the convict establishments.

In the Crimea they were in the Fourth Division, and were present at the Alma, at Inkerman, and in the various actions which preceded the fall of Sevastopol. At Inkerman General Cathcart, who led the Division, fell almost at the head of the 21st as he gave the word to charge. In the assault on the Redan, on the 18th of June, 1855, they were again engaged, and despite the unsuccessful nature of the attempt, elicited most favourable comments. After the Crimea the Royal Scots Fusiliers were again employed in the West Indies, and also in Burmah. The last name on their colours recalls the yet recent war in South Africa. They were amongst the reinforcements which reached Zululand in April, and a month or so after their arrival took part in the battle of Ulundi. Two companies, it may be added, had been previously left to garrison Fort Newdigate, under Colonel Collingwood of the regiment, while the rest of the regiment had occupied Fort Marshall. At Ulundi they were at the right rear angle of the square under Major Hazelrigge, and materially aided in repulsing the threatening charge made by the foe; later on, in the operations agaist Sekukuni, they were again employed, and bore a prominent part in the proceedings in November, a detachment on one occasion being under arms "twenty-four hours consecutively and without food." In the attack on Sekukuni's town, they were in the centre column under Major Murray of the 94th. The two regiments, we are told, made a rush at the stronghold in splendid order, vying each with the other which should be first, the pipers of the Fusiliers "filling the air with the breath of battle while playing with infernal energy." Under Captain Auchinleck they were actively employed in hunting and capturing the Basuto chieftain, and were fortunate enough to suffer comparatively little loss. At the outbreak of the Boer rebellion Captain Lambart was treacherously taken prisoner, and a treacherous and barbarous attempt made to kill him, under the circumstances mentioned in our notice of the 94th Regiment.

Fifty men of the Fusiliers had been before this organized as mounted infantry, and the remainder of the regiment were stationed at Pretoria and Rustenberg, where they were shortly afterwards besieged. A hundred or so were with Colley at the battle of Laing's Neck, and held the camp during that disastrous engagement. The garrison at Pretoria were under Colonel Gildea of the regiment, and during a sortie the Boers hoisted a flag of truce, and on the Fusiliers coming from cover, imagining they were dealing with civilised foes, fired upon them, killing or wounding twenty-one. "Colonel Gildea and his orderly while both bearing white flags in response were fired upon within sixty yards range, but both escaped. This was the third time the Boers had made a treacherous use of the white flag." It is satisfactory to record that on this occasion fourteen of the rebels were shot down and twenty taken prisoners. This was only one of the many gallant sorties made by the 21st from Pretoria, on one occasion Colonel Gildea being severely wounded. It is not remarkable that amongst the gallant soldiers who were fighting for life and honour against insolent and treacherous foes " a very bitter feeling was manifested against the conditions of peace concluded by the British Government with the Boers." Meanwhile at Rustenberg sixty of the 21st under Captain Auchinleck, who was wounded, were cooped up in a fort only twenty-five yards square, and kept the foe at bay for more than three months. It was by a detachment of the Fusiliers under Captain Burr that the heroic little band at Fort Mary was relieved. At Potchefstroom the regiment greatly distinguished themselves. Hostilities commenced by the Boers attempting to pull down the British flag. Captain Lambart of the 21st shot him in the arm, but was unfortunately taken prisoner. Then a regular fusilade began, and Captain Laurence Falls was shot dead. The commandant at Potchefstroom was Colonel Bellaris, and the officers of the 21st who were with him were Lieutenant-Colonel Winsloe, Lieutenants Lindsell, Dalrymple Hay, Kenneath Lean, and P. Brown. Major Thornhill and Lieutenant Rundle of the Royal Artillery were also present. On the 16th of December the Boers sent to demand surrender, but the only reply they received was two cannon shots. Throughout December, January, February, and the greater part of March the little force of three hundred men held the fort against an overwhelming number of the enemy.

On the 23rd of March, Lieutenant Dalrymple Hay with only ten men undertook to dislodge a party of some thirty rebels who had posted themselves in an annoying position. Three of his men were shot down at once; with the other seven he charged with fixed bayonets and drove the rebels away, killing about sixteen of them. From this incident may be gauged the value of all the nonsense written about the "courage" of the Boers. They were bold enough at a distance when they could bring their deadly marksmanship into play, but at close quarters *eight* men of the Fusiliers were more than sufficient to completely rout thirty of them. At last, when more than a third of the garrison were killed or wounded, when all provisions were exhausted, and after the allowance for each man had been some time reduced to "a pound of mealies and half a pound of Kaffir corn daily, with a quarter of a pound of tinned meat on alternate days," the garrison surrendered, claiming and obtaining full honours of war. The Boers knew that an armistice had been concluded *two full days before the capitulation*. Since the Transvaal war the Royal Scots Fusiliers have not had the opportunity of adding any distinction to their colours, though their recent achievements in Burmah give good evidence how well they still deserve the high estimation in which the regiment has ever been held.

THE CAMERONIANS (SCOTTISH RIFLES)*—Regimental District No. 26—which next engage our attention, consist of the 26th and 90th Foot. The 26th, from which the name is derived, were raised in 1689 from amongst those bands of stern Covenanters whom religious predilections had attracted to the cause of William and Mary. Their first colonel was the Earl of Angus, then apparently only eighteen years of age, and the conditions on which the men enlisted were curiously characteristic of their temperament. The officers were to be such men "as in conscience they could submit to;" a captain was appointed to the regiment, and an "elder" to each company; in each man's haversack was to be found a Bible. Their first engagement was at Dunkeld, where their gallant defence was for long the theme of universal praise. They were 1,200, whilst their assailants were more than four times as many; for four hours they fought desperately in street and house, by wall and market-place; when ammunition fell short they tore the lead from the roofs and converted it into slugs. At last the attacking force drew off, declaring that they "could fight men but not devils," and the Cameronians remained victors, having killed three hundred of the enemy and wounded "a vast number," while their own loss was under fifty. A Jacobite song of the period, quoted by Grant in his account of the siege, is higher praise than the compliments of troops of friends. Addressing the Cameronians, the poet says:

> "For murders too, as soldiers true,
> You were advanced well, boys;
> For you fought like devils, your only rivals,
> When you were at Dunkeld, boys."

At Steinkirke the Cameronians were in Mackay's brigade, and suffered severely in the terrible slaughter inflicted on them by the French Mousquetaires, their young colonel being killed at their head; at Namur they distinguished themselves under the brave Lord Cutts; at Blenheim their brigadier, the gallant Rowe, in whose division they were,

---

* The Cameronians bear as badge the Thistle on the glengary, and on the helmet-plate a mullet with bugle and strings. Surrounding this is a laurel wreath, on the leaves of which are the battles. On either side of the wreath are the sphinx and dragon. The whole has a coronet above. The motto is that of the Order of the Thistle. The battles inscribed are: "Blenheim," "Ramillies," "Oudenarde," "Malplaquet," "Mandora," "Egypt," "Corunna," "Martinique," "Guadeloupe," "China," "South Africa, 1846-7," "Sevastopol," "Lucknow," "Abyssinia," "South Africa, 1877-8-9." The uniform is green, with facings of dark green.

led them—as has been recorded—right up to the palisades, which he struck with his sword before giving the order to "Fire!" "At the battle of Ramillies the regiment, after being much exposed throughout the fight, was engaged in pursuit of the beaten foe till midnight;" they fought at Oudenarde and Wynendale, and in the battle of Malplaquet had four officers killed. Shortly after their return home they adopted the tartan trews, and, after serving in England for a few years, were ordered to the defence of Gibraltar in 1727. In 1767 the Cameronians were ordered to Canada, and throughout the American war fought under Lieut.-General Clinton.* They served at Alexandria, and at Corunna, where they were in the thickest of the fighting. A period of service with the Walcheren expedition so enfeebled the regiment through sickness that they were unable to take a very active part in the Peninsular war. But the chance for distinction came with the Chinese war of 1840, and they gladly seized it, though here again they suffered cruelly from sickness, losing their colonel and two hundred men. At Amoy Colonel Mountain, leading a body of the 26th, was the first of our forces actually over the wall, and at the capture of Chapoo distinguished himself by a hand-to-hand combat with a Tartar warrior. At the time the Tartar rushed at him "three balls struck him the same instant and three more passed through his haversack; of the former one furrowed the muscles of the spine, another hit him on the left side and passed out under the lower rib, the third struck him in the thigh, ran down the leg and came out at the knee; yet he killed his opponent and was soon fit for service." As an example of the severe loss the regiment incurred from fever, etc., may be mentioned the fact that scarcely one of those who started for the China war returned. Their number was nine hundred to commence with, nine hundred recruits were sent out, "yet only the original number remained when the regiment marched into the Castle of Edinburgh in 1843."

We must pass rapidly over the following years, during which the 26th served in Canada and India, and come to 1868, in which year they were with Napier's little army in Abyssinia. But even here their lot it was to learn that—

"They also serve who only stand and wait;"

for their duties did not bring them within actual fighting distance of the enemy. Since the Abyssinian war, though duty has been ever well performed, and the credit and high

* It is recorded that during this war a detachment of the regiment which had been embarked for some secret science was overpowered, but when capture appeared inevitable the colours were wound round a cannon shot and sunk in the river.

standing of the regiment well and thoroughly maintained, no foe has called for the stern lessons which these successors of the old Covenanters know so well how to give.

The 2nd battalion of the Scottish Rifles is the 90th, the Perthshire Volunteers of many a well-fought field. They date from 1794, when they were raised by Mr. Thomas Graham, somewhat to the annoyance of the 'Powers that be' near the Throne, who did not fancy a non-military man having too much to do with raising regiments. But "nice customs curtsey to great kings," and this volunteer of the Toulon expedition was to prove a veritable "king of men" in those Peninsular battles, where that "daring old man of a ready temper for battle" was to win renown as Sir Thomas Graham, afterwards Lord Lynedoch. Their first service was at Isle Dieu and Quiberon, and three years after they were at Minorca. Their first distinction was won in Egypt, where they won widespread praise for their gallant conduct at Mandora. Here, owing to their wearing brass helmets, they were mistaken by the enemy for dismounted dragoons, over whom an easy victory was to be anticipated. The withering fire with which they received the French cavalry proved the error of this surmise, but the fight was a stubborn and a severe one. Colonel Rowland Hill of the regiment was hit on the head and had to be taken off the field; at one time Abercrombie himself would have been taken prisoner but for the magnificent stand made by the 90th. Colonel Hill, it may be remarked, was taken on board the *Foudroyant*, and into the cabin occupied by him, slowly rallying from his severe wound, was the brave and well-loved Abercrombie brought to die. After Egypt the 90th served at Martinique, whence Captain Preedy of the regiment brought to the King the tidings of victory, and at Guadeloupe, where they captured an eagle. The following years were passed at home, at Malta, and in America. The records of the regiment contain an interesting account of the steadfast courage and discipline of the regiment on the occasion of a terrible shipwreck, and in 1846 they served under Lieutenant-Colonel Slade in the South African war of that date. Returning home in 1848, they landed in the Crimea in December, 1855, when amongst the Lieutenants was one Garnet Joseph Wolseley. On the occasion of the sortie of the 22nd of March Captain Vaughan, with about a dozen gallant fellows of the Perthshire Volunteers, beat back a formidable body of Russians; in the assault of the 7th of June, Colonel Campbell and Captain Wolseley were specially mentioned; a few days later Private Alexander won the Victoria Cross for bringing in wounded men, conduct which he repeated on the 6th of September following, when he helped to bring back the body of Captain Buckley of the Scots Guards.

In the final assault on the Redan a working party of one hundred men were under Captain Perrin. Colonel Handcock fell mortally wounded; inside the Redan were found the bodies of Captain Preston and Lieutenants Swift and Wilmer; Sergeant Moynihan "slew five Russians with his own hand" before it became necessary to retire. On the capture of the town Captain Vaughan of the regiment was found, terribly ill, in one of the hospitals. He said he had been brutally treated, and was about to be bayoneted in cold blood, but fortunately bethought him to make the Masonic sign, which was recognised by his would-be assassin who spared his life. Only for a few days, however, did Vaughan live after his rescue.

Scarcely was the Crimean War ended ere the 90th were ordered to India to assist in quelling the Mutiny. Their first exploit was the disarming of the disaffected cavalry at Berhampore. From there they were sent to reinforce Havelock, and with him marched to the relief of Lucknow. The first shot from the Alumbagh killed three officers, and about the same time, though elsewhere, fell the brave man Alexander, who had not yet received the V.C. he had so gallantly won in the Crimea. The splendid charge made by the 90th and 78th is recorded in any history of the events—how the Perthshire Light Infantry captured two guns, and how Colonel Campbell was saved from death by the Prayer-Book he carried in his breast arresting the course of a shot. Well known, too, is the gallant devotion to duty which earned the coveted Cross for Drs. Home and Bradshaw of the regiment, who, with only a handful of men, kept at bay hundreds of the rebels for nearly twenty-four hours. Three similar Crosses were won at the second relief of Lucknow by Major Guise, Sergeant Gill and Private Graham, when the regiment, under Major Barnston, did such great things. Throughout the Mutiny the 90th vied with the gallantest there in their endurance and courage, and before returning home had some further fighting in the Euzuffuzie expedition. Though the regiment itself did not participate in the Ashantee war, they may certainly claim a credit of connection in that campaign, for Wolseley and Evelyn Wood, and the gallant young Eyre, who fell at Ordahsu, were or had been all members of the Perthshire Light Infantry. In 1878 they were in South Africa, and early in the following year constituted the bulk of the infantry in No. 3 column under their own officer, Evelyn Wood, and served throughout the campaign; specially did they distinguish themselves at Inhlobane, where Lieutenant Lysons and Private Fowler were awarded the V.C., in clearing out a cavern whence the Zulus kept up a dangerous fire. Again at Kambula they were hotly engaged, eventually routing the foe with great loss, though Major Hackett was terribly wounded, and—trying to assist him—Lieutenant Bright, one of the most popular officers in the regiment, lost his life. They were with the flying column that fought so well at Ulundi, after which their more active participation in the operations going on in Zululand terminated, and with that termination we must perforce close our notice of the Perthshire Light Infantry, now the 2nd battalion of the Cameronians.

THE SEAFORTH HIGHLANDERS*—Regimental District No. 72—consists of the 72nd and 78th Foot. The former date from 1778, when they were raised by the then Lord Seaforth in recognition of the graceful act of the Government in restoring to him the forfeited title of his ancestors. By a somewhat strange coincidence the first number borne by the regiment was that of their present 2nd battalion, 78. The first years of the regiment were somewhat tempestuous; the relations between England and the Scottish Highlanders were still somewhat strained, and each side was only too eager to allege bad faith on the part of the other. From this feeling originated the affair of "the wild Macraes," a sept or small clan who had enlisted under Lord Seaforth. They refused to embark for foreign service, and with colours flying and pipes playing betook themselves to Arthur's Seat, where they continued for some days in a state of inaggressive mutiny. But this was got over by a little tact, and before long the brave Highlanders marched back to their regiment with their colonel and other officers at their head. They then set sail for India, but on the voyage out lost their Colonel—Seaforth—from illness, an occurrence which exercised a most depressing and fatal effect on his men, many of whom sickened and died. On arriving in India they joined Stuart's force and marched against Cuddalore, and at that place, as at Palghautchery, Savendroog and Outra Durgum, proved how valuable an acquisition the Seaforth Highlanders were to the British Army. Palghautchery and Outra Durgum may indeed be said to have owed their capture chiefly to the "heroic ardour" of the 72nd. At Seringapatam they were in the third column, to which was entrusted the storming of the Pagoda Hill, under Colonel Maxwell, and not a little of the credit of the day is due to the dashing manner

---

* The Seaforth Highlanders bear as badges the Coronel and Cypher of the late Duke of York and Albany on the Star of the Thistle, and the Elephant, with "Assaye," on cap and collar. The mottoes are "Cabar Feidh"—the clan cry of the Seaforth; "Tulach Ard," that of the Mackenzies of Kintoul; and "Cuidich'n Righ" ("Cuideach'd an Righ"). On their colours are "Hindoostan," "Assaye," "Cape of Good Hope," "Maida," "Java," "South Africa, 1835," "Sevastopol," "Persia," "Koosh-ab," "Lucknow," "Central India," "Peiwar Kotal," "Charasiah," "Kabul, 1879," "Kandahar, 1880," "Afghanistan, 1878-80," "Egypt, 1882," "Tel-el-Kebir." The uniform is scarlet with facings of yellow, with feather bonnet and kilt, the feather bonnet having a white hackle feather.

in which he carried out this plan. They also served at Pondicherry, and in Ceylon; after which, in 1798, they returned home.

In 1805 they embarked for the Cape of Good Hope, and at the Blaw Berg in the following year suffered somewhat severely, the list of casualties including Colonels Grant and Campbell of the regiment, while Lieutenant M'Arthur and thirty men distinguished themselves by engaging and repulsing a very superior force of Dutch. Three years later, in accordance with a "fad" of the government, the Seaforth Highlanders discontinued the wearing of the Highland costume, which, however, they have subsequently re-adopted. After this, for again we must pass over much, the 72nd were employed in the Mauritius and in India, about the time of Waterloo being employed in South Africa. During their sojourn here a somewhat characteristic incident occurred with the Boers. The latter appealed to the British for aid against the Kaffirs who were making raids upon their homesteads, and accordingly Captain Gethin of the regiment with some men went to the scene of a recent disturbance. Here they were surrounded by a body of Kaffirs in ambush and cut to pieces, Captain Gethin himself receiving no fewer than thirty-two wounds. It will surprise no one who has studied the history of the Boers to learn that the people whom Gethin came to help looked placidly on while he and his gallant men of the 72nd were being butchered. The regiment returned home in 1821, and two years after received the title of the "Duke of Albany's Highlanders," after the then Commander-in-Chief, his Royal Highness the Duke of York and Albany, at the same time receiving the Highland costume, only with trews instead of kilt. Their next service was again at the Cape of Good Hope, and during the operations against Macumo, the hostile Kaffir chief, they greatly distinguished themselves. After another interval of rest the Duke of Albany's Highlanders were dispatched to the Crimea, where they arrived in May, 1855, and from that date to the close of the war served in all the duties which our troops were called upon to perform. After the Crimea followed with deadly haste the Mutiny, where the 72nd earned lasting praise. Their chief exploits were while serving with Sir Hugh Rose's force in Central India, and at Kotah the fortune of war decreed that their chief opponents should be the revolted 72nd native regiment, whose uniform in some degree resembled that of the Duke of Albany's. The storming party was to abide the blowing up of the great gate, and owing to the unexpected delay in doing this found themselves exposed for some time to the fierce fire of the enemy. But when the explosion was heard, and the pipes struck up their martial tune, it required but a very few minutes to capture the town, thanks to the impetuous ardour of the 72nd and their comrades, who with a ringing shout—"Scotland for ever!" literally drove all before them. Throughout the struggles in Baroda the 72nd, who were subsequently with the Rajpootana Field Force, fought well and successfully, well meriting the unstinted meed of praise awarded to them. The next important campaign in which the 72nd were engaged was in Afghanistan in 1878. Here they were brigaded under General Roberts, and rendered most signal service at the storming of the Peiwar Kotal. Here the 72nd and the "brave little Ghoorkas" fairly divided the honours of the day between them, though Lieutenant Munro and several rank and file were in the list of casualties. During the march through the Sappri defile Sergeant Green gained his commission for the gallant defence he made of Captain Goad, and it is recorded by a Scotch writer that "a sick Highlander (of the 72nd), who was being carried in a dhooley, fired all his ammunition, sixty-two rounds, at the enemy, and as he was a good marksman, he never fired without getting a fair shot."

The following year they were still more actively employed, and round and about Cabul, under Roberts, came in for much fierce fighting, from which they gained a full sheaf of honours. Sergeants Macdonald, Cox, and M'Ilvean distinguished themselves at the assault of the Takt-i-Shah; Lieutenant Ferguson was twice wounded; Sergeant Jule (who was killed the next day) was the first man to gain the ridge, capturing at the same time two standards. Corporal Sellars, the first man to gain the top of the Asmai heights, gained a Victoria Cross; before that day's sun had set Captain Spens and Lieutenant Gainsford of the regiment had fallen fighting like heroes to the last; Lieutenant Egerton was badly wounded, and several rank and file put *hors de combat*. The regiment fought well in the attack on Sherpur, and in Roberts's famous march to Candahar were brigaded with the Gordon Highlanders and 60th Rifles. In the attack on Candahar Sir Frederick reported that "the 72nd and the 2nd Sikhs had the chief share of the fighting;" of the Second Brigade Colonel Brownlow, Captain Frowe and Sergeant Cameron were among the killed; Captain Stewart Murray and Lieutenant Munroe were badly wounded. In 1881 the regiment resumed the kilt, adopting the Mackenzie tartan, and were engaged in the Egyptian war of the following year, when they served with Macpherson's Indian Contingent; under Colonel Stockwell they brilliantly inaugurated their campaign by the capture of Chalouffe. At Tel-el-Kebir they were leading on the extreme left, "advancing steadily and in silence until an advanced battery of the enemy was reached, when it was gallantly stormed by the Highlanders" (*Sir G. Wolseley's Dispatch*), and after this they pursued the flying enemy and occupied the important town of Zagazig. Their losses were very slight, two men killed and three wounded, owing "to the excellent arrangements made by General Macpherson," and to the fact that the earlier attacks had so shaken the enemy that they could not withstand "the impetuous onslaught of the Seaforth Highlanders."

The 2nd battalion of the Seaforth Highlanders, consisting of the 78th regiment, the Ross-shire Buffs, also owes its existence to the loyal family of Seaforth, being raised in 1793 by the then head of the clan. Their first service was under the Earl of Chatham in the disastrous Walcheren Expedition, after which they took part in the campaign in Holland under the Duke of York. The value of the service rendered by the Highlanders during the terrible retreat to Bremen has been before mentioned; at Gildermalsen, however, the 78th ran a somewhat serious risk. "A regiment of the enemy's hussars, dressed in a uniform similar to that worn by the Emigrant regiment of the Duke de Choiseul in our service, pushed on, treacherously shouting 'Choiseul! Choiseul!' and got close to the 78th Highlanders undiscovered." They were, however, repulsed by some scathing volleys from the Black Watch. The 78th then served for a time at the Cape of Good Hope, and in 1797 were ordered to India,* where they gained the first of their many distinctions. Under Wellesley they assisted in the capture of the strong town of Ahmednughur, and under the immediate command of the same great leader fought with splendid courage at Assaye; they were on the left of the first line, and at the close of the day were led forward by Wellesley in person to clear out the village, which they did at the point of the bayonet after some desperate fighting. They fought at Argaum, and in 1811 were with the forces under Sir Samuel Achmuty in the operations in Java. On returning home they experienced the misfortune which our troops seem so often to have suffered, namely, that of being shipwrecked; the reports at the time speak in the most energetic terms of the courage and endurance displayed by the 78th, of whom, fortunately, not a man was lost. But the regiment had been reaping its harvest of honour in the West as well as in the East. Under Stuart they had been serving in Sicily, and are amongst the regiments whose colours bear the name "Maida." The record of the regiment narrates that the aspect of the regiment caused the general some apprehension, they looked so very young; quite six hundred of their number were under twenty-one. But there was nought of weakness or youthful instability in that splendid charge they made, led by their gallant Colonel, Patrick Macleod. Opposed to them was the French 42nd regiment of Grenadiers, led by a brave and skilful commander. But commander and

* A 2nd battalion.

troops alike were hurled back by the 78th. The retreat became a headlong flight, and so far did the Highlanders with fierce slaughter pursue the flying foe that an aide-de-camp was sent to bid them halt. "At the moment the order was delivered to Macleod he was incapable of speech, and was stooping from his horse on the shoulder of a sergeant of his regiment; a rifle ball had passed through his breast within an inch of the heart, inflicting a painful and perilous wound;" yet he never quitted his saddle or the field, but remained at the head of his Ross-shire Buffs during the remainder of the battle and the long pursuit that followed it. Again and again they charged during that day, and no regiment more nobly acquitted itself. In 1807 they fought in Egypt and gained undying fame at the disastrous conflict at El Hamet. Colonel Macleod with one company of the regiment and some of the 35th were surrounded and assailed by an overwhelming force. The colonel was killed; "there also fell Lieutenant Macrae with six more of his name; Sergeant John Macrae slew seven assailants with his claymore before his head was cloven from behind. Of Macleod's detachment, consisting of two hundred and seventy-five, all were killed to thirty, of whom fifteen only were unwounded." Strangely enough two of the prisoners of the 78th rose to high eminence in the land of their captivity. Ibrahim Aga, the famed governor of Medina and one of the Sultan's most able generals, was Private Thomas Keith on that dreadful day when his officers and comrades fell around him in El Hamet; Osman, "the learned leech" of Alexandria, who acquired a large practice and larger fortune, was a drummer boy in the 78th, whose medical training had been limited to assisting the regimental surgeon to tie bandages and mix medicines.

The Ross-shire Buffs have 'Persia' and 'Khoosh-ab' on their colours, words which recall their conduct in a campaign in which they earned a very high encomium from Sir Henry Havelock: they "behaved remarkably well at the battle of Khoosh-ab, ... and during the naval action on the Euphrates and the landing, their steadiness, zeal, and activity were conspicuous. They ... never seemed to complain of anything, but that they had no further chance of meeting the enemy. I am convinced that the regiment would be second to none in the service if their high military qualities were drawn forth; they are proud of their colours, their tartan, and their former high achievements." On the night preceding the battle of Khoosh-ab, the enemy attempted a surprise on our forces, but thanks to steadiness and discipline, the only result was to somewhat lessen the number of the morrow's assailants. During this midnight attack the 78th were exposed to a somewhat bewildering ruse on the part of the Persians, one of whose buglers had learned the "calls" used in our service, and repeatedly sounded "cease firing" close to the Ross-shires—fortunately, however, he entirely failed to mislead them. When the Mutiny broke out "the high military qualities" of the regiment were called forth with a vengeance, and the result proved how admirably General Havelock had gauged the calibre of the corps. We shall not attempt to follow *seriatim* the services the 78th rendered throughout the Mutiny; these services are matter of history, and will be recalled whenever the Indian Mutiny is mentioned. They were with Havelock in his march to relieve Cawnpore and Lucknow; marching in eight days a hundred and twenty-six miles, fighting four battles, and capturing a score of guns. As is sadly well known the force arrived too late at Cawnpore, despite their heroic efforts and splendid victories, and the terrible sight that met their eyes—mangled bodies, torn clothing, children's little frocks and toys, tresses of long hair torn out by the roots, all bedabbled with blood—lives yet, an awful memory. Not many years before, a poet had put into the lips of a singer of old Rome the stirring couplet which spoke of

> ... "the inexpiable wrong, the unutterable shame
> That turns the coward's heart to steel, the sluggard's blood to flame.'

There were neither cowards nor sluggards in this band of heroes, and men told at the time how the Ross-shire Buffs, finding amongst the blood-boltered débris a tress of black hair torn from the head of one of poor, murdered General Wheeler's daughters, divided it amongst their number, each vowing, like the Knight of Snowdon, to stain it deep in rebel blood. Splendidly did they fight at the Alumbagh, when, at last, Lucknow was taken. Two incidents are recorded by a countryman, each having for its hero a piper of the 78th. In one case the piper was wounded and a couple of his comrades were carrying him off, when they saw, to their dismay, a rebel trooper approaching with drawn sword. The position was critical, but the piper was equal to the occasion; "going through the ordinary manœuvres of loading a gun, he lifted the longest shank of his pipes to his shoulder and pointed it at the Sepoy's head." As a result the latter "turned tail and ran off." On another occasion—the capture of Lucknow—a piper found himself alone, lost in the tortuous streets, with gun discharged and bayonet unfixed. "To him enter," round a sudden corner, one of the rebel cavalry, who forthwith made at him. Whatever views may be held of the relative merits of sword and bayonet, there can be but one opinion as to the superiority of the former when the latter is not fixed. The days of the brave 78th man seemed numbered. "Suddenly," he wrote, "a bright idea struck me; all at once I seized my pipe, put it to my mouth, and gave forth a shrill note which so startled the fellow that he bolted like a shot, evidently imagining it was some infernal machine; so my pipe saved my life."

The 78th gained too many of those crosses inscribed "For Valour," for us to be able to do more than quote some of the circumstances. Private James Hollowell, 78th Highlanders, received the Victoria Cross for conduct officially described as follows:—
"A party on the 26th September, 1857, was shut up and besieged in a house in the city of Lucknow by the rebel Sepoys. Private James Hollowell, one of the party, behaved throughout the day in the most admirable manner; he directed, encouraged, and led the others, exposing himself fearlessly, and by his talent in persuading and cheering, prevailed on nine desperate men to make a successful defence in a burning house, with the enemy firing through four windows."

"Assistant Surgeon Valentine Munbee M'Master, 78th Highlanders, was recommended for the Victoria Cross for the intrepidity with which he exposed himself to the fire of the enemy in bringing in and attending to the wounded on the 25th September, at Lucknow. He had served in the Persian War and in all Havelock's operations for the succour of the Residency. After arriving at the latter place he accompanied many sorties and was wounded. He was with Outram's force at the Alumbagh, and took part in the Rohilcund campaign."

"Surgeon Joseph Jee was selected by his brother officers for the Victoria Cross. On September 25th, 1857, the 78th Highlanders had been left behind to protect the passage of the Char Bagh Bridge. The enemy, seeing their isolated position, gathered round them from every quarter, occupying all the neighbouring buildings. From the tops of these came a perfect hail of musket-bullets, while two heavy guns were enfilading the regiment with deadly accuracy. Ordered not to move till every bullock had crossed the bridge, the regiment for a long time remained halted. At length, becoming desperate, they charged the guns, dashing up the street with a loud cheer, led by their Adjutant, whose horse had been shot under him. They were received by a volley, and men dropped in numbers; but the survivors persevered, reached the guns, and after a short, sharp struggle captured them. Dr. Jee contrived, by great personal exertions, in getting the wounded who had been hit in the charge carried off on the backs of their comrades, till he had succeeded in collecting the dhooly-bearers who had fled. He is said to have exposed himself in the most devoted manner. Later on, while trying to reach the Residency with the wounded under his charge, he was obliged to throw himself into the Moti Mehal, where he remained besieged the whole of the following night and morning."

The official account says that he repeatedly exposed himself to a heavy fire "in proceeding to dress the wounded men who fell while serving a 24-pounder in a most exposed situation. He eventually succeeded in taking many of the wounded, through a cross-fire of ordnance and musketry, safely into the Residency, by the river bank, although repeatedly warned not to make the perilous attempt."

The gallant Adjutant who led the 78th Highlanders in the brilliant charge abovementioned was Lieutenant Herbert Taylor Macpherson, afterwards the Sir Herbert Macpherson who commanded the Indian contingent in the Egyptian War, and is now a C.B.

After Lucknow the 78th joined the Rohilcund Field Force, where they, needless to say, did yeoman's service. The following years were passed in Gibraltar, Canada, and Ireland; after this they served under General Phayre in Afghanistan, but were not actively engaged. No important operations coming within the scope of this sketch have since that date fallen to the lot of the gallant Ross-shire Buffs.

THE KING'S (SHROPSHIRE) LIGHT INFANTRY*—Regimental District No. 53—is composed of the 53rd and 85th Regiments of the line. The former, the 53rd, date from 1755, when they were raised by Colonel Whitmore, and first numbered the 55th. The first duty on which they were engaged was that of garrisoning Gibraltar, where they stayed twelve years. In 1776 occurred the fighting under Burgoyne in and about Quebec, and in this campaign the 53rd gained considerable credit, especially at Crown Point and Ticonderoga, where the flank companies were engaged, and shared, with so many others of the royal troops, the discomforts of imprisonment. Returning to England in 1789 they fought, four years later, in Flanders, where they gained their first distinction in "Nieuport," previously to which, however, they had made an honourable name for themselves at Famars and Valenciennes. The 53rd are the only regiment that bear Nieuport on their colours, and it is recorded that Major R. Matthews of the regiment "particularly distinguished himself," while their conduct was such as to elicit very eulogistic mention in the dispatches of the commander. The following year they fought at Vaux, Prémont, Landrécies, Cateau, Tournay, and other less notable engagements,

* The King's (Shropshire) Light Infantry bear as badges the monogram K.L.I., with a bugle on a star on the cap, and a bugle on the collar. The motto is "Aucto Splendore Resurgo." On the colours are : "Nieuport," "Tournay," "St. Lucia," "Talavera," "Fuentes d'Onor," "Salamanca," "Vittoria," "Pyrenees," "Nivelle," "Nive," "Toulouse," "Peninsula," "Bladensburg," "Aliwal," "Sobraon," "Punjaub," "Goojerat," "Lucknow," "Afghanistan, 1879–80," "Egypt, 1882," "Suakin, 1885." The uniform is scarlet, with facings of blue.

and with the 14th and 37th Regiments were known as the "Fighting Brigade." Right well did they earn the sobriquet! On one occasion, on the road between Lisle and Roubaix, the fighting Brigade kept at bay an overwhelming mass of the enemy, but for close upon *half* their gallant number it was the last of all their glorious fields. At Tournay, again, the regiment, under Major Wiseman, was severely engaged and suffered considerable loss; their conduct, however, earned the special praise and thanks of the Commander-in-Chief. They returned to England in 1795 after sharing in that terrible retreat so often, perforce, referred to, and shortly after were ordered to the West Indies. At St. Lucia they were with the future hero of Corunna in the splendid attack which captured Morne Chabot, after which they rendered signal service in the Carib War in St. Vincent, and added the capture of Trinidad to their already crowded list of achievements. They returned to England in 1802, and the year following a 2nd battalion was formed, which represented the gallant Shropshire in the Peninsular Campaign. We will, however, before dealing with them, pursue the career of the 1st battalion, which, in 1805, was ordered to India, and for many years bore a conspicuous part in the many fierce encounters fought with the native princes. At the storming of Callinger, for instance, a fortress of immense strength, surrounded by seemingly impassable defiles and ravines, and itself recalling the lonely hamlet which the poet describes as being—

> "Like an eagle's nest
> Perched on the crest
> Of purple Apennine,"

Colonel Mawby, who commanded them, declared that "he had not words to express his admiration of the conduct of every officer and soldier in the 53rd," while the General Orders echoed his eulogy in their reference to "the exemplary exertions, zeal, and persevering courage of officers and men." In 1813 and the following year, the 53rd were with Sir Robert Rollo Gillespie in Nepaul, and at the capture of Kalunga—another fortress standing, as Sir Robert himself described it, "on the summit of an almost inaccessible mountain and covered by an impenetrable forest"—again won universal praise. Colonel Mawby, Major Ingleby, Captain Coultman, Lieutenants Young, Anstice, and Harrington are some of those of the 53rd whose names were in men's mouths as those who had done gloriously, and had in many cases won honour only at the cost of life or limb. For many years they fought in India and returned home in 1823, having lost 350 officers and 1,167 privates, who had been killed or had succumbed to wounds or disease, and nearly 500 of all ranks invalided.

We must now retrace our steps somewhat and glance at the doings of the 2nd battalion, which, as has been said, was formed in 1803. The first six years of their existence were passed in Ireland, whence, in 1809, they were dispatched to the Peninsula. Here they were brigaded with the 7th Fusiliers under General A. Campbell, and commenced their warlike career with the combats about Oporto. It was not to be long before they added the famous name of "Talavera" to the roll of the regiment's honours. The historian of the war records that on Campbell's division the French fell with infinite fury, yet "the English regiments, putting the French skirmishers aside, met the advancing columns with loud shouts, broke their front, lapped their flanks with fire, and giving them no respite pushed them back with a terrible carnage." They were not actually attacked at Busaco, but took part in the investment of Almeida and in the battle of Fuentes d'Onor. They were employed in covering the siege of Badajoz and the operations at Almaraz; in the capture of the fortified convents before Salamanca they elicited unstinted admiration; at the battle of Salamanca itself no regiment was for a time more hardly pressed than "that brave regiment," as Napier styles the 53rd. In vain Boyer's Dragoons thundered down upon their flank, exposed by the retreat of the Portuguese regiments; though many of the 53rd were actually cut down by their sabres, steadily and unflinchingly did they stem the surging tide; the crisis of the day thus passed favourably to the British, and before many hours the important battle was won. The regiment served in the siege of Burgos, Lieutenant Frazer distinguishing himself in one of the assaults; they fought in the centre column at Vittoria, took part in the blockade of Pampeluna, and showed how stubbornly they could struggle till they conquered in the wild warfare that took place on the slopes of the towering Pyrenees. The regimental record states that there were volunteers from the regiment present at St. Sebastian; at Nivelle they "evinced great courage" and captured a field-piece; at Toulouse, that "needless battle," they suffered very severely. The last duty of the 2nd battalion of the 53rd was to garrison St. Helena, where the Emperor—officially known as 'General Buonaparte'—was placed that the world might have peace. Here they gained the respect and admiration of their mighty captive, and we cannot better bid farewell to this brave regiment—which was disbanded in 1817—than by quoting the words used by a Minister in his place in Parliament. "Whatsoever," averred Lord Bathurst, "the General could say in praise of that corps was not adequate to its merits."

For twenty-one years the 53rd (1st battalion) served at various home stations, and in 1844 returned again to India, there to win fresh honours. Plenty of fighting had they on the Sutlej. At Aliwal they were on the extreme left and carried the village of Boondree at the point of the bayonet, being referred to by Sir Harry Smith as 'a young regiment, but veterans in daring gallantry and regularity.' At Sobraon the 53rd were in Sir Robert Dick's Division under Brigadier Stacy. The attack made by the brigade in the teeth of a withering fire will long be remembered by the eulogists—and they are many—of British Infantry, and the official records of the regiment show how highly the General esteemed their share in the warfare. At Goojerat they were in reserve, and for the following years were engaged in the desultory fighting along the Peshawur frontier. During the mutiny they were, as beseemed men with such traditions, of invaluable service. After being for some short time at Fort William they were attached to Campbell's force which marched to relieve Lucknow. In the attack made by the enemy on the advance guard on the 12th of November, the 53rd were foremost in inflicting the repulse which resulted, and in the assault on the Secunderbagh the regiment, under Captain Walton, vied with the Sikhs and Highlanders in exacting a terrible recompense from the merciless, murderous foe. At Furruckbad they were attacked while crossing the river to support an advanced picket, and shared in inflicting the crushing defeat on the rebels. In the battle of Cawnpore, the siege of Lucknow, the subsequent operations in Oude, and the final crusade under Colonel Walker of the Bays, which completed the subjugation of the terror-stricken rebels, the 53rd were well to the fore. At the assault of Meangunge they especially distinguished themselves.

"The Light Company of the 53rd, under Captain Hopkins, were thrown forward in a plantation which approached the walls near enough to check the musketry fire from the fort, and some Punjaubees to the right of the guns in another plantation. About a couple of hours' pounding brought down a piece of the wall large enough to let four men abreast enter, when the 53rd were ordered up to be ready to assault, and the General spoke a few encouraging words to them. Soon Anson was sent to order the 53rd to the assault, the cannonade ceased and they immediately debouched from the plantation, headed by their gallant Colonel, and marched as steadily as if on parade towards the breach. In a second the leading files of the 53rd were up, Hopkins getting first to the breach, and turning to our left down a street, we were directly among the enemy, chopping and sticking as hard as we could. About this time poor Brockhurst of the 53rd was shot through the body."

The 53rd were, indeed, well to the fore. It would be a lengthy task to detail in full the many instances of valour which the regiment and individual members of it displayed, but in the annals of those who have won the Victoria Cross few accounts are more eloquent in their plain unadorned narration than the following:—

"At Chota Nagpore, on the 2nd October, 1857, the mutineers were, after a hard struggle, defeated, but not till they had killed or disabled one-third of our weak force. Two of the enemy's guns caused great havoc and affairs looked critical, when, with Sergeant Denis Dynon of the 53rd, Lieutenant Daunt rushed forward and, pistolling the artillerymen, drove them from their guns. Again on the 2nd November, at Nomeelah Behar, Daunt, with a few of Rattray's Sikhs, pursued a large body of mutineers of the 32nd Bengal Native Infantry into an enclosure, in driving them from which he was severely wounded. The Victoria Cross was awarded both to him and Dynon."

"The 53rd regiment at the capture of the Secunderbagh did not enter by the breach, but by a gate which was opened for them after the 93rd and Sikhs had got in. Nevertheless, in driving the Sepoys out of the numerous buildings in which they had taken refuge the 53rd had a good deal of fighting, for the enemy was only conquered by being absolutely exterminated. The regiment also distinguished itself on the 17th November. To it, therefore, were assigned four Victoria Crosses, the recipients to be selected by their comrades. The names of those thus decorated were Lieutenant Alfred Ffrench, Sergeant-Major Charles Pye, and Privates J. Kenny and C. Irwin. Lieutenant Ffrench, in command of the Grenadiers, was one of the first to enter the building. The whole company bore testimony to his conspicuous gallantry on this occasion. Sergeant-Major Pye was remarked for the steady and fearless manner in which he brought up ammunition under fire on the 17th November, and on every occasion on which his regiment had been engaged. Kenny obtained the Cross for conspicuous courage at the taking of the Secunderbagh, and for volunteering to bring up ammunition to his company under a very severe cross-fire. Irwin also displayed great bravery at the capture of the Secunderbagh and, though severely wounded, was one of the first men of his regiment who entered the building under a heavy fire." (*Victoria Cross in India.*)

The 53rd returned home in 1860, and from that time to the commencement of the Egyptian War of 1882 were quartered in the United Kingdom, Canada, and the Bermudas. In the disposition of the forces at Alexandria the 53rd were in the Second Division under General Hamley, and shared in the various operations which culminated in the capture of the lines of Kafr Dowar and the surrender of Damietta. It was by an escort of the 53rd under Major Rogerson that Abdellah, the Pasha who had vowed that he would never yield to the infidels, was conveyed to Cairo. At the conclusion of the war the 53rd remained for a time to garrison Cairo, and in the operations of 1885 added to their list of distinctions, under circumstances of too recent date to need enumeration here.

The 2nd battalion of the King's (Shropshire) Light Infantry, the 85th, dates from 1793, when it was raised, and known, from the place of recruiting, as the Bucks Volunteers. The first service of the regiment was in 1794, when the Bucks Volunteers were ordered to Walcheren and had their share of fighting; they were then for a time at Gibraltar, and after again visiting Holland, where they very greatly distinguished themselves, returned home. After being employed in Madeira and Jamaica they again served at Walcheren in the discreditably planned expedition of 1809. They then repaired to the Peninsula, and fought with credit at Fuentes d'Onor, having been previously engaged in many of the less known combats and skirmishes which so frequently took place. On the occasion of the first storming of the Fort Christoval at Badajoz, the stormers were led by Major McIntosh of the 85th; the effort was fruitless, but if valour alone could have won that terrible breach, of a surety it would have been won that night. They fought at the Nive and at Barrouilhet, and then proceeded to America. Perhaps seldom have troops fought under greater disadvantages than those which here confronted the 85th and their comrades. "These troops, badly provisioned, slenderly supplied even with ammunition, and, after their hardships in the Peninsula, many of them requiring repose and attendance in hospital, rather than exposure in battle," numbered perhaps four thousand; " except those belonging to General Ross and the staff officers, there was not a single horse with our troops;" and the three "toy guns" which constituted our artillery were drawn by seamen. During the march towards Bladensburg, many fell out of the ranks, faint and utterly exhausted; nine thousand Americans with twenty guns occupied a position of great strength and commanding altitude; yet in a few minutes this force—double ours in numerical strength, and composed of fresh, unwearied men, fighting in their own country and protected by the fire of their own well-placed guns—fled before the impetuous charge of the British, headed by " the gallant 85th under Colonel Thornton." They fought at Baltimore, the following September, with similar gallantry though with heavy loss, and at New Orleans again acquitted themselves in such wise that the records of that unfortunate expedition mention again and again the brave deeds of "Colonel Thornton and the gallant 85th."* For many years after this, only peaceful duties engaged their services. They served in England, Ireland, Canada, the Mauritius and other places till 1856, when they were ordered to South Africa, where the growing power of Panda, father of Cetewayo, compelled the Imperial Government to observe a watchful attitude. In 1868 the 85th were ordered to India, and eleven years later took part in the operations of the Cabul Field Force, their services in which are evidenced by the distinction, "Afghanistan, 1879—80."

THE PRINCE ALBERT'S (SOMERSETSHIRE LIGHT INFANTRY),†—Regimental District No. 13—consisting of the famous old 13th Foot, date from 1685, when the threatened invasion by Monmouth induced the King to increase the strength of the army. At the time of the Revolution the sympathies of the regiment were divided, their Colonel, Lord Huntingdon, remaining loyal to King James, while others of the officers advocated the cause of the Prince of Orange. When the country had settled down under the new régime the 13th were employed in Scotland, taking part in the operations against Edinburgh and in the battle of Killiecrankie. On the latter occasion, under Colonel Hastings, they shared with the 25th the praise of being the only regiments that did not behave badly,‡ the commander stating that in the thick of the fight he saw "Hastings on the right sustaining the reputation of the British lion."§ They fought at the Boyne and other Irish battles, and in 1701 commenced the career of foreign service in which they have won so great a renown. They fought at Mineguen and assisted at the sieges of Venloo, St. Michaels, Ruremonde, Liege, and others. In 1704 Barrymore's Regiment, as the 13th were then called, were sent to Gibraltar to assist the Prince of Hesse Darmstadt who was defending Gibraltar, and during the siege Major Moncall of the regiment rendered most important service. A selected party of French Grenadiers forced their way some distance into the defences when Major Moncall led his men to the charge and

---

* It was a few months previous to this that they received their motto of the Duke of York's Own Regiment of Light Infantry. This was subsequently changed to the King's Light Infantry Regiment, a title which obtained till the most recent change gave to the amalgamated corps the name they now bear.

† The Prince Albert's Somersetshire Light Infantry bear as badges a mural crown with "Jellalabad" over it, underneath it a bugle with the cypher of the late Prince Consort on cap and collar. The motto is that of the Garter. On the colours are: "The Sphinx," "Dettingen," "Egypt," "Martinique," "Ava," "Afghanistan," "Ghuznee," "Jellalabad," "Cabool," "Sevastopol," "South Africa, 1878—9." The uniform is scarlet with blue facings; on the gold lace of the officers' tunic is a black stripe.

‡ See ante, page 286.

§ This brave officer, it is sad to relate, was subsequently cashiered for irregularity connected with the supplies which it was then the duty of colonels of regiments to provide.

drove the bold assailants off. The 13th then served at the siege of Barcelona and the relief of St. Matheo. Shortly after the bulk of the regiment were, at the instance of Lord Peterborough, converted bodily into dragoons. The nucleus returned home to recruit, and the following year returned again to Portugal, when they fought most gallantly at Caya. In 1727 they took part in the defence of Gibraltar, after which they remained comparatively inactive till 1743, when they fought at Dettingen, the first name they bear on their colours. They suffered heavy loss at Fontenoy, after which they returned home and took part in the engagements with the adherents of Prince Charles Edward. In 1746 they went abroad, and at Roucoux and Val were distinguished for their "heroic conduct." Passing over the intervening years, during which they were not engaged in any war of importance, in 1790 we find the 1st Somersetshire Regiment—to use the title given in 1782—ordered to the West Indies, where, notably at Fort Bizzeton, in St. Domingo, they very greatly distinguished themselves. They returned home "a regimental wreck" in 1796, and after taking part in the suppression of the Irish rebellion went, in 1800, to Egypt. Here they were brigaded under General Cradock, their own Colonel being Colonel Colville, and at the battle and blockade of Alexandria earned high praise. Their next fighting of importance was at Martinique, where, as well as at Guadeloupe under General Skinner, they again distinguished themselves. The 13th were not engaged in any of the Peninsular battles, but in 1813 were ordered to Canada, where they had their full share in what fighting was to be had. After a few years at home they were ordered, in 1823, to India, and the following year played a glorious part in the Burmese War. Most interesting would it be to follow at length the brave deeds which are commemorated by "Ava," but a very brief recapitulation of them must perforce serve our purpose. In the capture of Rangoon Major Sale of the regiment killed the Burmese commander in single combat, and took his gold-hilted sword and scabbard. When fear lent prudence to the councils of the "Lord of the White Elephant" the European captives were released, but "Major Sale, of the 13th Light Infantry—the future hero of Jellalabad—found Mrs. Hudson, of missionary celebrity, bound to a tree and immediately released her."

Throughout the campaign Major—soon afterwards Colonel—Sale was with his brave 13th, foremost wherever fighting was, and almost invariably the same dispatch that recorded his courage added the ominous words, "severely wounded." At Mellone the 13th, with the 38th, formed the storming party. "By these two British regiments, weakened in numbers by war and pestilence to nearly half their proper strength, fifteen thousand well-armed men were hunted, in one confused mass, from the strongest works they had ever constructed." So fierce and irresistible was the assault that the total casualties of the storming column were only five killed and twenty wounded. Returning to India, the 13th had a period of repose for twelve years or so, after which their prowess found another opportunity for assertion in the Afghan War of 1839. Well, indeed, may the regiment glory in the recollection of Jellalabad, and, like their ancestors of Agincourt,

"Stand a-tiptoe when that day is named."

At Ghuznee they captured two standards. There were a few of the 13th amongst the unfortunate captives from Cabul; Lady Sale, the wife of their gallant Colonel, was wounded by a musket-ball, and sent back—happily for her—as a hostage; it was Colonel Dennie* of the 13th who, when rumours of trouble first came from Cabul, foretold with such terribly literal accuracy the ghastly catastrophe that came to pass:— "You will see that not a soul will escape from Cabul *but one man, and he will come to tell us that the rest are all destroyed.*" Meanwhile, at Jellalabad, the gallant Sale and the 13th were stemming the fierce torrent of murder and conquest, and when the time came for the Army of Vengeance to start on its righteously stern mission, the command of one of the divisions was given to him. At Jugdulluck, the 13th, with whom were the 9th, "scaled the heights, turned the position, and bayoneted the defenders with dreadful slaughter, neither side asking quarter nor hoping for it." At Tizeen, that decisive battle that occupied only a few minutes, and where the might of the British power was indelibly written in grim and blood-red letters, the 13th operated in extended order on the right, and when the central gorge was passed, "closed in by companies, fixing their bayonets as they came cheering down to the charge." When the rescued captives were brought in under an escort led by Sir Robert Sale in person, it is difficult to read without emotion how " the gallant 13th Light Infantry crowded with loud cheers round the wife and widowed daughter" of their beloved chief. On their return to India, the brave regiment that had fought so splendidly were received everywhere with praise and applause; garrisons presented arms to them as they passed; public and private bodies vied in doing them honour; and they received from their Sovereign the title of her Consort's regiment, the right to wear the Royal facings, and the special badge of the "Mural Crown."

Many were the officers of the 13th who distinguished themselves in that Afghan

* Colonel Dennie was killed in the famous and brilliant sortie from Jellalabad.

War,* and amongst them was one whose name a few years later was on the lips and in the hearts of all his countrymen—Sir Henry Havelock.

The 13th returned to England in 1845, and for a few years enjoyed well-earned repose. In the Crimean War they were attached to the Fourth Division, but did not take part in any of the three famous battles whose names appear on the colours of other regiments; they bear, however, the comprehensive distinction of "Sevastopol." In October, 1857, they arrived in India, where they shared in the relief of Azimghur, and "subsequently saw some service in the Jugdespore jungle, and in the Trans-Gogra districts during the years 1858—9." After a sojourn at home and in Gibraltar, the Prince Albert's Light Infantry were ordered to the Cape, and were in the third column of Lord Chelmsford's army, under Sir Evelyn Wood—subsequently the Flying Column—their own chief being Colonel Victor Gilbert. At the battle of Kambula, on the 29th of March, 1879, they experienced some severe fighting, and greatly distinguished themselves, they and the 90th "vying with each other in noble rivalry, and beating back the hordes of Zulus upon the two most exposed flanks." They fought gallantly at Ulundi, where they unfortunately lost Lieutenant Pardoe, who was mortally wounded, and in July received orders to return to England, their departure effecting the disintegration of the famous Flying Column which had done such great things.† Since the Zulu War, the only active service in which the Somersetshire have been engaged has been with the Burmah expeditionary force, the details of which are of too recent date to come within the scope of this work.‡

THE PRINCE OF WALES'S (NORTH STAFFORDSHIRE REGIMENT§)—Regimental District No. 64—is composed of the 64th and 98th Foot. In 1758 the 2nd battalion of the 11th Foot was constituted the 64th Regiment, and the newly formed corps were speedily under orders for the West Indies, where they were engaged at Martinique. Returning home in 1763, they went to America in 1770, and served there till 1782, during which period occurred the revolt of the colonies against British rule. After a short time at

---

* The gallant Sir R. Sale was killed at Moodkhee, where, by a strange coincidence, also fell Sir John M'Caskill, who commanded the other division of Pollock's Army of Vengeance.

† Amongst the Victoria Crosses gained in the Zulu War was one awarded to Captain Knox, late of the 13th, serving with a body of Irregulars, for gallantly rescuing Lieutenant Smith at Inhlobane.

‡ The 2nd battalion of the Thirteenth dates from 1858.

§ The Prince of Wales's North Staffordshire Regiment bear as badges the Prince of Wales's Plume with Staffordshire Knot on cap, and Staffordshire Knot on collar. The motto is that of the Prince of Wales. On the Colours are the Dragon and "St. Lucia," "Surinam," "China," "Punjaub," "Persia," "Reshire," "Bushire," "Koosh-ab," "Lucknow." The uniform is scarlet with facings of white.

VOL. II.

home, they went in 1793 to Barbadoes and again took part in the operations directed against Martinique and Guadaloupe, subsequently gaining the distinction of "St. Lucia" on their colours. They were engaged a few years later under Brigadier Hughes at Surinam. Duties elsewhere prevented their taking part in any of the Peninsular battles, but they were for some time in the army of occupation in France, from which time till 1856 only peace duties occupied their services. In the latter year, however, the Persian War broke out, and brought to the 64th an opportunity of showing they were no whit behind regiments which had been more actively employed. "Bushire," "Reshire," "Koosh-ab,"—all speak to the courage and endurance of the 64th, in the operations in which they were engaged. A yet more serious warfare awaited them in India; the moment they landed they marched under Havelock to Cawnpore, and had some sharp fighting at Futtehpore. At the capture of Cawnpore, the conduct of the 64th under Major Stirling provoked the greatest praise. After capturing four villages and seven guns, our wearied troops were checked by a 24-pounder which the rebels had placed in position on the road. The 64th were ordered to take it, and, despite the heavy loss they had incurred, they charged up to the grinning muzzle, captured it, and dispersed the rebels. In the General Order issued by Havelock, he addressed the 64th in the following words: "Your fire was reserved till you saw the colour of your enemies' moustaches—this gave us the victory."

It is impossible to avoid mentioning in connection with this incident the somewhat aggrieved feelings that were naturally aroused amongst the officers and men of the 64th by the fact of Lieutenant Havelock—now Sir H. Havelock Allen—heading them at the final charge, and being, therefore, recommended by his father for the Victoria Cross. No one who remembers the General's previous reticence as to his son's valour will accuse him of paternal bias. No one who recalls the previous and subsequent career of Lieutenant Havelock will deny that he was brave amongst the brave. But it is not difficult to understand that the 64th were hurt at even an apparent suggestion that their own officers were not competent to lead them, no matter how desperate the venture. Perhaps the most dispassionate account of the incident is that contained in the work, "The Victoria Cross in India," from which we have before quoted.

"At the final action previous to the entry into Cawnpore, affairs at one time looked rather bad. The British guns, owing to the fatigue of their cattle, could not come up quickly enough to reply to a 24-pounder placed on the road, which was doing great execution. This gun was guarded by a large body of rebel infantry. Havelock ordered his exhausted infantry to make a last effort. They responded to the appeal, and advanced. The 64th regiment was more immediately opposite to the gun than the other regiments. Major Stirling commanding the 64th had lost his horse, but was gallantly leading his men on foot. No other mounted officer was present. Perhaps observing this fact, perhaps only obeying the dictates of his own courage, Lieutenant Havelock placed himself in front of the regiment, and steered steadily for the 24-pounder, which fired round-shot up to 300 yards, and grape afterwards, with great precision and rapidity. Coolly the 64th drew nearer, losing men at every step, and equally coolly did Lieutenant Havelock ride at a foot's pace straight for the muzzle of the gun. At length, with a rush, the latter was captured; the enemy then fled, and the day was won."

They remained under General Wyndham to garrison Cawnpore, and in the attack made by the rebels on the 28th of November were greatly distinguished. Encouraged by a temporary success they had obtained, the rebels fought with redoubled vigour, hoping, doubtless, to revel in another massacre. The 64th frustrated the fiendish hope. "Captain Wright, with only thirty men of the 64th, held the Baptist chapel and the old burial ground. Finding that the enemy were surrounding him he drew off his men in skirmishing order and stopped the advance of the Sepoys by a fire of musketry. About this time he saw a wing of his own corps, about two hundred and fifty strong, commanded by Colonel Wilson, marching by order of General Wyndham to capture four guns that were playing with fatal precision on the British left. Rallying his small force, Wright instantly led it as a sort of advanced guard to Wilson, on whose men the enemy now turned, their guns doing terrible execution. The brave 64th never wavered, but with a ringing shout rushed on the cannon, spiking three of them before the gunners had recovered from their surprise; but it was alike impossible to retain or carry them off, for the foe were ten to one. Colonel Wilson and Major Stirling were shot, Captains Murphy and M'Crea were cut down at the guns, while Captain M'Kinnon and Lieutenant Gordon were severely wounded, taken prisoners, and murdered in cold blood. The slaughter was great among the 64th." During this episode, Drummer Thomas Flinn, of the 64th Regiment, was wounded; but, nevertheless, he persisted in remaining with his comrades, and engaged in a hand-to-hand encounter with two of the rebel artillerymen. Later on the regiment was engaged against Tantia Topee and in Rohilcund, and throughout the mutiny gained deservedly the reputation of being a gallant and dashing regiment. Since then no warlike duties of importance have fallen to their lot.

The 98th, the 2nd battalion of the North Staffordshire, dates from 1824, and is, according to Colonel Archer, the sixth regiment which has borne that number. Their first duty was in South Africa, where they served for several years, after which they fought in the China War of 1840—41, their officer being Colonel Campbell. In 1846 they repaired to India and bear the distinction "Punjaub" in commemoration of the services they rendered during that anxious time. In 1850 they took part in the campaign against the fierce Afridis, and in the fighting in the Kohat Pass rendered signal and meritorious service. Returning home in 1855, a couple of years later saw them again in India, sharing in the operations under General Cotton against the Ensufzies. For many years the 98th remained in India, finding from time to time plenty of occupation in the occasionally irksome duties devolving upon the army in "our Great Dependency;" and after a stay in England, whither they returned in 1867, the Afghan troubles of 1879—80 caused them again to seek "the tented field," though their participation in the operations was limited to the steps taken after the taking of Candahar. No subsequent warfare has fallen to their lot, but amongst the minor military services which from time to time occupy our forces; the Zhob Valley Expedition of 1884 broke for the 98th the spell of inaction.

THE SOUTH STAFFORDSHIRE REGIMENT*—Regimental District No. 38—is composed of the 38th and 80th Regiments of the line. The 38th Regiment dates from 1702, when it was raised in Ireland, and for many years known as Colonel Luke Lillingstone's Regiment of Foot. Five years after its formation the regiment went to the West Indies and served there "an unprecedented period of, it is said, nearly sixty years, during which detachments of the corps served at the capture of Guadaloupe in 1759, and of Martinique in 1762." (*Archer.*) On their return home the 38th—as they were numbered in 1751—served in the American War, after which the flank companies were employed at Martinique in 1794, and subsequently at St. Lucia. The regiment as a whole, after taking part in the campaign in Holland, served under Sir D. Baird at the Cape of Good Hope in 1805, and the following year at Buenos Ayres. At Monte Video in 1807, under Colonel Vassal, they formed part of the assaulting party, and greatly distinguished

* The South Stafford Regiment bear as badges the Sphinx and "Egypt" over the Staffordshire Knot on the cap, and the Staffordshire Knot on the collar. On the waist-plate is borne Windsor Castle between these two badges. The Motto is that of the Garter. On the colours are "Egypt," "Monte Video," "Roleia," "Vimiera," "Corunna," "Busaco," "Badajoz," "Salamanca," "Vittoria," "St. Sebastian," "Nive," "Peninsula," "Ava," "Moodkee," "Ferozeshah," "Sobraon," "Pegu," "Alma," "Inkerman," "Sevastopol," "Lucknow," "Central India," "South Africa, 1878—79," "Egypt, 1882," "Nile, 1884—85," "Kirbekan."

themselves, Colonel Vassal being mortally wounded. The 38th then took part in the Peninsular War, fighting at Roleia and Vimiera, sharing in Moore's splendid victory at Corunna, and gaining for their colours the eloquent legend of "Busaco." At Badajoz, when a temporary discomfiture caused Walker's brigade to fall back, the pursuing French found themselves checked by "two hundred men of the 38th, who had been kept well in hand by Colonel Nugent," and who, after a fierce volley, charged with the bayonet. They fought at Salamanca and Burgos under Graham, they conquered at Vittoria, they shared in the ghastly victory at San Sebastian, forced the passage of the Bidassoa, and fought in the conquering ranks at the Nive. They were not at Waterloo, but joined the army of occupation after it was won. In 1818 they served in South America, and in 1822 repaired to India and were engaged in the first Burmese War, gaining the distinction of "Ava" for their colours. Returning to England in 1836, the following fifteen years were spent in various places, including Central America. In the Crimea the 38th were in Sir Richard England's (Third) Division, and—for we must needs leave much untold—bear "Alma," "Inkerman," and "Sevastopol" on their heavily emblazoned colours. From the Crimea they were ordered to India, where they arrived in November, 1857, and after fighting valiantly at Lucknow, took part in the subsequent campaign in Oude. They returned to England in 1872, and enjoyed a peaceful interval between that date and 1882, when they were ordered to Egypt.

Few regiments can boast a better record than the South Staffordshire during the campaigns of 1882, and 1884—85. The 38th, with the 3rd battalion of the 60th, were the first regiments to land in Egypt after Sir Beauchamp Seymour's ultimatum, and on the 22nd of July took part in the first skirmish of the war in connection with the destruction of the Ramleh Isthmus. In the final arrangement of the forces they were in the 4th brigade (Second Division), and took part, under Colonel Thackwell, in the reconnaissance at Mahalla, where they had one man wounded.* During the whole of the operations they ably carried out their part in the various duties which devolved upon the Second Division, duties none the less important because they did not include the more familiarly known of the engagements. They formed part of the force under General Earle, and at Kirbekan they highly distinguished themselves. Early in the day fell their gallant Colonel Eyre,† leading his men against a ridge held by an overwhelming force of fierce fanatics; "the Arabs fought

---

* He was shot through the cheek, "but went on fighting as if untouched."
† Colonel Eyre had been promoted from the ranks in recognition of his valour in the Crimea.

at bay with the courage of desperation, having the vantage-ground everywhere. And thus, against desperate odds our gallant soldiers, in spite of a withering fire all round, gained rock after rock, fastness after fastness, behind which the well-directed aim of the Arabs dealt death at every shot. Inch by inch, with fearful odds against them, do the Highlanders on the left and the South Staffordshire men on the right press forward and gain ground." After General Earle had fallen the 38th were ordered by General Brackenbury to storm "a steep and rocky hill four hundred feet high, held by a body of the Soudanese," a difficult task which they brilliantly accomplished after incredible toil and severe fighting. And so, with the freshly added lustre shed by the latest Egyptian War, ends the record of the services of the brave South Staffordshire.

The 2nd battalion of the South Staffordshire, the 80th Regiment, dates from 1793, when it was raised by Lord Paget. The following year, the Staffordshire Volunteers, as the regiment was then called, joined the Duke of York's army in Flanders, and during their sojourn there lost more than half their number. A few years later they formed part of Baird's army, which, with a view to joining Abercrombie, made the march across the desert which has been before referred to, and by this participation in the campaign gained the Sphinx and "Egypt" for their colours. After this they were for several years in India, gaining warriors' craft in the many battles by which the British rule was consolidated, and thus missed participation in any of the Peninsular battles, as they did not return to England before 1818. After a stay here of some sixteen years or so, they were ordered to Australia, and during the years 1836—1844, were more or less busily employed in the not very congenial task of suppressing convict riots. Their next station was in India, during their voyage to which occurred a most extraordinary incident. "Part of the corps," says Colonel Archer, "during the voyage was shipwrecked under very remarkable circumstances, being cast high and dry by a stormwave in the dead of night on the top of a wood or jungle in the Little Andamans." Arrived in India, they were fortunate enough to participate in some of the most important events which the stirring history of British arms in India has to chronicle. They fought at Moodkee, where night alone saved the foe from total destruction. At Ferozeshah they earned a reputation for courage and discipline of which any regiment might be proud.

"About twelve o'clock at night, the Sikhs finding that Sir Harry Smith had been forced to retire from the village, and that their batteries were not occupied, brought some guns to bear upon our column, the fire from which was very destructive. The Governor-

General mounted his horse and called to the 80th Regiment, which was at the head of the column, 'My lads, we shall have no sleep until we have those guns.' The regiment deployed immediately, advanced, supported by the 1st Bengal Europeans, and drove a large body of Sikhs from three guns, which they spiked. The regiment then retired, and took up its position again at the head of the column as steadily as if on a parade, much to the admiration of the Governor-General and Commander-in-Chief, the former of whom exclaimed, as they passed him, 'Plucky dogs! plucky dogs! we cannot fail to win with such men as these.'"

To the brilliant victory of Sobraon they contributed not a little, and it was at the head of the 80th that the gallant Sir Robert Dick received his death wound. They bore a brilliant part in the second Burmese War in 1852. In the attack on the Grand Pagoda four companies of the 80th under Major Montgomery formed the advance, driving the enemy steadily before them, while in the attack on the eastern entrance the assaulting force comprised a wing of the 80th under Major Lockhart. In the attack on Pegu, the one company of the 80th that were present were commanded by Captain Ormsby, and ably performed their part in the singularly easy and bloodless victory achieved by our troops. After the war in Burmah, the next fighting in which the 80th shared was in India, where they gained "Central India" as a distinction. Those familiar with the military history of that time know how much severe and splendid fighting those words commemorate. They assisted at the capture of Calpee, shared in the arduous task of the pacification of Oude, and a few years later took part in the Bhotan Expedition,* which was found so much more difficult than had at first been anticipated. The regiment returned home in 1866, and were represented nine years later in the expedition to Perak. The next important war in which they were engaged was that in South Africa of 1878—79. They were in garrison at Luneburg under Major Charles Tucker, and in March, 1879, a company under Captain Moriarty was ordered to meet some supplies which were being forwarded. Owing to some delay the Intombe River which had to be crossed grew swollen with the rains, and some question seems to have been raised as to the judgment with which the encampment was laid. However that may be, in the early morning of the 12th some four thousand Zulus, led by the Chief Umbelini, swept down upon the little band of seventy-one. Across the river, Lieutenant Harward had been posted with some thirty men; in a few moments all that remained of the entire company scarcely numbered more. Captain Moriarty was killed the moment he left

* Three companies only were engaged at the commencement of the campaign.

his tent; in some cases his men were assegaied before they could leave theirs. Lieutenant Harward's party opened a brisk fire on the Zulus, but naturally it could have no effect on such a mass, and at least two hundred of them crossed the river. Lieutenant Harward ordered his men to fall back upon a farmhouse, and then he did a thing which, fortunately, is without a parallel in military history—rode off himself to obtain succour from Luneburg! Probably the severest critics of this infatuated action would acquit Lieutenant Harward of anything approaching cowardice, but the error was none the less a terrible one. Fortunately, dark though the hour was, with it came the Man.

"Sergeant Booth, the senior non-commissioned officer present, now assumed command, rallied the small group of men, and endeavoured to cover the retreat of the few soldiers upon the opposite bank, who were trying to escape across the river towards him. The little band, to avoid being assegaied at close quarters, were compelled to fall back. This small knot of gallant men fought the Zulus for three miles in retreat, but Sergeant Booth and his men showed a bold front on every side. They kept close together, firing volleys at their pursuers as they prepared to rush upon them. The party gallantly checked the Zulus, and finally completed its retirement without losing a man. Sergeant Booth's heroic conduct enabled several fugitives who had safely crossed the river without arms or even clothes to escape and reach Luneberg."

The *Gazette* informed his countrymen "that had it not been for the coolness displayed by this non-commissioned officer, not one man would have escaped."

The observations made by Lord Chelmsford in commenting on the decision of the Court Martial held on Lieutenant Harward included some remarks which deserve a place in any record of British regiments. After referring to the "monstrous theory that a regimental officer, who is the only officer present with a party of soldiers actually and seriously engaged with the enemy, can, under any pretext whatever, be justified in deserting them," his Lordship went on to say:—"The more helpless the position in which an officer finds his men, the more it is his bounden duty to stay and share their fortune, whether for good or ill. It is because the British officer has always done so, that he occupies the position in which he is held in the estimation of the world, and that he possesses the influence he does in the ranks of our army. The soldier has learned to feel that come what may, he can in the direst moment of danger look with implicit faith to his officer, knowing that he will never desert him under any possible circumstances. It is to this faith of the British soldier in his officer that we owe most of the gallant deeds recorded in our annals."

On another and previous occasion had a V.C. been gained in this savage African warfare, by a man of the 80th. "On the 22nd January, 1879, when the camp at Isandhlwana was taken by the enemy, Private Wassall, 80th Foot, retreated towards the Buffalo River, in which he saw a comrade, Private Westwood of the same regiment, struggling and apparently drowning. He rode to the bank, dismounted, leaving his horse on the Zulu side, rescued the man from the stream, and again mounted his horse, dragging Private Westwood across the river under a heavy shower of bullets."

Some five companies of the 80th were at Ulundi, where they led the advance, and subsequently the regiment was represented in Colonel Clarke's column. In the operations against Sekukuni, Major Creagh did valuable service, and in the final attack upon the chief's stronghold, the 80th were in the centre column. The regiment returned home in 1880, and have not since then been engaged in any important warfare.*

THE SUFFOLK REGIMENT †—Regimental District No. 12—is composed of the two battalions of the old 12th Foot. In 1661, Windsor Castle was garrisoned by several independent companies, from which was formed the 12th Regiment, which, however, did not receive the numerical distinction till twenty-four years later. It was with the 12th Regiment that James II. made the experiment which was to give him such unwelcome proof of the unwillingness of the army as a whole to assist in his contemplated return to subservience to Rome. Advancing to their head he called upon all who would not support the proposed repeal of the Test clauses to lay down their arms. With a very few exceptions the whole regiment complied with most disconcerting alacrity. James paused for a few minutes and then bid the soldiers take them up again, moodily observing he would not do them the honour of consulting them again. The Colonel of the 12th—Lord Lichfield—remained, however, loyal to his misguided sovereign.

Till after the Revolution no particularly important service seems to have fallen to the lot of the 12th; in 1689 Wharton's Regiment, as they were then generally called, followed the veteran Schomberg to Ireland, where, the following year, they fought in the battle of the Boyne. After this they were employed on the coast of France and in

---

* It is to the 80th that the South Staffordshire owe the badge of Windsor Castle, which was granted by William IV.

† The Suffolk Regiment bear as badges the Castle and Key in a laurel wreath with a Crown above and "Gibraltar" below on cap and collar. The motto is " Montis Insignia Calpe "—"The badges of Mount Calpe" (Gibraltar). On the colours are "Dettingen," " Minden," " Gibraltar," " Seringapatam," " India," "South Africa, 1851—53," " New Zealand," " Afghanistan, 1878—79." The uniform is scarlet with facings of white.

Flanders, being amongst the regiments which the cowardice of the Dutch governor compelled to surrender at Dixmude. Colonel Brewer of the 12th vehemently protested against this shameful action, counselling that the fortress should be defended to the last extremity; he was, however, overruled, but his protest secured his immunity from the disgrace and punishment awarded to the other officers who supported the governor's views. Their next service was in the West Indies, on returning from whence they were employed in the dyke-cutting operations about Ostend, and in Minorca. They were then ordered to Scotland, where they formed part of General Wade's expedition, and, twenty years or so later, gained their first distinction at Dettingen. Splendid was their courage at Fontenoy, while they were in Ingoldsby's Brigade, where their loss was more than that of any other regiment.* Three hundred and seventy-one officers and men fell, yet when their colonel and half their number were *hors de combat*, the splendid English regiment fought on, refusing to believe till the last that the army to which they belonged was beaten. The 12th subsequently repaired to Germany, where they took part in the Seven Years' War, being one of the six British Infantry Regiments who bear Minden† on their colours, and of whose bearing at that battle it was written—"Such was the unshaken firmness of these troops that nothing could stop them, and the whole body of French cavalry was routed."‡ They fought at Kirch Denkern, Grobenstein, Lutterberg, Homburg and Cassel, after which their next important service was that from which is derived the badge of the "Castle and Key," the ever-memorable defence of Gibraltar. Though the adage that "the world knows nothing of its greatest men" holds true, *mutatis mutandis*, with regard to achievements, yet the story of this defence of Gibraltar, the endurance, the heroism, the indomitable British pluck it called forth, is, we are glad to think, familiar to all. Under Colonel Trigge the regiment, numbering 29 officers and 570 rank and file, rendered sterling service, notably in the famous sortie, and thanks to them and their brave comrades the mountain Tarif§ still remains a mighty witness to the power of Britain. During the siege the total loss of the regiment was a hundred and seventy-four of all ranks. It is noted as a coincidence that on the occasion of the sortie of the night of the 26th of November, 1761, the only two complete regiments were the 12th and Hardenberg's, which had fought side by side at Minden. Lieutenant Tweedie of

* Of the line; the Scots Guards are said to have lost 437 of all ranks, killed and wounded.
† At Minden the 12th were commanded by Lieutenant-Colonel Robinson.
‡ About this time the 2nd battalion of the 12th was formed into the 65th regiment.
§ Such is the derivation of the word Gibraltar, Gib-el-Tarif, "Tarif" being a renowned Moorish chieftain.

the regiment was the only officer wounded in this enormously successful operation, which effected destruction to the value of £2,000,000 sterling. As indicative of the straits to which, in the earlier part of the siege, the garrison was reduced, the following extract from Major Drinkwater's history may be of interest:—

"Provisions of every kind were now becoming very scarce and exorbitantly dear: mutton, 3s. and 3s. 6d. per pound; veal, 4s.; pork, 2s. and 2s. 6d.; a pig's head, 19s.; ducks, from 14s. to 18s. a couple; and a goose a guinea. Fish was equally high, and vegetables were with difficulty to be got for any money; but bread, the great essential of life and health, was the article most wanted. It was about this period that the Governor made trial what quantity of rice would suffice a single person for twenty-four hours, and actually lived himself eight days on four ounces of rice per day."

After Gibraltar the 12th served for some time as Marines, while the flank companies were engaged at Martinique and Guadaloupe, where they were almost annihilated. They fought again in Flanders and shared in the disastrous retreat of Bremen, after which, in 1796, they proceeded to the Cape, and thence to India. Here they were the senior King's Regiment, and were required by General Order to be always ready to turn out, night or day. At Seringapatam, under Lieutenant-Colonel Shaw, they were the leading regiment in Baird's column, and on one occasion were ordered forward to occupy an important position midway between our camp and the fortress. Scarcely had they approached the required posts when the enemy sent off showers of rockets and blue lights which illuminated the surrounding country and showed the movements of our men with alarming distinctness. Twenty thousand of the enemy are said to have been showering these missiles, at one time "no hail could be thicker; with every blue light came a shower of bullets, and several rockets passed through the column from head to rear, causing death and dreadful lacerations. The cries of the wounded were awful." Yet still the 12th pressed on, firing not a shot, in obedience to the order of "brave old Colonel Shaw"—"All must be done with the bayonet." At last, when a fresh attack was commenced on his flank, the Colonel ordered his men to lie flat down, with the result that the enemy, supposing their withering fire had destroyed the column, "ventured forward to make sure with the bayonet, to be greeted with the words, 'Up 12th and charge,'" and to be driven back to their positions. At the final assault the 12th formed part of the storming party, and by their adroit rear attack on Tippoo's desperate band undoubtedly saved much loss to our force. In the attempted sortie made by the fierce tyrant, a volley from the light company of the 12th gave him his

P 2

mortal wound. "Covered with blood and dying now, the fallen Sultan was raised by a faithful few and placed in his palanquin, where he lay faint and exhausted, till some of the 12th, climbing over the dead and dying, reached him. A servant who survived the carnage related that one of the soldiers seized Tippoo's sword-belt, which was exceedingly rich, and attempted to drag it off, and that the Sultan, who still grasped his sword, made a last cut with it, wounding in the knee the soldier, who shot him through the temple and killed him on the spot."

The career of the regiment after the fall of Seringapatam may be shortly epitomised by stating that they were actively employed in "Wynaad, in the Carnatic, against the Polygars, in Cochin and Travancore—services commemorated by the word 'India' on their colours." The mention of these places recalls the prowess displayed by the 12th at Quilon in 1808, under circumstances which read like a romance. When the hostile attitude of the Rajah of Travancore threatened Quilon, the 12th, who were stationed at Cannamore in Malabar, were ordered to the support of the garrison, and under Colonel Picton, brother of the Peninsular hero, they embarked. On the way more than half of the regiment were belated, and on arriving off Quilon with the rest, Colonel Picton was received with the intelligence that the whole country was in arms, and that to land would be to court absolute annihilation. "In defiance of this the 12th landed in small boats that would only convey three or four men at a time," and proceeded to make good their position. The next morning—utterly regardless that they numbered units as against the hundreds of the enemy—the gallant Suffolk proceeded to storm the palace of the Rajah's prime minister, after accomplishing which they returned to their camp. This, however, they were compelled to evacuate, as a force of some forty thousand of the enemy, led by European officers, were advancing against them, and they accordingly took possession of an old fort. By this time the 12th were reduced to two hundred and fifty men; there were about twelve hundred Sepoys and some ten thousand followers; and to add to their discomfort a terrible tropical storm came on directly they got into the dismantled fort, "rusting the fire-arms, and rendering much of the ammunition unfit for service." Despite this it was determined to regain the camp at the bayonet's point, and at that critical juncture the missing six companies were hailed approaching with some native troops they had picked up *en route*. They brought with them tidings which stimulated to fever point the already furious rage of the 12th against the barbarous foe. Some thirty men of the regiment under Sergeant-Major Tilsby had been in a small vessel and so escaped the hurricane which had delayed the others. They had landed near Alepe, and mistaking it for Quilon had marched in. They were beguiled with falsehoods, induced to pile their arms in what they were told was the English barracks, and invited to drink and fraternise with their foes. The arrack was drugged: "They soon became intoxicated and stupefied, and while in this state were easily secured by the Travancorians, one of whom, with a heavy iron bar, broke the two wrists of each soldier, smashing the bones hopelessly to atoms; then, tightly tying their hands behind them, and binding their knees and necks together, they precipitated them into a loathsome dungeon." They were left like this four days and nights, without food or drink, the savages around them derisively mimicking their groans; then they were taken out, and dragged to a deep pool, into which—with heavy stones tied to the neck of each—they were flung in to drown "amid shouts, laughter, and the clapping of hands." No wonder that when the day of battle came the avenging fury of the 12th was irresistible. They carried a strong battery of guns, and hurled aside a force of at least ten thousand of the enemy who strove to retake them. "The 12th were inspired by a degree of fury beyond description, and never ceased to shout 'Remember Alepe! Remember Alepe!' One thrust his bayonet with such force into his adversary's body as to fix it in the back-bone so firmly that he had perforce to leave it. "Lieutenant Thomson of the 12th charged five thousand of the enemy, with only fifty men, three times, and fell to rise no more, covered with wounds."

The 12th served in the Mauritius, and the years that elapsed between the warfare signalised by "India" and 1851 were passed in various places, no fighting of any magnitude coming in their way. In 1851 they were ordered to South Africa to take part in the Kaffir War, in which they greatly distinguished themselves.* For some time they were employed in Australia, and took part in the Maori War in New Zealand.

Passing over the following few years we come to the Afghan Campaign of 1878—80, the last in which the gallant Suffolk have been engaged, and in which they acquitted themselves in such manner as to win the final distinction for their colours, and to give evidence of the fact that one of Her Majesty's oldest and most efficient regiments has deteriorated no whit from the heroes of Minden and Gibraltar.

* It was the 2nd battalion engaged in South Africa. Sixteen men of the regiment went down in the *Birkenhead*.

THE EAST SURREY REGIMENT*—Regimental District No. 31—is composed of the 31st and 70th Regiments. The 31st were originally Marines, and were formed into a regiment of foot in 1715. Their first important fighting was at Dettingen, where they gained the approbation of George II., and at the same time as a consequence the sobriquet of the Young Buffs, the king having mistaken them for the famous 3rd Regiment. Fierce fighting, too, did they have at Fontenoy, where, it is recorded, only eleven men of the grenadier company came out of action. Four years later they served at Minorca, then, after a short sojourn at home, in Florida, and the Carib War in St. Vincent, where they did good service. In 1776 they were quartered in Canada, some garrisoning Quebec, others participating in the misfortunes which attended General Burgoyne's army at Saratoga.† In 1794 the flank companies served at Martinique, Guadaloupe and St. Lucia, and returned home in 1797, "reduced to a mere company." Soon after a 2nd battalion was formed, which obtained, for the East Surrey the Peninsular distinctions on their colours.

They fought at Talavera; at Albuhera the 31st alone of the four splendid regiments that charged against the advancing column of the enemy "being formed in column, stood their ground," and escaped the disastrous onset of the French cavalry. Yet their loss was very heavy, and—as has been recorded in connection with the "Die-hards,"—"at the close of the action the dead and wounded men of our gallant 31st and 57th Regiments were found lying in two distinct lines on the very ground they occupied when fighting." In his account of the action, Lord Wellesley wrote: "This little battalion alone held its ground against all the *colonnes en masse.*" The story of "Vittoria" and "The Pyrenees," of "Nivelle" and the "Nive," has before been told, and the 31st bear these names on their colours. At St. Pierre they formed part of the right wing under General Byng, and the important part they played in that most brilliant victory may be gauged by the fact that when their gallant leader was elevated to the peerage as Earl of Strafford, the regimental colours of the regiment formed a portion of his coat-of-arms. They fought at Orthes, and bear that name as well as the "Peninsula" on their colours. Like many other 2nd battalions they were disbanded at the Peace, leaving a record

* The East Surrey Regiment bear as badges the arms of Guildford surrounded by the Garter surmounted by the Crown on a star of eight points on the cap, and the arms of Guildford on the collar. The motto is that of the Garter. On the colours is the Tudor Rose, and "Dettingen," "Guadaloupe," "Talavera," "Albuhera," "Vittoria," "Pyrenees," "Nivelle," "Nive," "Orthes," "Peninsula," "Cabool, 1842," "Moodkee," "Ferozeshah," "Aliwal," "Sobraon," "Sevastopol," "Taku Forts," "New Zealand," "Afghanistan, 1878—79," "Suakim, 1885." The uniform is scarlet with facings of white ; a black line is worn in the officers' gold lace.

† During this period they received the county name of "Huntingdonshire."

of services of which any corps might be proud. The 1st battalion meanwhile had been serving in Sicily, Egypt, Spain, Genoa, and various other places, all of them witnesses to the courage and discipline of the regiment, though the names of none of them are found amongst the distinctions. In 1824 they were ordered to India under Colonel Pearson and Major McGregor, and were on the ill-fated *Kent* East Indiaman when she foundered. As the official record expresses it: "In the midst of dangers against which it seemed hopeless to struggle—at a time when no aid appeared, and passively to die was all that remained—each man displayed the manly resignation, the ready obedience, and the unfailing discipline characteristic of a good soldier." Fortunately the great majority were saved, only seventy-six out of a total of nearly five hundred being lost. During their stay in India they took part in the Afghan and Sikh Wars, and were with Pollock's avenging army after the massacre of Cabul. They fought at Moodkee; at Ferozeshah fell Major Baldwin of the regiment; at Aliwal they were remarked as being "emulous for the front;" "Sobraon" gives the final gleam to the lustre of their Indian achievements. Then followed a period of comparative peace till, in May, 1855, they arrived in the Crimea. In this war they took part in the assaults on the Redan of the 18th of June and 8th of September, and bear "Sevastopol" in commemoration of their gallant conduct. After peace was declared they were dispatched to the Cape and in 1858 to Bombay, their next service of note being the China Campaign of 1860. Here they were in the First Division, and after the fall of the Taku Forts marched to Tientsin, detachments being subsequently stationed at Ho-see-woo and Yung-tsan to keep the road clear between that city and our camp. The regiment returned home in 1863, since which date they have not been engaged in any operations which call for notice.

The 70th—the 2nd battalion of the East Surrey Regiment—was formed in 1756 from the 2nd battalion of the 31st, so that the recent amalgamation has replaced it in its original position. Colonel Archer cites the fact that a few years after the incorporation of the regiment, "five companies were embarked on board a naval squadron as reinforcements for Madras, but nothing more is known of them." In 1764 the 70th were ordered to the West Indies, where they remained for some ten years, subsequently serving for four years in Canada, during which time they received the territorial designation of "The Surrey Regiment." To anticipate for a moment the order of events, we find that in 1812 they were officially styled the "Glasgow Lowland Regiment," but during a subsequent sojourn in Canada—namely in 1825—they received their original and present title again. In 1794 they took part in Sir Charles Grey's expedition in

Martinique, and during the operations connected therewith gained the distinction of "Guadaloupe." For many years following their sphere of duty lay mainly amongst our various colonies and possessions, chiefly in Canada. In 1848 the 70th were ordered to India, and during the Mutiny were engaged on the Peshawar frontier. In 1863 they were with Sir Duncan Cameron in New Zealand, and took part in the attack on the Gate Pah, the evacuation of which by the Maories was discovered by Major Greaves of the regiment, who, regardless of the possible fatal result to himself, made a reconnaissance of the position. Returning to England in 1866, they remained in this country for some five years, in 1871 being again ordered to India. In the Afghan campaign of 1878—79 the 70th were in the Candahar column, and afterwards served with the Thull Field Force. Their last active service was in the Egyptian campaign of 1884, during which they acquitted themselves with great credit, under General Graham, in the fighting which took place round Suakin, Hasheen, and Tamai.

It is a very famous Regiment that next calls for notice, being none other than the QUEEN's (ROYAL WEST SURREY REGIMENT)*—Regimental District No. 2.

One of the oldest, as it is one of the most famous of Her Majesty's regiments, its proud title, *The Queen's*, recalls the epoch of the Merry Monarch, when Tangiers became the property of the crown of England, as the marriage portion of Catherine of Portugal. So valuable a possession necessitated an efficient garrison, and accordingly, in 1661, Lord Peterborough's regiment was raised for the purpose, and the following year received the title of "The Queen's," with the badge of the Paschal Lamb, one of the armorial bearings of Portugal, and started for our new African possession. Here the Queen's was recruited from the garrison of Dunkirk, composed of veterans who had fought for the King during the late rebellion, and the First Tangier Regiment, to use the alternative title, became in a military sense a *corps d'élite*. They soon had opportunity to prove their metal. A body of twenty-four thousand Moors, notwithstanding a treaty of alliance, made, in June, 1663, an attempt to surprise the Tangier garrison, and would probably have succeeded, but for the stubborn defence made by Major Ridgert of the Queen's, who with

---

* The Queen's Royal West Surrey Regiment bear as badge the Paschal Lamb, granted by Queen Catherine, wife of Charles II. and daughter of King John of Portugal. The mottoes are "Pristinæ Virtutis Memor" and "Vel exuviæ triumphant." On the colours are the Royal Cypher in the Garter, and the Sphinx, with the following names: "Egypt," "Vimiera," "Corunna," "Salamanca," "Vittoria," "Pyrenees," "Nivelle," "Toulouse," "Peninsula," "Afghanistan," "Ghuznee," "Khelat," "South Africa, 1851-2-3," "Taku Forts," "Pekin." The uniform is scarlet with facings of blue. "The Queen's are the only regiment that still possess a third colour." Some other regiments, such as the 5th and 74th, also preserve a third colour, but do not carry it on parade.—(*Perry*).

only forty men held the foe at bay till the garrison could turn out in force. From this time skirmishes, sometimes assuming the proportions of battles, were of frequent occurrence, and in one of them the Earl of Teviot, who had succeeded Lord Peterborough in the colonelcy of the regiment and governorship of the garrison, was killed. In 1668, Lord Middleton became colonel, and during his tenure of the post, the Queen's had the honour of numbering amongst its volunteers the man who afterwards became the most successful and most celebrated general of his age, " the man who never fought a battle which he did not gain, or besieged a town which he failed to reduce—John Churchill, Duke of Marlborough." Mr. Churchill was at this time about twenty years of age, and held an ensign's commission in the Foot Guards, but made his first essays in actual service beneath the walls of Tangiers. Passing over the intermediate years, during which "the Queen's Regiment had, almost single-handed, maintained the important fortress, and many and various had been their warlike exploits against the barbarians," we come to 1682, when the colonelcy of the regiment was given to Colonel Piercy Kirke, whose name was for so long connected with the Queen's.

Four years later, as Parliament most unaccountably failed to provide for the support of this most important possession, the King was reluctantly compelled to destroy the fortifications at Tangiers, and recall the garrison, and the Queen's arrived in England in 1684. The following year at Sedgemoor, we read that "Kirke's regiment did good service." Then followed the period of repression, to which common tradition attributes the origin of the nickname of "Kirke's Lambs," with an implied character for cruelty. It is indeed more than probable that the colonel did not unduly temper justice with mercy, but the historian of the regiment well points out that had the cruelty of the regiment been so excessive as commonly reported, " it is not very probable that in the short space of four years it would have been so lost sight of, as to admit a demonstration of joy on the occasion of Kirke relieving Derry, when the people of Taunton devoted an evening to drinking his health in public." With regard to the epithet "Lambs" as applied to the regiment, assumedly in an unfavourable and ironical sense, the assumption is entirely demolished by the fact, noted by writers of the time, that the sobriquet was in use long before the alleged "atrocities" in the West. Shortly after the Revolution,* the Queen Dowager's Regiment, as they had been called after the death of Charles II., were ordered to Ireland, where they fought at the Boyne, Limerick,

* It is recorded that when overtures were made to Colonel Kirke to embrace the Roman Catholic faith, he replied that " he was pre-engaged, for he had promised the Emperor of Morocco that if ever he changed his religion, he would turn Mahommedan."

Athlone, Aghrim, and other places, and in 1692 joined the army in Flanders. At Landen they fought with signal gallantry. The Royal Scots were being forced back by the brilliant charge of the French, when "the Queen Dowager's Regiment, through smoke and flame and a storm of shot, came rushing with charged pikes to the succour of their Scottish comrades." Soon, though after desperate fighting, the enemy were driven back, and the two splendid regiments which before now had stood side by side at Tangiers when the dense hordes of the Moorish Cavalry swept round them like a whirlwind, once again "stood triumphant at the end of the village they had won, and were thanked for their gallantry by the King." They were with the army which took Nassau, where they lost several officers, and where their colonel, Selwyn, was promoted to the rank of Brigadier-General. Early in the next reign they shared in the operations at Cadiz and Vigo,* and the following year joined Marlborough's army in the Netherlands. Here, at Tongres, they gained the status of a *Royal* Regiment and their motto, "Pristinæ Virtutis Memor."†

The Queen's and another regiment, since disbanded, were the only force garrisoning Tongres, the speedy reduction of which was necessary to the plans of the French. Accordingly *forty thousand men*, under Marshals Villeroy and Boufflers, made a night march to seize it, and "attacked it with great vigour; but the two regiments defended themselves with extraordinary bravery for *twenty-eight hours;* and when at length reduced to surrender they had secured time for Marshal D'Auverquerke to collect his forces in so strong a position that the enemy declined a general engagement." They were shortly after exchanged, and took part in the various battles in Spain under the Earl of Galway, at Almanza losing twenty-two officers killed or prisoners. Portmore's Regiment (as the 2nd Foot were at this time called) had suffered so much during the campaign, that after Almanza their serviceable men were transferred to other regiments, and the headquarters sent to England to recruit. With the exception of an abortive attempt on Quebec in 1711, and some garrison duty in Gibraltar in 1740 and subsequently, the Queen's had no active service till 1793, when they were employed as Marines in Lord Howe's fleet, and, in the glorious victories gained over the French, experienced some slight loss.‡ In 1794, a 2nd battalion was formed, and under Lord

* Colonel Bellasis, who then commanded the regiment, made rather too free with the plunder, for on his return he was tried by court-martial and dismissed the service.

† Such is the generally accepted view; it has, however, been suggested that the second and unexplained motto, "Vel exuviæ triumphant," may commemorate Tongres, while the former may, as in the case of the 5th Royal Irish Lancers, allude to their prowess in Spain.

‡ On the accession of George I. the regiment was called "Her Royal Highness the Princess of Wales's own Regiment of Foot," receiving its former and present designation of "The Queen's Own" on the accession of George II.

Dalhousie proceeded almost immediately to the West Indies, where, so great had been their sufferings, at the end of 1795 all that remained of the ten companies which originally composed the battalion were a hundred and sixty-two men. In that year the 1st battalion was also ordered to the West Indies, but owing to a tempest only six companies arrived, under Lieut.-Colonel Harris, where they were incorporated into the 2nd battalion, which after the capture of Trinidad returned to England. The 1st battalion, which had been reformed, served in Ireland during the rebellion there, and afterwards joined the Duke of York's army in Holland, where they greatly distinguished themselves at the Helder and Egmont-op-Zee. During one of the incursions on the coast of France, then so much in vogue, the Official Record relates that "Major Ramsay, of the Queen's, seized several sloops and gun-vessels and burned a corvette of 18 guns."

The following year, 1801, was to gain for the regiment the first of their "distinctions," if we except the motto before referred to, in the sandy plains of Egypt, when "the fate of Asia was to be decided on the shores of Africa, by the two most powerful European nations." They besieged Aboukir and fought at Alexandria, Rosetta and Rahmanie, and on the conclusion of the treaty of Amiens repaired to their familiar quarters at Gibraltar, returning to England in 1805. In 1808 they were ordered to proceed to the Peninsula, in General Acland's brigade, and arrived there a few hours before Vimiera, the second name they bear on their colours. In the winter campaign in Spain which terminated in Corunna, the Queen's bore a gallant part, being brigaded on that eventful 16th of January, 1809, under General Hill, on the left of Moore's position.* The rearguard, to which was assigned the duty of covering the retreat of the army and keeping the enemy in check till the embarkation was completed, was under the command of Colonel Kingsbury of the regiment. After Corunna the regiment returned to England, though a detachment under Captain Gordon was fortunate enough to share in the battle of Talavera. The regiment as a whole shared in Lord Chatham's Walcheren expedition, and in 1811 joined the Sixth Division of Wellesley's army. After some sharp service round Salamanca, they participated in the memorable battle which bears that name. The advance of the Sixth Division to restore the wavering fortunes of the day forms one of the most dramatic scenes of that glorious war piece. Despite

The numerical title was given in 1751. In 1783, the regiment was for a while commanded by the Duke of Kent, father of Her present Majesty.

* An occurrence preserved by the Official Record is of sufficiently extraordinary a nature to merit mention. A private named Samuel Evans was wounded at Corunna. "He was landed in England, and died in the Military Hospital at Plymouth, on the 30th of January. A post-mortem examination showed that he had been *shot through the heart*, yet had survived *sixteen days*. His heart is preserved in the museum of the above hospital.

the concentrated fire of twenty-one guns, and a perfect tempest of well-directed musketry, the Queen's and their gallant companions pressed on, and the battle of Salamanca was won. So heavy was the loss to the Queen's, that "towards the close of the action, a subaltern officer, Lieutenant Borlase, had the honour of commanding the regiment." In consequence of the loss on this occasion the head-quarters of the regiment with six attenuated companies returned to England, the remaining four companies being attached to Lowry Cole's Division, and sharing with it the honours of "Vittoria" and the "Pyrenees." At "Nivelle" the Queen's particularly distinguished themselves, leading the attack of the centre columns against the enemy's position, and before the war ended, once more rendered themselves splendidly conspicuous at the battle of Toulouse. The regiment was in England when Waterloo was fought, and early in the following year proceeded to the West Indies, where the gallant heroes of Egypt and the Peninsula found in the terrible climate a foe more deadly than the legions of Napoleon, losing in three months, from fever, eleven officers and two hundred men. They returned to England in 1821, and four years later were ordered to India, where they remained for many years, during which they were enabled to add "Afghanistan" to their distinctions, with the sequent names of Ghuznee and Khelat. They were also engaged in the intermittent warfare with the Mahrattas. After this, their next warfare of note was in South Africa, where they rendered signal service. In the attack on the Waterkloof the Queen's were brigaded with the 6th and 91st, under Colonel Michell, and experienced some severe fighting, Captain Addison of the regiment being severely wounded. Passing over the following few years, which were spent in South Africa, the gallant Queen's were next engaged in the war in China, where they were in the second brigade of the First Division, which was the first to disembark. A reconnaissance was determined on, and the Queen's were the British regiment chosen to perform this arduous undertaking. For three-quarters of a mile their road lay over a "flat of soft, sticky, slippery mud," into which the men sank ankle-deep. "Nearly every man was disembarrassed of his lower integuments, and one gallant brigadier led on his men in no other garment than his shirt." In the final advance on the Taku Forts the Queen's were on the left of the advance column, and in the comparatively bloodless victory then gained, admirably performed the important duties allotted to them, at Tangku and Chang-chai-wan especially distinguishing themselves. Before they quitted the Celestial kingdom the Queen's had seen Pekin surrendered to the allied forces, and gained thereby the last name which appears on their colours. Since the campaign in China they have not been engaged in any war, their services having been those of peaceful occupation in the East and West Indies, Canada, and the Ionian Islands.

THE ROYAL SUSSEX REGIMENT*—Regimental District No. 35—consists of the old 35th and 107th Regiments. The 35th was raised in Ireland in 1701, and in the following year placed on the British establishment as a "Regiment of Foot for sea service." Before long Lord Donegal's Regiment, as the 35th were then styled, had plenty of active work at Cadiz and the West Indies, and in the defence of Gibraltar in 1704. The following year they served "with Peterborough in Spain," and at the capture of Barcelona—"one of the most gallant actions performed by that little army in Spain"—and its subsequent defence suffered severely, losing their colonel in one of the stubbornly contested engagements. The disastrous battle of Almanza ended for a long time their career of foreign service, the next forty years or so being passed in Ireland. In 1758 the 35th formed part of General Amherst's expedition against Louisburg, where they acquitted themselves in such wise as to gain the first distinction on their colours. At Quebec, the following year, they won the distinctive badge of the Feather for their heroic conduct in defeating the Royal Roussillon Grenadiers of France. Throughout the war which resulted in the subjugation of Canada to the British Crown the 35th were engaged, remaining in the Dominion till 1761, when they were ordered to Martinique, and rendered good service there and at the Havannah. After a short sojourn at home they were ordered to America, and took part in many of the engagements between the royal troops and colonists. They fought at Bunker's Hill, Brooklyn, New York, and other places, the flank companies being with General Burgoyne in the expedition to Ticonderoga in the spring of 1777. For sixteen years or thereabouts they were quartered in the West Indies, after which they were represented—by two battalions —in the fighting in Holland in 1799. Passing over a few years we find the Sussex Regiment—as they were called in 1805—gaining for themselves a lasting reputation at Maida, where a hundred and fifty picked men of the regiment, under Major Robinson, were in that famous right wing which Colonel Kemp led against the French Light Infantry with the result that "the enemy became appalled; they broke and endeavoured to fly, but . . . . were overtaken with most dreadful slaughter." Some of the regiment,

* The Royal Sussex bear as badges the Cross of St. George on an eight-pointed star placed on a feather on cap, and the Cross of St. George in a wreath on a Maltese cross placed on a feather on collar. The motto is that of the Garter. On the colours is the Tudor Rose with the following names: "Louisburg," "Quebec, 1759," "Maida," "Egypt, 1882," "Nile, 1884-85," "Abu Klea." The uniform is scarlet with facings of blue.

too, formed part of the little band of two hundred, which, under Colonel Robertson, held the castle of Scylla against the overwhelming forces of Regnier. On one side was the sea, whose terrors were attested by fact and fable alike; on the other a force of six thousand French, "with five 24-pounders, four battering mortars, and many field-pieces." Yet, when after three days and nights of desperate fighting the heroic garrison was embarked by the war-ship *Electra;* cries of derision and mockery from the retreating boats greeted the ears of the enraged enemy, who " purchased only a pile of ruins at the expense of several hundred lives, while the loss of the British was only eleven killed and thirty-one wounded." The following year they fought in Egypt, where they lost more than half their numbers. Under Stuart and Oswald they marched against Rosetta, and when the attacking force, having lost two-fifths of its number, had to fall back, a company of the Sussex were with Colonel Macleod, of the 78th, when he was surrounded by the Albanians.* For the following seven years the 1st battalion of the 35th were busily employed in various duties on the Continent, distinguishing themselves in the capture of Santa Maura in the Ionian Isles, the conquest of Lissa, and numerous other engagements, which, owing to the Titanic struggle waging in the Peninsula, are apt to be lost sight of. A second battalion, which had been raised on the renewal of the war, took part in the Walcheren expedition, and, after serving in Holland, were in reserve at Huy during the battle of Waterloo, after which they joined the army of occupation. For many years the record of the 35th, though indicative of plenty of hard work, does not present any very noteworthy incident. From Waterloo till just before the Mutiny in India their duties were divided between Italy, the West Indies, Corfu, and the Mauritius. In 1854 they were ordered to Burmah, and during the latter half of 1857 were in garrison at Calcutta, subsequently taking part in the sundry engagements incident to the final suppression of the Mutiny. The years which intervened between the Mutiny and the recent Egyptian war were passed by the Royal Sussex at home, in our West Indian and European dominions. When military operations in Egypt were resolved upon, the 35th were assigned to the Second Division, under Sir Evelyn Wood, and occupied the Antoniades estate at Alexandria, which they transformed into a most effective and strong position. It will be noted that by a strange coincidence the Royal Sussex of our days found themselves, under Colonel Vandeleur, Major Grattan, and other officers, quartered not far from the spot where, three-quarters of a century ago, their predecessors had fought and died under the brave Macleod. After Kafrdowar

* See p. 83.

they remained in garrison at Ramleh, and when the first phase of the war terminated were amongst the troops left to occupy Cairo. When hostilities again broke out they were ready to hand and proved themselves worthy successors of the heroes of Maida. Under Major Sunderland they were on the right flank of Stewart's square at Abu Klea, where there was need, if ever there was, for British soldiers to heed well the counsel of the valiant Philistine of old—to "be strong and quit themselves like men." After the battle a hundred and fifty men of the regiment were left to guard the wells of Abu Klea. Again at Abu Kru they fought, and throughout the remainder of the war rendered sterling service, returning home on its termination.

The 2nd battalion of the Royal Sussex Regiment, the 107th, was originally the 3rd Bengal European Infantry in the employ of the East India Company, and dates from 1854. Needless to say that their matriculation in the stern school of war was provided by the Mutiny, during which they were widely employed. At Agra, in October, 1857, the 107th were in garrison when the enemy, ignorant of the fact that Greathead's column had arrived, attempted a surprise. "As soon as the firing was heard in the fort of Agra, the 3rd Bengal Infantry rushed forward to the assistance of their comrades (of Greathead's force) and eagerly joined in the pursuit, which lasted for twelve miles." Throughout the Mutiny they were of the utmost service, and in 1861 were incorporated into the Imperial army. It was not, however, till 1875 that they came to England. The subsequent services of the 107th have been confined to garrison duty at Malta and Cairo.

The SOUTH WALES BORDERERS*—Regimental District No. 24—are composed of the 24th Foot. Despite their Welsh designation, they were raised in Ireland in 1689, almost immediately after which they were transferred to England. Under Sir Edward Dering, their first Colonel, they fought at the Boyne and probably at all the Irish battles. They are said, too, to have served with King William's army in the Netherlands, and to have taken part in the siege of Namur. In 1702, the famous Marlborough was appointed to the colonelcy of the regiment, which, under his generalship, fought at Schellenberg, Blenheim and Ramillies, Oudenarde, Lisle, and Malplaquet. In 1791,

* The South Wales Borderers bear as badges the Red Dragon of Wales in a laurel wreath with Crown over on cap, and the Sphinx with "Egypt" on collar. The motto is that of the Garter. The Queen's Colour has a silver wreath on the Staff in memory of Isandhlwana. On the Colours are the Sphinx and "Blenheim," "Ramillies," "Oudenarde," "Malplaquet," "Egypt," "Cape of Good Hope, 1806," "Talavera," "Fuentes d'Onor," "Salamanca," "Vittoria," "Pyrenees," "Nivelle," "Orthes," "Peninsula," "Chillianwallah," "Goojerat," "South Africa, 1877-8-9." The uniform is scarlet with facings of white.

they took part in the expedition under Lord Cobham against Vigo, and after a comparatively uneventful period of something over twenty years, fought as "Wentworth's Regiment" at Carthagena. After this most unsatisfactory performance, they were for some time in Cuba, with the result that they lost four-fifths of their number. After a short stay in Jamaica, they returned home, and found their next active employment, with the exception of the attempted capture of St. Malo in 1758, in the Seven Years' War in Germany, where they fought under Lord Granby at Warbourg, Corbach, Kirch Denkern, and Wilhelmstahl. After a few years at Gibraltar, they were ordered in 1776 to Canada, where they fought at Stillwater and the subsequent actions. After a brief sojourn in England, the 24th, then called the South Warwickshire, again repaired to America, where they remained till ordered to join the army in Egypt, where they gained another distinction by the part they took in the siege of Alexandria. Their next employment was in South Africa in 1806, when the 1st battalion formed part of Sir David Baird's force, after which they proceeded to India, incurring the misfortune of having a considerable number of their body taken prisoners by a French fleet. This, however, was not accomplished without a struggle. The transports were three East Indiamen named respectively the *Ceylon*, the *Wyndham*, and the *Astell*, and the last named probably owed its escape to the gallantry of the 24th under Major Foster, with whom were Captains Gubbins, Craig, and Maxwell, and Ensign D'Aine.

Meanwhile the 2nd battalion had joined the British army in the Peninsula, and fought with distinction at Talavera, Fuentes d'Onor, Salamanca, Burgos, and Vittoria, experiencing such heavy losses "that only four weak companies remained, which were formed, with four others similarly situated, as the 2nd battalion of the 58th, and so fought throughout the remainder of the war." They greatly distinguished themselves under Colonel McLean at the siege of St. Sebastian. They had to ford the Urumea River, which ran so deep that the men had to hold their cartridge-boxes above it. A terrible shower of grape was poured upon them when they were in mid stream, "many were killed, and more sank wounded to drown miserably. But closing in shoulder to shoulder the survivors moved steadily on." Their point of attack was the great breach, where the struggle raged with fearful ferocity, so that "it could hardly be judged whether the hurt or unhurt were most numerous." Then came the explosion which opened the mighty walls of the stubborn fort, and the 24th with their comrades poured in through the chasm, victors at last. When peace was declared, the 2nd battalion of the South Warwickshire was disbanded. The 1st battalion had during this time been engaged in India, notably on the Nepaulese frontier. After a short stay in England they were ordered to Canada, where they stayed some years, and were of great service during the troubles in 1837. Sterner warfare awaited them in India, whither they were sent in 1846. After fighting at Sadoolapore early in December, 1848, they were present in Colin Campbell's division at the disastrous conflict of Chillianwallah, the following month. Under Colonel Brooks, they effected a most brilliant charge on the enemy's guns. Despite the six hundred yards across which they had to double, they drove away the gunners, and were in the act of spiking the guns, when several regiments of the enemy lying in ambush poured upon them "a concentrated fire that no troops could withstand." They fell literally in heaps, and at this critical moment the Sikh Cavalry swept down upon them. "Pennycuick and his son, both officers of the 24th, fell just as they reached the guns. A stalwart Sikh was seen leaning over the helpless father, prostrated by a shot, and inflicting fresh gashes on his body, when the boy ensign of seventeen, worthy of such a noble father, stepped forward and dealt an avenging blow. The heroic boy strode across his parent's corpse, and bade defiance to the savage multitude; but numbers soon overwhelmed him, and he fell dead." (*Thackwell*). Not the least of the disasters of the day was the loss of the colours of the gallant 24th, but, as if in melancholy anticipation of a similar heroic episode of more recent date, "one was afterwards found, wrapped round the dead body of the ensign who had borne it into action." That day no fewer than 13 officers and 227 men of the regiment were killed, and 310 of all ranks wounded. A month later was fought Goojerat, the last Indian distinction which the 24th bear, though for many years after the North-west Frontier and the Punjaub witnessed innumerable evidences of their courage and warlike prowess. The years which intervened between the suppression of the Mutiny and the Zulu War were passed by the 24th in various places, in most of which something of active service fell to their lot. India, Burmah, West Griqua-Land, and the Gauka country were severally the spheres of their duty.

While they were in Burmah, a detachment was despatched to the Little Andamans to rescue the captain and some of the crew of a British vessel, who it was but too truly surmised had fallen victims to the savages. About twenty men formed the small force under Lieutenant Much, who was accompanied by Surgeon Douglas and Lieutenant Glassford, the last-named as a volunteer. On arriving at their destination, they landed under a discharge of arrows, and soon found conclusive evidences that their unfortunate countrymen had been barbarously murdered. When they wished to return it was found that their boats were so seriously damaged as to be useless. Efforts were made to get off on a raft, but the nature of the coast rendered this impossible. "Seeing the evil plight of their comrades, Dr. Douglas, Privates Murphy, and Cooper, Bell, and Griffiths, of the 24th Regiment, manned the second gig, and made their way through the surf almost to the shore. Finding their boats half filled with water, they returned, but only to make a second attempt which proved successful, Dr. Douglas and his crew managing to convey five of the party which had landed safely, through the surf to the boats outside. On a third trip he removed the remainder, all being rescued with the exception of Lieutenant Glassford, who was drowned." The official report eulogises the "intrepid," "cool," and "collected" manner in which Dr. Douglas and his companions achieved their heroic task, and it is satisfactory to record that the statutes of the Order were for this occasion a little strained, to enable these five gallant men to receive the guerdon of the Victoria Cross.

It is a mere truism to say that wherever and whenever the Zulu War is mentioned, two names spontaneously suggest themselves. One, immortalised by the melancholy romance of his life and death, is that of the Prince Imperial of France, the other is that of the 24th Regiment individually and collectively. It is with the latter part of the Zulu War that we shall chiefly deal, premising that the 1st battalion of the 24th was already *in situ* when hostilities began (having been, as has been mentioned, engaged in Griqualand), and that the 2nd battalion arrived in 1879. Both battalions were attached to the second column, the command of which was entrusted to Colonel Glynn of the regiment, and, in January, 1879, were encamped at Rorke's Drift on the Buffalo River, where they had one or two successful skirmishes with the enemy. Two companies were left at Helpmakaar, and two at Rorke's Drift, when, on the 20th of the same month, the column moved on to the hill of Isandhlwana. By dint of false reports the enemy succeeded in disarming all suspicion, and the camp at Isandhlwana was weakened by the dispatch of various parties on reconnaissances. Before there was a suspicion of danger, with the awful suddenness of a tropical tempest, the Zulus, numbering many thousands, swept down upon the devoted garrison. Before "Mostyn's and Cavaye's companies of the 24th had time to form rallying squares, or even to fix their bayonets, they were slaughtered to a man." No hope was left; death at the hands of a savage foe was inevitable, yet probably never throughout their long and brilliant career had the 24th more nobly vindicated the honour and valour of British warriors. Calmly, as if the yelling savages were but a London crowd thronging to see a review, Colonel Pulleine turned to Melvill with the words: "You, as senior lieutenant, will take the colours, and make the best of your way from here," and, with a farewell hand-shake with his subaltern, addressed the handful of his gallant regiment who were about him: "Men of the 24th, here we are, and here we stand to fight it out to the end." The end was terribly near. "The light was darkened with flying assegais thrown from near with deadly effect. In a few minutes Colonel Pulleine, every officer, and every man of the gallant 24th lay upon the ground dying or dead. The two companies* who had been skirmishing on the left by the skirts of the 'Ngata Range, were never seen or heard of again . . . . Instantly surrounded, every man was laid dead upon the ground. Not one was left alive." † Lieutenants Melvill and Coghill, with Private Williams, dashed on till they came to the Buffalo River. Here Williams was drowned. Melvill's horse was shot, and the colours slipped from his hand. Coghill had reached the other side in safety, when, looking back, he saw his companion clinging to a rock, trying in vain to recover the colours. He rode back to his assistance, and then his horse, also, was shot, and the two doomed officers struggled on, literal targets for the enemy. Let us quote Captain Parr to learn the last of these heroes of our own days. "There are, not many hundred yards from the river's side, two boulders within six feet of each other, near the rocky path. At these boulders they made their last stand, and fought until overpowered. Here we found them lying side by side, and buried them on the spot where they fought and fell so gallantly." Ten days after, the colours were found in the bed of the river by Major Black of the regiment. Many are the incidents gathered, some of them from the Zulus themselves, relating to that terrible struggle. A corporal of the regiment "slew four Zulus with his bayonet, which stuck for a moment in the throat of his last opponent; then he was assegaied." The Zulus described how the "red soldiers taunted them to come on," and how when our ammunition was all exhausted, the cunning savages hurled the bodies of their own dead against the gleaming fence of bayonets, and then rushing in, assegaied every man. Another account describes the tortures and mutilations inflicted on the wounded: "The men who returned with the General saw enough of it—one poor little drummer-boy held up on a bayonet."

Of the 24th there fell that day five entire companies of the 1st battalion with ninety men of the 2nd. Meanwhile one company of the 2nd battalion had been left at Rorke's Drift under Lieutenant Bromhead. The splendid defence made by him and Lieutenant Chard has been before referred to,‡ so we will here only notice a few of the deeds of valour performed by men of the 24th. When the enemy set fire to the hospital,

* Under Lieutenant Younghusband. † Major Elliott. ‡ See p. 137.

the garrison defended it step by step as they brought out as many of the sick as possible. Privates Williams and Hook held a room in the hospital for about an hour, "one holding the enemy at bay with his bayonet, while the other broke through three more partitions to the inner defence, and got eight sick men safely out of the hospital. Privates Williams and Robert Jones in like manner rescued six men; Corporal Allen and Private Hitch held a most dangerous post commanding the communication between the hospital and inner defence. Exposed to fire from both sides they were severely wounded, yet when their injuries rendered them incapable of handling their arms, they had their wounds dressed by the surgeon, and then returned to the defence and handed out cartridges to their comrades." Throughout the war the gallant 24th, who were subsequently reinforced, rendered sterling service, and in the retreat from Inhlobane, Lieutenant Brown of the 1st battalion gained the Victoria Cross for rescuing under heavy fire two soldiers who would otherwise have been captured by the closely pursuing Zulus.

Since the Zulu War the South Wales Borderers have not been engaged in any warfare which comes within the scope of this work. The silver wreath on the Queen's colour of the regiment is a permanent memorial of the wreath of immortelles fastened by Her Majesty on the colours, to save which Melvill, Coghill, and Williams gave their lives, and will remain to all time an eloquent testimony of the honour in which Sovereign and nation hold one of the most gallant and distinguished regiments of the Queen's army.

THE ROYAL WARWICKSHIRE REGIMENT*—Regimental District No. 6—consists of the old 6th Foot, and dates from 1673, when a body of English soldiers was raised for the service of the States General, and placed under the command of Sir Walter Vane, Colonel of the Buffs. Of this body of troops, the regiment now known as the Royal Warwickshire formed part. It is not within our province to follow the deeds of the regiment while fighting purely as auxiliaries in the service of another power. The histories of the time have few more enthralling passages than those which tell of the prowess of those gallant English who alike in court and camp, in battlefield and Presence Chamber, held their own against all comers, and gained honour and fair fame as well for themselves as for the imperial Island, "compassed by the inviolate sea," whose warrior sons they

* The Royal Warwickshire bear as badges a white antelope with gold collar and chain (in the Garter), surrounded by a laurel wreath, on cap; and the Bear and Ragged Staff, the cognisance of the Earls of Warwick, on collar. The motto is that of the Garter, though it would seem that "Nec aspera terrent" and "Vi et Armis" have also been used as mottoes. On their colours are the Tudor Rose on crown, and "Roleia," "Vimiera," "Corunna," "Vittoria," "Pyrenees," "Nivelle," "Orthes," "Peninsula," "Niagara," "South Africa, 1846—7," "South Africa, 1851—2—3." The uniform is scarlet with facings of blue.

were. When Monmouth's claims began to alarm King James, he required the return of the regiments in the service of the States, and the 6th, then known as Bellasis' Regiment, arrived in England in July, 1685, returning, however, shortly after to the Netherlands. When they next came to England it was in the train of the Prince of Orange, who a few weeks later assumed the style of King of England. On the voyage hither, four companies of the regiment were captured by Captain Aylmer, whose ship, the *Swallow*, had not yet migrated to the new *régime*. The next employment of the 6th was in Ireland, where the adherents of King James still held together, and in this service they fought at Charlemont, the Boyne, Athlone, Ballymore, Aghrim, and other battles. In 1692 the 6th—then known as Hesse d'Armstadt's Regiment, the Prince of that name being appointed to the colonelcy—were ordered to Holland, and fought in Holland. "The 6th nobly sustained their reputation, and fought manfully, resisting the superior numbers of the enemy with signal firmness: their commanding officer, Lieutenant-Colonel Foxon, fell mortally wounded. The French legions—dragoons, musketeers, pikemen, and grenadiers—crowded round this devoted corps in great numbers, and it sustained considerable loss." When at last a retreat was ordered, the 6th withdrew from the field "a mere skeleton." After being recruited, they served at Namur, again with considerable loss, and after various unimportant operations, took part in the expeditions against Cadiz and Vigo. They joined Lord Peterborough's army in Spain in 1705, and greatly distinguished themselves at the siege of Barcelona, the grenadiers of the regiment, under Lieutenant-Colonel Southwell, leading the assault upon the strong detached fort of Montjuich. After most strenuous and gallant fighting, the attack proved successful: the garrison surrendered to the "intrepid Southwell," who was embraced by King Charles of Spain and appointed Governor of the citadel. Barcelona fell soon afterwards, and the regiment continued, under the immediate direction of Lord Peterborough, to share in all the exploits performed by our troops, exploits so brilliant and heroic as—to quote the words of the historian—to "carry with them the appearance of fiction and romance rather than sober truth," but which nevertheless are as well attested as any other historical fact. Two years later they fought at Almanza, needless to say with gallantry, but with heavy loss: nine officers, including the lieutenant-colonel, were killed, and fourteen wounded or prisoners. In 1708 they took part in the subjugation of Minorca, Fort St. Philip—the only fortress which made any serious resistance—being captured by the headlong gallantry of "the grenadiers of the 6th and another corps."

They fought at Saragossa, their colonel, Thomas Harrison, being commissioned to carry home the news and spoils of the victory to Queen Anne. It is probably to their achievements in Spain that the 6th owe their badge of the Antelope. So at least says tradition, which, however, is not supported by any documentary evidence. They fought at Brihuega in 1710, where several were taken prisoners, soon, however, to escape or be exchanged, and in 1714 the regiment returned home. In 1719 they took part in the Vigo expedition, after which their next service of importance seems to have been in the West Indies in 1741, from whence they returned the following year sorely reduced by pestilence. They were actively engaged in the "affair of '45," fighting at Ruthven and Preston Pans, where they were amongst those battalions of infantry who stood their ground, and as a consequence "had nearly every man killed, wounded, or taken prisoner." After this, with the exception of garrison duty in Gibraltar, the 6th were chiefly at home till 1772, when they received orders to proceed to St. Vincent, where they were engaged with credit to themselves in the operations against the Caribs. After a sojourn in England and in Canada they went to Martinique in 1794, and took part in the fighting which there took place. After assisting in suppressing the rebellion in Ireland, during which irksome service—notably at Castlebar—they most gallantly acquitted themselves, the 6th proceeded, in the summer of 1808, to join Lord Wellesley's army in Portugal. They were brigaded with the 32nd Regiment under General Bowles, and on the 17th of August took part—though not "seriously"—in the battle of Roleia, the first name which, despite their long and arduous service, appears on their colours. Two days later followed Vimiera, after which they were attached to the army under Sir John Moore, "the only general," as the vaunting Buonaparte declared, "worthy for him to contend against," and under him fought in the ill-fated field of Corunna. Their losses here were about four hundred, and the Walcheren expedition, in which they took part, still further swelled the list of casualties. In 1812 they again joined the Allied Army in the Peninsula, being brigaded under General Barnes in Lord Dalhousie's Division. They arrived at Vittoria after the battle had begun, but their gallant conduct there was conspicuous, as it was in the subsequent sanguinary engagements in the Pyrenees. At Echelar in particular they were the observed of all observers—and they were not a few—of that "terrible drama called war." "Barnes," wrote an officer present, "set at the French as if every man had been a bull-dog, and himself the best bred of all;" "The attack on the enemy," wrote Lord Wellesley, "is the most gallant and finest thing I ever witnessed."

The regiment were partially engaged at the Bidassoa, and under Beresford carried the strong redoubts on the enemy's left centre at the Nivelle. The next year at Orthes they suffered severely, and on the termination of the war in the Peninsula proceeded to Canada, where they immediately took part in the siege of Port Erie, particularly distinguishing themselves under Major Taylor in the repulse of a sortie in force made by the Americans in September, 1814. Joining the Duke of Wellington after Waterloo, the 6th remained for some months with the army of occupation, returning to England towards the end of 1818. From that date till 1846 they were stationed in various places, including South Africa and India. In 1846 they were engaged in the Caffre war, and a few years after in the renewed hostilities with the same gallant but barbarous foes. In the latter campaign they were in Colonel Michell's brigade, and had their full share of the severe fighting that ensued. In the attack on the Waterkloof, Lieutenant Morris of the regiment was mortally wounded, and in the final assault the 6th formed part of the centre column, and by their courage and endurance well deserved their final distinction in South Africa, 1851—2—3.* In 1857 they were ordered to India, and were actively engaged in the Oude campaign of 1858, and many of the subsequent years have been passed by the regiment in the same country, the Hazarah expedition and the "little war" on the Punjab frontier providing something of active service. A second battalion was raised in 1858, but has not yet been engaged in warfare of any magnitude.

Foremost amongst the famous regiments of Her Majesty's Army are the ROYAL WELSH FUSILIERS,†—Regimental District No. 23—the old 23rd of warlike renown. The Royal Welsh Fusiliers were raised almost immediately after the Revolution had transferred the royal authority from the hands of King James to those of his daughter

* At Fort Cox the Grenadier company particularly distinguished itself.

† The Royal Welsh Fusiliers bear as badges the Red Dragon of Wales on a grenade on cap, and a grenade on collar. On the cap plate, waist plate, and buttons is the Prince of Wales' Plume. The mottoes are "Ich Dien" and "Nec aspera terrent." The Royal Welsh Fusiliers are the only regiment that retain the "flash" (five black ribbons some nine inches long, hanging from the back of the collar), a survival of the days when queues were worn, and when the flour and grease used in them played havoc with the tunics. The 23rd were abroad when the queue was abolished, and on their return their commanding officer obtained leave to retain the "flash." The "Regimental Goat" is also accorded by Royal Warrant. Grose, in his "Military Antiquities," says that the Royal Welsh Fusiliers "have a privileged honour of passing in review preceded by a goat with gilded horns, and adorned with ringlets of flowers . . . and the corps values itself much on the ancientness of the custom." On the colours are the Rising Sun, the Red Dragon, the White Horse, the Sphinx, and the following names : "Blenheim," "Ramillies," "Oudenarde," "Malplaquet," "Dettingen," "Minden," "Egypt," "Corunna," "Martinique," "Albuhera," "Badajoz," "Salamanca," "Vittoria," "Pyrenees," "Nivelle," "Orthes," "Toulouse," "Peninsula," "Waterloo," "Alma," "Inkerman," "Sevastopol," "Lucknow," "Ashantee." The uniform is scarlet with facings of blue, and fusilier cap.

and son-in-law. Raised in Wales and the adjoining counties in 1689, the 23rd in August of that year arrived in Ireland, where the aforesaid transfer of power was not yet an accomplished fact. At the battle of the Boyne they satisfied the critical eye of William, who is reported to have watched with some anxiety the effect of their first fire on his newly raised regiments; and to the present day the Welsh Fusiliers preserve a memento of this their first battle. "The spurs won by Major Toby Purcell (of the 23rd) at the battle of the Boyne are still preserved in the regiment, in possession of the senior major for the time being" (*Cannon*). After the fall of Aghrim, at which the regiment suffered severely, Major Toby Purcell became colonel, *vice* Colonel Herbert, their first commander, who fell into the hands of the Irish and was inhumanly murdered. Passing over the melancholy category of the battles in Ireland, we find the 23rd—then known as Ingoldsby's Regiment—amongst the reinforcements which joined King William's army in Holland in the early part of 1694, and the following year they took part in the siege of Namur, during which they suffered very severely. On the final capitulation the 23rd were ordered to take possession of the gates. After the peace of Ryswick the regiment returned to Ireland, remaining there till June, 1701, when they again embarked for Flanders, to take part in the memorable campaigns of Marlborough. After sharing in numerous battles and sieges they were present at the battle of Schellenberg, where they vied in gallantry with the Foot Guards and Royals, losing five officers and sixty-six rank and file killed, eleven officers and a hundred and sixty others wounded. Then came Blenheim, where the 23rd were in Rowe's brigade, which commenced the action, and where, "amidst the storm of war, they had repeated opportunities of distinguishing themselves." They fought at Huy and Neer Hespen, and after some less important engagements were in the right of the British line at Ramillies. Again—passing over subordinate incidents in the long war—we come to Oudenarde, to which few regiments can refer with greater pride than the Royal Welsh Fusiliers. It was they who, under Brigadier Sabine, headed the brilliant attack on the village of Heynem, when seven battalions of the enemy were taken prisoners; and it was they who, after driving another body of French from their position, repulsed a body of cavalry which attacked them in front and flank. At the siege of Lisle the attacking force included the 23rd, again led to victory by the brave Sabine; they shared in the siege of Tournay, and in September, 1709, took part in the battle of Malplaquet, where the loss of life was greater "than at the battles of Blenheim, Ramillies, and Oudenarde put together." On this occasion they were in Count Lothum's Division, to which was allotted the severe and trying task

www.ingramcontent.com/pod-product-compliance
Lightning Source LLC
Chambersburg PA
CBHW020808230426
43666CB00007B/917